THE TRUTHS OF PSYCHOANALYSIS

FIGURES OF THE UNCONSCIOUS 18

THE TRUTHS OF PSYCHOANALYSIS

Edited by
Jasper Feyaerts and Paulo Beer

LEUVEN UNIVERSITY PRESS

Published with the support of
São Paulo Research Foundation (FAPESP) – processes 2016/03096-7 and 2018/09753-5;
Center for Contemporary European philosophy (CCEP), Radboud University;
Centre de Recherches Psychanalyse, Médecine et Société (CRPMS), Université de Paris

ISBN 978 94 6270 300 1
e-ISBN 978 94 6166 416 7
D/2022/1869/5
NUR: 770
https://doi.org/10.11116/9789461664167

Cover design: Daniel Benneworth-Gray
Lay-out: Friedemann Vervoort

GPRC
Guaranteed
Peer Reviewed
Content
www.gprc.be

Table of Contents

The Truths of Psychoanalysis
Introduction

Jasper Feyaerts & Paulo Beer

Truth has always been at the forefront of political, epistemological, and ontological debates. At once the most uncompromising yet fragile and defenseless of all philosophical categories, it has mobilized thinkers from all intellectual traditions, producing a distinct array of heterogeneous approaches. These range from traditional Aristotelian correspondence views in which truth results from thought adequately reflecting external reality and Spinozist coherence theories in which truth derives from the internal consistency of propositions to constructive, historicized, and performative accounts in which truth is never a given, but the dynamic outcome of material and structural conditions that simultaneously generate what is to be counted as true.

Thinking about truth today, however, is almost impossible without immediately including a reflection on its continuous debasement and effacement. Alternative truths and facts have become truth's most faithful companion, generalized obscurantism its most immediate reflection. In this respect, our political post-truth epoch seems to announce a significant rupture with respect to traditional critical metaphysics. While the value, attainment, or power of truth has been incessantly contested—most notably by the three classical masters of suspicion: Nietzsche, Marx, and Freud—such demystifying critiques only ever set out to destroy imaginary pretentions in order to expose, rebuild, and decipher a truth that was regarded to be located elsewhere. While self-consciousness—to name but the most maligned philosophical concept—might have been systematically attacked as a structural place of self-deception and as the ever-productive site of self-serving illusions, critical deconstruction went hand in hand with constructive proposals that opened the way for different epistemological procedures to disclose and to attain what was hitherto deemed obfuscated and misrecognized. In short, "false consciousness" had to be radically questioned, interpreted, and exposed, yet only from within the liberating perspective of truth itself.

Political and ideological deconstruction today, however, seems to have abandoned this *Sorge* for a different or more adequate conception of truth. What counts in the present ideological context is not the distinction between truths and falsehoods, but rather the efficacy of political discourse to produce and evoke identifications and affects. At first sight, of course, this observation seems to contain nothing radically new: addressing and seducing public opinion has always been more effective by appealing to personal affects and by generating sentiments of recognition, rather than by inviting the neutral and detached deliberation of facts. However, contemporary post-truth politics does not seem to rely on affective identification to attain or produce an ultimately more truthful *Weltanschauung*, it focuses first of all on exposing truth itself as a fundamentally impotent, inert, and inessential category. This seems to be the Trumpian lesson for ideology critique today: our current political situation demonstrates that ideology does not even require the *appearance* or *semblance* of truth to realize its objectives (whatever those may be). On the contrary, the unconcealed and playful disregard for truth constitutes an essential part of its efficiency and appeal. In post-truth politics, we encounter a form of false consciousness that pleasurably admits and reveals its own falsity, thereby simultaneously degrading classical ideology critiques to seemingly outdated and obsolete relics of the past.

Rather than drifting along with the numbing sense of critical disillusionment it inspires, these observations invite a renewed reflection on the affective and libidinal vicissitudes underlying truth and its effacement, which leads us back, once again, to the enduring relevance of psychoanalysis. Psychoanalysis has dealt with the unruly nature of truth from its inception. As soon as Freud began to question the truthfulness of his patients' stories, truth, in close conjunction with the notions of fantasy and reality, became central to psychoanalytic theory and practice. In the most general sense, what can be gleaned from psychoanalysis's instructive attempts to clarify its own distinctive relation to truth is a seemingly insoluble yet productive tension that transpires within the works of both Freud and Lacan.

In Freud's case, there can be no doubt, on the one hand, that psychoanalysis, at least in aspiration, was destined to become a new rigorous science of the *psyche*. It may well be that others before Freud were observationally acute enough to observe and detect unconscious desires and resistances at work in the psychopathologies of everyday life. As is already apparent from his early *Project for a Scientific Psychology* (Freud 1950[1895]), Freud's novelty derived from his obstinate determination to investigate such resistances in a systematic scientific fashion, accompanying his inquiry with more or less plausible hypotheses and postulates that would be tested, modified, and replaced on the basis of his psychoanalytic experience. While much has been said about the actual scientific and methodological adequacy of Freud's procedures, the traditional *ideal* of science is a basic motivation underlying Freud's work.

However, it is equally clear that, beyond his traditional scientific realism, Freud also attests to a different, more modern conception of truth whenever he considers the translation and the efficacy of psychoanalytic knowledge within psychoanalytic practice. While the early Freud, following the initial trauma theory of seduction, still conceived psychoanalytic work within the straightforward perspective of "reality-testing," hence as geared toward recovering and retrieving "lost" memories of real material events, complications arising in practice would eventually lead him to abandon this traditional scheme. As Verhaeghe (1996: 26) put it, Freud discovered that "the neurotic defends himself not only with, but also against, falsified memories and fantasies," thereby leading him to the conclusion—as Freud expressed in a letter to Fliess—"that there are no indications of reality in the unconscious, so that one cannot distinguish between the truth and a fiction cathected with affect" (Freud in Masson 1985[1887–1904]: 264).

The significance of this disconcerting discovery for psychoanalytic theory is, first of all, that the particular theory of truth that would be able to account for psychoanalytic practice could no longer be conceived within a classical perspective of correspondence theories, if only because what constitutes "reality" in the context of this practice seems itself entirely affected by fantasies. Yet the intricacies of the analytic encounter also don't lead to any easy wedding with more permissive constructionist or hermeneutic coherence theories, because these phantasmic constructions seem at once to hint at a more intimate and foreign kernel, a new kind of adverse objectivity, that is neither readily reducible to any internal narrative truth nor to any externalist perspective outside of these narratives. This is what ultimately distinguishes the psychoanalytic conception of fantasy from its more common-sense rendition. Within a common-sense perspective, fantasies correspond to a subject's most intimate and direct self-experience with regard to which the subject furthermore enjoys an unparalleled first-person authority. In psychoanalysis, by contrast, the notion of fantasy confronts a subject with a dimension of irreducible strangeness and inaccessibility that radically subverts the classical idea of first-personal intimacy or immediate self-acquaintance. At the same time, this observation opens toward a new epistemological terrain that traverses the classical distinction between subjectivity and objectivity and which sets out to account for the distinctive *kind* of truth that emerges from this phantasmic inaccessibility.

A similar tension between audacious scientific aspiration and a subverted notion of truth permeates the work of Lacan. On the one hand, far from expressing reservations with respect to what intellectual contemporaries such as Sartre or Ricoeur denounced as Freud's indigestible "mechanistic cramp" (Sartre 1979[1972]: 37) issuing forth from his supposedly misguided "scientism,"

Lacan insisted on preserving that part of the psychoanalytic heritage. In effect, Lacan's structuralist-materialist reworking of Freudian metapsychology in terms of his "logic of the signifier" seems to have been driven by an even more fierce ambition to finally establish psychoanalysis as a rigorous scientific endeavor, grounded in the Koyréan ideal of mathematical formalization (Eyers 2012; Tomšič 2012). In Lacan's hands, the Freudian unconscious was to be purified even further from any remaining residues of metaphysical humanism and its associated anthropomorphic terminology, the better to emphasize man's radical displacement by the gripping effects of the signifying chain, "a form in which the subject is inserted at the level of his being" (Lacan 1993: 179).

All the same, this austere scientific rhetoric did not prevent Lacan from retaining and elaborating a concept of truth that differs from a traditional scientific perspective, yet one that would nonetheless be co-extensive with structuralism's recasting of human subjectivity as a structured effect rather than a constitutive origin. As Lacan recognizes early on:

> Freud was exploring a line of research which is not characterized by the same style as other sciences. Its domain is that of the truth of the subject. The quest for truth is not entirely reducible to the objective, and indeed objectifying, research of the normal scientific method. It is a matter of the realization of the truth of the subject, as a specific dimension which must be detached in its originality from the notion of reality. (Lacan 1988: 21)

To be sure, while psychoanalysis might diverge from other objectifying sciences in seeking to preserve a certain "truth of the subject," it is clear that, given Lacan's definition of this subject as "caught up in a constituting division" (2006: 727), the truth envisaged to be at stake here can neither simply be a matter of subjective nor phenomenological truthfulness, of a subject honestly nor authentically expressing its desires, experiences, and beliefs. While "true speech," at least for a certain period within Lacan's teaching, might have constituted a regulative ideal for psychoanalytic practice, the subject's radical decentering by the Freudian unconscious significantly complicates the forms in which such exemplary speech could be attained. If it is not me who means things with words, but rather the words that come to define the meaning in which I am implicated—if I am not the intentional agent subtending my speech acts, but rather a retroactive illusion emerging from linguistic determination, how could this fact about myself be expressed in the most truthful way? In effect, this is perhaps Lacan's most basic question: What happens to the idea of truthful speech when the nature of the speaking subject is essentially derived? Is there a stylistic form of *parole vraie* that could authentically transmit the subject's inauthentic nature? Is there a way to conceive a *bien-dire* that aesthetically perfects the *mi-dire* of the subject of truth?

With varying degrees of authenticity and truthfulness, yet with consistent theoretical and clinical ingenuity, the essays collected in this book address the nature of truth within psychoanalysis. Offering both new and sustained reflections on the wide variety of manifestations and forms of truth in and beyond psychoanalysis, this book condenses seminal and innovative work by international specialists spanning several continents. As such, all contributions collected here aim to renew our understanding of the meaning, significance, and elusiveness of truth, thereby also appealing and responding to an urgency permeating global society today.

The book is divided into three sections. The first, "Truth in Psychoanalytic Theory and Practice," provides a combination of more immanent readings of the nature and role of truth in psychoanalytic theory, psychoanalytic anthropology, clinical practice, and implications of psychoanalytic reflections on truth and authenticity for gender issues and sexual identity. The second section, "Psychoanalysis and the Philosophy of Truth," assembles a rich variety of essays that help to rethink the nature of truth in philosophy from a psychoanalytic perspective, while also employing philosophy to enlighten the appearance and forms of truth in psychoanalysis. The last section, "Toward a Psychoanalytic Politics of Truth," demonstrates how psychoanalysis's conception of truth can be productively employed in the field of politics, enabling us to think through the paradoxes of contemporary ideologies and to advance a form of truthful emancipation and revolutionary action.

The first section opens with Carin Franzén's "The Virtue of Truth, Ignorance, and Love: A Reflection on Lacan's Theory of the Subject." Franzén offers a pointed reflection on the ethical dimensions of truth and love starting from the Socratic virtue of self-conscious ignorance and Lacan's qualified praise of this virtue as something that, "in its finest successes, does not always succeed" (Lacan 2015: 80). Throughout this chapter, Franzén discusses how the truth of the nonexistence of the sexual relation is obfuscated yet skillfully displayed through the romantic procedures of courtly love, while being offered a more feminine, and therefore perhaps more truthful, articulation in the works of Marguerite Duras and Marguerite de Navarre. The essay concludes by demonstrating how the ethical implications of this truth about love sustaining psychoanalytic practice can serve as a counterdiscourse to the constant neoliberal injunction according to which anything—and hence nothing—is possible.

In "Where the Truth Lies in Psychoanalysis: The Role of Fictional Construction," Derek Humphreys zooms in on the role of "fiction" in psychoanalysis and why this fictional epistemological departure does not necessarily entail that the psychoanalytic approach would be arbitrary or dismissive of any reference to truth. Nonetheless, Humphreys shows how Freud's reference to the metaphor of archaeological excavation to compare and enlighten the psychoanalytic process of truth-finding is confronted with an essential limit. As is often the case with Freud, Freud self-consciously deconstructs his own metaphor by pointing out euphemistically "that psychological objects are incomparably more complicated than the excavator's material ones" (1937: 260). In fact, further imploding the metaphorical reference, Humphreys shows that the psychoanalytic method precisely begins where the archaeological procedure ends. Psychoanalysis is not so much focused on deciphering the final meaning of symptoms and to expose it once and for all—its particular form of truth-finding is intrinsically dynamic and singular, determined by the multiplicity of unconscious meaning and the affective textuality of language. Humphreys helpfully illustrates this specificity of the psychoanalytic method with a clinical case study at the end of his chapter.

In chapter 3, "Feminine Identification and Infinite Mourning," Christian Dunker offers a new perspective on Freud's theory of mourning by emphasizing the difference between phallic types of "finite mourning" that presuppose a dialectic of identification and disidentification, and feminine types of infinite mourning that transcend predicative and symbolic determination. In developing this distinction, Dunker revisits his earlier arguments regarding the necessity of a concept of "non-identitarian identification" within psychoanalytic anthropology, substantiating his point by referring to new developments in perspectivist anthropology that extend beyond Lévi-Strauss's influential structuralist paradigm. As in the rituals of the Indigenous people of the Arawetés, some kinds of mourning are determined not so much by imaginary or symbolic forms of kinship and identification, but by an animistic tendency toward identity-dispossession and indeterminate self-annihilation. Dunker situates this infinite and indefinite form of mourning and its eventual therapeutic solution within Lacan's logic of sexuation, and as in the preceding chapter, Dunker lively demonstrates its clinical validity by means of a detailed case study.

The next chapter—Peter Jansson's "The Truth of the Real"—continues this anthropological reflection by elaborating how the concept of the "Real" introduces a new understanding of truth in psychoanalysis and the way it plays out in what Jansson calls—in a Heideggerian vein—the different "existential structures" of neurosis, psychosis, perversion, and sublimation. Jansson shows how each of those structures harbors a distinctive way of dealing with the truth of the Real and how psychoanalysis can assist in supporting the relation the subject entertains with this dimension of truth.

In chapter 5, "Truth and Sexuality: Foucault, the Genealogist of Psychoanalysis," Laurie Laufer starts from Michel Foucault's incisive observations regarding the historical emergence of an essential link between truth and sexuality in the nineteenth century. Foucault emphasizes how truth became intrinsically entangled with sex, as if the latter, more so than any other identifying features, could reveal the truth about oneself and one's desire in the most original and authentic way. With Foucault, Laufer critically questions this concern and fascination with the truth of sex, denouncing the confessional tendency to locate and search for truth in whatever happens to contingently organize one's sexual preferences and desires. Laufer illustrates this timely lesson with the tragic historical case of Herculine Barbin. Yet, against Foucault, Laufer shows how psychoanalysis is not merely another confession science, because it abstracts from the verity regime of sexual identity in favor of the radical contingency that results from depsychologized pleasure. Pleasure harbors no meaning or norm, a truth that guides psychoanalytic practice in exposing the fictional structure of sexual identity.

Further exploring the concepts of realness, truth, and authenticity with regard to gender identities, in chapter 6, "Yearning to Be: Authenticity and Truth in Clinical Psychoanalytic Practice," Patricia Gherovici takes us on a journey along Janet Mock's memoirs, *Redefining Realness* (Mock 2014), to make room for a concept of realness that transcends the traditional philosophical opposition between appearance and reality. In her close reading of Mock's work, Gherovici critically interrogates what it means to authentically "pass" as a credible transgender, pointing out that the more decisive criterion is not situated between realness and unrealness, but between life and death. Those who undergo gender transition are less concerned with problems of sexual identity and the permeable border between male and female than with the ontological search for a livable embodiment that enables to defer death as our ultimate frontier. Gherovici, like Laufer in the preceding chapter, sets out to dismantle our current pathological obsession with sexual identity and the prevailing imperative to be or become one's authentic (sexual) self. Resisting this ideal, however, doesn't diminish the value of speaking one's truth. Even while this truth cannot be defined along existing symbolic categories, even while attesting to this truth can only be expressed by a "what the fuck?," the only thing that is more frightening than not speaking one's truth is not speaking at all.

In the final chapter of this section, "The Truth of Gender: Psychoanalysis's Unthinkable Trauma," Nicolas Evzonas extends this critical questioning of the epistemological privileges of cis identity, and in particular its persistence within psychoanalytic metapsychology. Evzonas shows how psychoanalytic metapsychology is often bound by the historical and cultural normative doxa in which it is situated, especially when it comes to the thorny issue of trans identities. As Evzonas points out, it is no mere coincidence that Freud identified the *trouble générateur* behind Schreber's psychotic complaints as a case of "repressed homosexuality." In a similar way, one of psychoanalysis's founding myths—the Oedipus complex—rather than constituting a transcendental cornerstone of psychosexual development, is more likely to be a contingent mythical fiction whose main function is to restrain the anarchy of the primary partial drives. Evzonas thoughtfully cites Jean Laplanche's indictment of the Oedipal complex as not situated "on the side of the repressed but rather on that of the repressing" (Laplanche 2003: 212). Evzonas concludes by offering some therapeutic suggestions for psychoanalysis to overcome its countertransferential transphobia.

In the first chapter of the second section, "Psychoanalysis and the Philosophy of Truth," Mladen Dolar's "Sophist's Choice" opens with the founding choice of philosophy: that between true knowledge and its semblance, truth and the rhetoric of discursive persuasion, or between philosophy and its inner perversion, in other words, sophistry. There seems to be a choice to be made between these opposing terms, a choice that also runs through psychoanalysis: discourse vs. matheme, the feminine side of senseless enjoyment vs. the sturdy masculine logic of formalization, *lalangue* vs. language. This division is equally present in two different guises of Lacan: Jaques the sophist vs. Jacques the philosopher. It soon becomes clear that this choice should be resisted. The Lacanian-Hegelian wager is to stress their speculative identity: not by sublating their incommensurable difference, but by positing the identity of their own internal divisions. *Lalangue* is another way to point toward the paradoxes of logic, just as the impasses of formalization indicate the truth of *lalangue*. Psychoanalysis empathically chooses for this nonchoice, safeguarding its errant truth from the conceptual oppositions in which that truth is nevertheless most faithfully expressed.

In chapter 9, Augusto Ismerin continues this conceptual division in his "Consistency and Contradiction: The Two Logical Aspects of Truth in Psychoanalysis." Ismerin sets out to investigate an unresolved (or perhaps unresolvable) tension between classical and paraconsistent paradigms of truth within psychoanalysis. The tension derives from the fact that psychoanalysis seems wedded to both paradigms at once. On the one hand, unconscious productions seem to defy traditional consistency demands—it is at the essence of what psychoanalysis calls a symptom that contradiction must be allowed, hence pointing to the need to embrace some sort of paraconsistent approach of truth. On the other hand, some of psychoanalysis's predictions are straightforward enough to be subsumed under the classical heading of traditional logic: either a patient is neurotic or not, either the name of the father is present or foreclosed. Ismerim shows how this epistemological contradiction survives in contemporary forms of Lacanian theory: conventional post-Lacanianism has continued the paraconsistent strategy of Lacan, seeking to develop a specific epistemology able to account for the peculiar behavior of truth in the psychoanalytic domain; Lacanian neuropsychoanalysis, on the other hand, emphasizes its compatibility with ordinary empirical science and shares its traditional conception of truth. Ismerim concludes his chapter by pointing out the question that confronts psychoanalysis today: What would solving or preserving this contradiction within psychoanalysis mean and entail?

This section concludes with Jasper Feyaerts's essay "On Saying More than One Knows: Psychoanalysis, Truth, and Subjectivity," which revisits Freud's ambiguous therapeutic advice "to tell more than one knows" in the analytic cure. Feyaerts situates this advice within the conceptual couple of "enunciation" and "enunciated" emphasized by Lacan to present four successive theses on the nature of truth, subjectivity, and the unconscious in psychoanalytic theory. The criterion for truth in psychoanalysis is specifically determined by its conceptualization of the speaking subject: only for a subject internally divided by its own speech acts would it make sense to propose a dialectical opposition between knowledge and truth. On the other hand, the nature of this truth is strictly determined by the disjunctive form of the speaking subject. Feyaerts concludes by elaborating the difference of this psychoanalytic conception of truth from both classical correspondence theories and the phenomenological principle of appearance qua appearance.

The third section, "Toward a Psychoanalytic Politics of Truth," opens with the chapter "The Politics of Truth and Its Transformation in Neoliberalism," in which Nelson da Silva Junior, following Hannah Arendt's entrustment to the intellectual of responding to what is seemingly incomprehensible in a given society, offers such an attempt in relation to the most recent elections in Brazil. Silva Junior revisits Foucault's elucidation of the "politics of truth" to explain the sudden rise of conservatism and moralism in Brazilian society. Following Nietzsche's critique of Western idealism, Foucault's approach to truth is strictly materialistic: truth is not approached as something transcendent or absolute, but as radically worldly and inseparable from the political and historical context in which it is situated. Furthering this materialistic principle, Silva Junior describes how common man has become the primary figure who is appealed to in order to decide and discern what is true. Neoliberalism elevates common man as the new subject-supposed-to-know to strengthen its pastoral hold on individuals, effectively submitting subjects to its political project by offering them the sentiments of free choice and individual freedom. Within this paradoxical form of domination, as Silva Junior shows, the legitimization of truth by common man, and his recognition as an actor who should autonomously decide on the truth of his situation, is a central effective mechanism. Yet this comes at a certain price: the individual experience of knowing the truth seems inseparable from the constant intuition of being deceived. Therefore, the form of knowledge handed down to common man is essentially paranoid: all established knowledge must be put under suspicion, even if that means denying what is in man's best interest.

In chapter 12, Paulo Beer's "Resistance and Truth: Between Psychoanalysis and Politics" offers a comprehensive overview of the dynamic and dialectically related concepts of truth and resistance in the works of both Freud and Lacan. Through his close reading of these central concepts and their evolution in psychoanalytic theory, Beer seeks to address the critique (famously put forward by Adolf Grünbaum, among others) according to which psychoanalysis—through its therapeutic focus on the interpretation of resistance—would involve yet another form of power domination, effectively creating the problems it suggests to cure. Beer argues that resistance in psychoanalysis is not merely considered an obstacle to treatment, but as a dialectical concept that minimally implies three moments: "truth *of* resistance," "resistance *to* truth," and "truth *as* resistance." In the latter moment, truth entails resistance to the idea that a final form of desire, of the self, of knowledge, would be possible. As Beer demonstrates, the articulation between truth and resistance only leads to the critique regarding the interpretation of resistance (and psychoanalysis) as a tool for domination within a particularly reductive reading. Formulating their dialectical intertwinement therefore shows itself to be an eminently critical procedure, one in which truth nevertheless resists.

The next chapter—Vladimir Safatle's "Revolution and Liquidation of Transference: The Subjective Destitution as a Procedure of Social Emancipation"—provides a reading of Lacan's seminal contribution with respect to the nature of a psychoanalytically informed politics, in other words, "Proposition of October 9, 1967 on the Psychoanalyst of the School." Safatle argues that Lacan's decision to eventually dissolve the school he established was closely informed by the problematic of the end of an analysis and the accompanying dissolution of transference. The central question that guides Lacan's reflections in this text is how psychoanalysis can contribute to a form of structural emancipation that is truly revolutionary and escapes the conservative tendency toward repetition and the restoration of previous orders. Safatle points out that this is the political importance of the concept of the "analytic act": it allows us to think the formal dimension of transformation and change that a revolution must produce to be recognized as such. This transformation is not primarily about attaining new knowledge or about gaining autonomy and independence, but rather follows the displacement and depersonalization that the experience of jouissance entails. Because of its essentially transgressive character with respect to the symbolic, the recognition and assumption of enjoyment can give rise to a transformative and singular destitution surpassing the existing orders. Moreover, it is in this light, as Safatle argues, that Lacan's act to dissolve the school should be revaluated: not as attesting to a mere failure of institutional organization, but as pointing toward the truth of clinical revolutions.

The book concludes with Samo Tomšič's "Critique of Epistemic Economy (Fragments)." The chapter offers a reading of psychoanalysis's troubled relationship with the natural sciences, revolving around a tension that mobilizes the concepts of truth, knowledge, and the role of science in the modern world. Tomšič elucidates the Lacanian-Koyréan epistemic perspective on scientific discourse as an autonomous, anonymous, and foreign body that abstracts from human knowledge and its ideological position as the centering subject. Modern science's modus operandi consists in an accumulative process of knowledge extraction wherein the subject ceases to appear as a speaking being. In this way, as Tomšič shows, the natural sciences intersect with the modern economic regime in which the same extractivist logic can be discerned. As in Silva Junior's contribution, Tomšič emphasizes how the subjective effect of this extraction leads to a paradoxical increase of uncertainty and lack of knowledge. *Plus-de-savoir*, the dialectical intertwinement of knowledge and unknowledge, emerges at the core of the process of both scientific and capitalist accumulation. At the same time, the Lacanian-Koyréan epistemology allows for the conception of the "split of science," science's antagonistic impossibility, as an emancipatory horizon for the formation and transformation of subjectivity.

The Truths of Psychoanalysis intervenes in current debates about the nature, value, and efficacy of truth; its ideological appearance, challenge, and deformation; its modern and postmodern rendition; its relation and opposition to (self-) knowledge; its troubled link with ideals regarding authenticity and identity; and its transformative and political potential, while also offering a comprehensive overview and reassessment of the status and role of truth in psychoanalytic theory and clinical practice. All essays in this book aim to demonstrate that psychoanalysis, because of its complex, layered, and at times perturbed relation with truth, might be considered the discipline par excellence from which the contemporary refractory appearance of truth can be productively clarified and revalued. If Lacan's famous answer in *Science and Truth* to the question whether psychoanalysis is a science consisted in boldly claiming that psychoanalysis may in fact enlighten us about what we should understand by science, we hope that the current collection of essays will tempt the reader to consider a similar answer with regard to the notion of truth.

References

Eyers, T. 2012. "Bachelard, Lacan and the Impurity of Scientific Formalization." *Paragraph* 35(3): 320–337.

Freud, S. 1950[1895]. *Project for a Scientific Psychology. The Standard Edition*, 1.

Freud, S. 1950[1937]. *Constructions in analysis. The Standard Edition*, 23.

Lacan, J. 1993. "The Psychoses." In *The Seminar of Jacques Lacan: Book III 1955–1956*, edited by J. A. Miller. London: Routledge.

Lacan, J. 1988. *The Seminar 1954–1955, Book II, The Ego in Freud's Theory and in the Technique of Psychoanalysis*. Cambridge: Cambridge University Press.

Lacan, J. 2006. *Écrits*. London: Norton.

Lacan, J. 2015. *Transference. Seminar VIII*. Translated by B. Fink. Cambridge: Polity Press.

Laplanche, J. 2003. "Trois acceptions du mot « inconscient » dans la cadre de la théorie de la séduction généralisée." In *Sexual: La Sexualité élargie au sens freudien*, 195–214. Paris: PUF, 2007.

Masson, J. M. 1985. *The Complete Letters of Sigmund Freud to Wilhelm Fliess 1887–1904*. Translated and edited by J. M. Masson. Cambridge, MA: Harvard University Press.

Mock, J. 2014. *Redefining Realness: My Path to Womanhood, Identity, Love, and So Much More*. New York: Atria Books.

Sartre, J. P. 1979[1972]. *Between Existentialism and Marxism Situations VIII and IX*. New York: Morrow Quill.

Tomšič, S. 2012. "Three Notes on Science and Psychoanalysis." *Filozofski Vestnik* 33: 127–144.

Verhaeghe, P. 1996. *Does the Woman Exist? From Freud's Hysteric to Lacan's Feminine*. London: Rebus Press.

PART 1

Truth in Psychoanalytic Theory and Practice

Chapter 1

The Virtue of Truth, Ignorance, and Love
A Reflection on Lacan's Theory of the Subject

Carin Franzén

In *Seminar VIII* (Transference), Lacan points to the dimension of truth as essential in psychoanalytic practice by a commentary on Plato's *Symposium*. Lacan uses the ancient text to clarify what is at stake in the analytic relationship, and it is rather obvious that it also regards the function of discourse in this "talking cure" when he says that what Socrates "brings out or detaches, is that discourse engenders the dimension of truth" (Lacan 2015: 80). Yet, from the beginning of this seminar on transference from 1960 to 1961, Lacan makes clear that the dimension of truth engendered by discourse is related to ignorance. For instance, he underlines that "Socrates claims to know nothing, except how to recognize what love is" (Lacan 2015: 8), and, talking about the philosopher's famous elenctic method, he states: "To show everyone that they know nothing is a path that is in itself revealing—it reveals a virtue which, in its finest successes, does not always succeed" (Lacan 2015: 80). An idea of the character of this virtue is also given by Lacan when he compares himself with Socrates: "As for what it means to love and to know what it is to love, I must at least, like Socrates, be able to credit myself with knowing something about it" (Lacan 2015: 16). To be sure, this specific Socratic knowledge does not impede Lacan from referring to a long philosophical and literary Western tradition that speaks about love and that precisely has Plato's *Symposium* as one of its cornerstones.

In this chapter, I would like approach the question of the relation between truth, ignorance, and love in Lacan's work by returning to some of his many historical references. I will also try to demonstrate how Lacan's way of historicizing the psychoanalytic theory of the subject differs from Foucault's assessment of the history of Western subjectivity, namely, as formed by Christianity and its obligation to confess and to put one's truth into discourse. While Foucault defines this self-technique as "one of the basic forms of our obedience" in his Collège de France course from 1979 to 1980 *On the Government of the Living* (2014: 313), Lacan's many turns to history—to ancient philosophers, medieval poets and theologians, early modern moralists, etc.—seem to highlight a constitutive limit at the core of this very obligation.

Michel Senellart, editor of Foucault's course, points out that

> truth-telling about oneself in the framework of the psychoanalytic relationship cannot be reduced to the Christian practice of confession, as if the former derived directly from the second. They are truth acts that no doubt present structural analogies [...] but which nonetheless fall under very different regimes of truth. (Foucault 2014: 354)

I would like to highlight the specificity of the psychoanalytic regime of truth by demonstrating how Lacan's theory of the subject puts ignorance in relation to a dimension of truth that only love can harbor and transform into an ethical and political virtue. In this way, I would also like to suggest that Lacanian psychoanalysis could serve as a resistance to the imperatives of enhancements that surrounds us in neoliberal society. In other words, if the neoliberal subject is driven by ideas of perfection or fulfillment, the subject of the unconscious can work as a springboard for a thinking that resists these fatiguing demands.

As a basis and frame for this suggestion, I will take Lacan's uses of courtly love and its relation to a "locus of truth." This term appears in a text paying homage to Marguerite Duras (Lacan 1987), in which Lacan also refers to Marguerite de Navarre, who he mentions both in *Seminar VII* (Lacan 1992: 131) and *Seminar VIII* (Lacan 2015: 25, 29). As a matter of fact, these female writers could be said to play a similar role for Lacan as Diotima does for Socrates in the *Symposium*—the woman from whom the philosopher claims to have learned the truth about love. At any rate, by focusing on Lacan's indirect way of dealing with two female writers that appropriate courtly love in ways that differ from the male subject and his desire—according to Lacan's more explicit explanation of this medieval code to which I also will return—I hope to better clarify the relationship between truth, ignorance, and love in the theory of the subject of the unconscious.

Ignorance and Love

"Alas! I thought I knew so much about love, but really, I know so little," sings the Occitan troubadour Bernart de Ventadorn in the twelfth century, expressing a certainty of not knowing that could be paralleled with Socrates's reversed insistence on his fundamental ignorance of everything except love in the *Symposium*. The troubadour's love of a Lady who never responds leaves him in a state of ignorance and loss that only increases his love and desire, as the lines goes:

Alas! I thought I knew so much
about love, but really, I know so little.
For I cannot keep myself from loving
her from whom I shall have no favor.
She has stolen from me my heart, myself,
herself and all the world.
When she took herself from me, she left me nothing
but desire and a longing heart
(Bernart de Ventadorn 1962: 168)

The Lady, according to the courtly code, gives her lover nothing, and it turns out that the lover, left with "desire and a longing heart," ends up (after a long complaint about Ladies' general mercilessness) deciding to hide from love: "I forsake and renounce singing, and I seek shelter from joy and love" (Bernart de Ventadorn 1962: 168).

The courtly love code has often been understood as an expression of male desire in a social context in which women are subjugated to men. As medievalist Howard Bloch puts it: "the deprecation of the feminine lurks just below the surface of the courtly idealization of women" (Bloch 1991: 148). Or with Slavoj Žižek's more psychoanalytic description, the courtly codes' "elevation of woman to the sublime object of love equals her debasement into the passive stuff or screen for the narcissistic projection of the male ego-ideal" (Žižek 1994: 108). However, instead of going deeper into the misogynic aspect of courtly love, I would like to stress the fact that the code was also appropriated by premodern female writers and that it functioned in a *dialogical* discourse in which women played central roles. From this perspective, the troubadour's complaints about a Lady from whom the lover "shall have no favor" and who "left me nothing" appear as discursive elements in a game of love in which the position of the Lady illustrates rather well Lacan's definition of love in *Seminar VIII*: "that love is giving what you don't have" (Lacan 2015: 34).

Furthermore, the troubadour, with his "desire and longing heart," who knows so little about love, could serve to highlight the analysand's relation to the analyst, namely, as a desire for a subject-supposed-to-know. As Lacan puts it in *Seminar XX*: "I love the person I assume to have knowledge" (Lacan 1999: 67). In this sense, the Lady's position could also be equated with the analyst, or the subject-supposed-to-know, but who in fact could be said to occupy a Socratic position: if he "knows anything, if there is anything about which he is not ignorant, it is about matters of love" (Lacan 2015: 137). If we continue this comparison between the codes of courtly love and the analytic relationship, we can also say that the troubadour's desire to be loved by the Lady parallels the fact that the analysand's desire is also "to be found lovable" (Fink 2016: 46). As Lacan puts it, "the subject is introduced as worthy of interest and love," but he underlines that, on a latent or structural level, the analysand's object of desire is still "in the Other" and that this desire is related to "his non-science," or his ignorance (Lacan 2015: 193).

What kind of paradoxical relation of knowledge and ignorance are we dealing with when one does know "so little" of love and the other is supposed to know at least about "matters of love"? Or, as Bruce Fink puts it: "If the lover and the beloved have anything in common, it is that neither one knows something that seems to be of very great importance" (Fink 2016: 40).

I would like to suggest that, what is sensed in this kind of mutual ignorance or "non-science" (Lacan 2015: 193), is the effects of a constitutive limit or lack in the subject of the unconscious that is articulated in a beautiful way by Bernart de Ventadorn when he sings of the lovers' complaints and decision to seek shelter from love, joy, and songs. As a matter of fact, in *Seminar VIII*, this foundational lack it further enlightened by the myth of Psyche and Amor, as we find it in the Roman author Apuleius's novel *The Golden Ass*.

A Foundational Myth

As this story goes in a Lacanian framework, Psyche first dwells in a harmony that could be equated with a kind a paradise where all needs and desires are fulfilled—a dream of completion reminiscent of a time before culture and language. The subject's entrance into this symbolic order comes with a loss, which the myth indicates when Psyche violates the prohibition from seeing Amor and lights up the bedroom. From that moment, Psyche is separated from Amor. And Lacan reads her following quest for reunion as "nothing other than the relations between the soul and desire" (Lacan 2015: 225).

Thus, this crucial transition from harmony to loss in the myth can be used to illustrate symbolic castration as a condition for the subject, which Lacan here describes in more premodern terms:

> The birth of the soul is, in both the universal and in the particular, for all of us and for each of us, an historic moment. It is from this moment on that the dramatic story with which we are faced unfolds in all its consequences. (Lacan 2015: 227)

And these consequences are nothing other than the search for completion of a desire that no longer stays in its place.

As Lacan retells the myth, Psyche's adventures begin "at the moment at which the desire that fulfilled her slips away and takes flight" (Lacan 2015: 226). Thus, if symbolic castration is a condition for the becoming of the subject, it could also be argued that there is a denial of this condition in contemporary neoliberal discourse, which creates an illusion that everything is possible, it is "only up to you to fix it." I will come back to this contemporary form of subjectivity at the end of my chapter.

What symbolic castration does, and what the Psyche and Amor myth demonstrates in Lacan's reading, is the "endless perpetuation of the subject's desire" (Lacan 2005: 262) that not even the sexual relationship can remedy. To quote Lacan's famous formulation from *Seminar XX*, "there's no such thing as a sexual relationship" (Lacan 1999: 34). Love, in its many forms and disguises, comes to make up for this lack and endless desire, but it does not always succeed in doing so.

To outline a consequence of Lacan's aporetic formulations of love as giving what we do not have and of the absence of sexual relationship—to love is to make manifest one's latent lack to another subject that is looking for completion of its own lack. Needless to say, the adventures of Psyche are therefore often misled by dreams of fulfillment or completeness of different sorts. These misleading paths are nevertheless crucial in the analytical experience, which Jean-Pierre Klotz defines as follows:

> Lacan emphasizes the dimension of love that lies or misleads, suggesting that this misleading belongs, as such, to the dimension of truth. Lacan develops the idea that it is impossible to encounter the dimension of truth without being misled. Love is the point of encounter, i.e., transference is the point of encounter which introduces the dimension of truth into analytic practice itself. (Klotz 1995: 92)

I will not expound upon this highly dense quote, but I use it as an inspiration to further explore the dimension of truth in psychoanalytic experience by returning to courtly love as a discursive form that can mislead but also function as a "point of encounter" where precisely the subject of the unconscious reveals itself. Now, I will more closely examine Lacan's references to Marguerite de Navarre and Marguerite Duras to make this specific dimension of truth more tangible.

Love and Truth

Lacan refers to the twentieth-century author and the Renaissance queen on different occasions. He does it most explicitly in a text paying homage to Marguerite Duras, in which he says that both women through their texts bear witness of a certain form of love that he designates with the term *charity* (Lacan, 1987: 128):

> It seems quite natural to me to find in Marguerite Duras that severe and militant charity that animates the stories of Marguerite d'Angoulême, when they can be read free from those prejudices which are intended solely to screen us off from their locus of truth.

To "free" the stories from prejudices, he uses historian Lucien Febvre's study of Marguerite de Navarre (her name after her marriage to Henry II). According to Lacan, Febvre is the one who modifies the reading of her stories as "gallant" by tracing them back to the "techniques of the convention of courtly love" before they were made into a "mere fictional account" in sentimental novels (Lacan 1987: 128).

In his study, Febvre stresses courtly love as cultural impediment to the realization of desire by what he calls a negative ideal—that is, by not satisfying it sexually. Thus, Febvre sees the courtly love code as a way to handle dissatisfaction, and he calls this an "ethical revolution" in Western civilization (Febvre 1944: 228). In *Seminar VII*, on the ethics of psychoanalysis, Lacan draws on Febvre when he assesses the ethical function of courtly love in terms of a specific technique that counteracts "the purposes of the pleasure principle" (Lacan 1992: 152), through a postponement of the imaginary wish for completion. Sentimental novels and, more generally, romantic love could therefore be said to be misleading in this context by representing completion as a goal—the happy end of every romantic myth or story—or, as Lacan puts it in *Seminar VIII*, "the romantic confusion concerning this sublimation" (Lacan 2015: 87). Here, Lacan is also referring to the idea that love is to find your other half, as Aristophanes puts it in the *Symposium*. In other words, while romantic love turns this myth of union into its very essence, the configuration of love in Marguerite Duras's novels and Marguerite de Navarre's novellas articulates a dimension of truth that both seem to have learned from courtly love.

To better understand this truth, let us return to *Seminar XX*, in which Lacan describes this medieval cultural and literary code among the feudal aristocracy. He describes it as a "highly refined way of making up for the absence of the sexual relationship, by feigning that we are the ones who erect an obstacle thereto," making clear that the "we" he is referring to is male: "Courtly love is, for man—in relation to whom the lady is entirely, and in the most servile sense of the word, a subject—the only way to elegantly pull off the absence of the sexual relationship" (Lacan 1999: 69). In this approach, the courtly love code is regarded as a specific solution to the structural lack in the constitution of the subject's desire, which the other is supposed to fulfill. Needless to say, the Lady in courtly love is this other for the desiring male subject.

How, then, is the courtly love code treated by the two Marguerites—by their "strange way of loving," as Lacan writes in his homage (Lacan 1987: 128)—and why do they reveal a dimension of truth while the male troubadours that invented the code just "pull it off" in an elegant manner? I think it is rather clear that it has to do with their responses to and less illusionary way of dealing with the male subject's desire.

From a sociological perspective, it is clear that women have used the idealized figure of the Lady as a support and a protection against social and psychological debasement that is its other side, also pointed out by Lacan: "The lady is entirely and in the most servile sense of the word, a subject" (Lacan 1999: 69).

The position of the Lady in courtly love is a highly debated topic, and feminist readings have assessed the code and its literature as a construction in an antifeminist tradition that, in the final analysis, serves to establish the male subject's ego. As Howard Bloch argues, courtly lyric demonstrates "a desire for the absolute, which [...] subtends a profound wish for identity with the other, for self-identity" (Bloch 1991: 151). To be sure, this "self-identity" is one of the ways that love takes when it serves the interests of the ego.

It is not necessary, however, to reduce the courtly love code to narcissism or to this specific function of male desire. As a matter of fact, in its appropriated forms by female writers, the figure of the Lady or the Other can be understood as the point of encounter where a dimension of truth is introduced. Because, if the male position in courtly love covers up the subject's lack by creating an object—the idealized woman—for his desire, the feminine position in the courtly love code is the impediment to this imaginary dream of fulfillment. And it is clear that it is in this impediment to the imaginary dream of fulfillment that Lacan sees the ethical dimension of courtly eroticism. When female writers, in their appropriation of the courtly love code, reveal this dimension of truth, they also deconstruct "the narcissistic overestimation of the subject, of the subject assumed to reside in the beloved object" (Lacan 2015: 87).

The Process of Love

Courtly love is a main topic in Marguerite de Navarre's collection of stories, the *Heptameron* (posthumously published in 1559). The work is modeled on Boccaccio's *Decameron*, but it is the elevated, Neoplatonic form of love that the author seems to defend throughout the stories. In a male hegemony, this configuration of love also functions as a point of resistance, a part of the interplay of power relations, as in Marguerite de Navarre's tenth novella, in which the courtly setting is evident. Febvre sees this novella as representative of the conception of love in the entire collection (Febvre 1944: 191). In the story, the knight Amador falls in love with Florida and serves her for many years in conformity to the courtly code, but his aim is, from the beginning, to possess the young Lady. When it becomes clear that he wants more than courtly love, Florida says "Alas, Amador! What is it that drives you to seek that which can give you no satisfaction, and to cause me the greatest sorrow anyone could ever cause me? [...] seek that which you know you cannot find" (Marguerite de Navarre 2004: 147). Amador answers by acting out his desire and tries to rape her. At the end of the story, Florida's husband, whom she has been forced to marry, and her lover die, and she chooses to enter a convent. The Lady's choice is a paradigmatic solution to feminine subjugation in medieval and early modern society, but Marguerite de Navarre uses the elevation of love as something more than a social protection against rape and sexual abuse. This can be sensed in the discussions of each novella, where the storytellers play out their judgments of what has been narrated. In the tenth novella, the female audience is, for example, asked "to be less harsh, and not to have so much faith in men that you end up being disappointed when you learn the truth" (Marguerite de Navarre 2004: 152). In other words, the courtly code is conceived as a convention in need of a more concrete or pragmatic experience of the relation between love and power. Paraphrasing Foucault, one can say that the Renaissance queen puts courtly love into a process that impedes it to work as a general system of domination (Foucault 1998: 92). The playful use of the code could furthermore be related to what Lacan calls the ethical dimension of courtly eroticism.

This is a dimension that Lacan also discerns in Marguerite Duras's writing from the modern period. He pays homage to her for making her writing practice converge "with the workings of the unconscious" (Lacan 1987: 124). If this work is not easy to grasp, it is nevertheless clear that, when Duras writes about love and desire, she often criticizes a conception of romantic love as a dream about an everlasting relation in which two become one. Let us take a quotation from her novel *The Lover*, which, in a rather straightforward way, could be said to illustrate that there is no such thing as a sexual relationship. In the scene, we find the narrator as a young girl just after her meeting with the Chinese man—the lover:

> He's desirable. I tell him of this desire. He tells me to wait awhile. Talks to me, says he knew right away, when we were crossing the river, that I'd be like this after my first lover, that I'd love love, he says he knows now I'll deceive him and deceive all the men I'm ever with. (Duras 1997: 42)

Among all the resonances in the quotation, I would like to stress the formulation "I'd love love," which can be traced to Augustine's *Confessions*, in which he states that "I was not in love as yet, but I was in love with love [...] I was looking for something to love, for I was in love with loving" (Augustine 2002: 31), as well as to the tradition of courtly love in which the obstacles to love can be said to "enable the passion to progress" (Rougemont 1983: 42).

When Duras lets the lover in this story inscribe the young girl in these traditional discourses on love, the author nevertheless also turns them around and deconstructs their idealization of love and its object by instead highlighting sexual dissymmetry. To spell it out, one can say that Duras cuts through the symbolic and the imaginary dreams of union, revealing the impossible ground as a condition for every union. On a more general level, Duras's writing—and other discourses that, in this way or another, engender the dimension of truth—have the potential to disrupt postulations of completion or self-identity promoted in a world dominated by an imaginary belief that one can have it all. As Paul Verhaeghe puts it: "We are living in a discourse that tells us that there should be no lack whatsoever, that everything is available, that everything is predictable and controllable" (2019: 17).

As an antidote to such a contemporary situation, Duras's themes of impossible love echo the "severe and militant charity that animates the stories" of Marguerite de Navarre. And I believe that it is this "strange way of loving" that constitutes the dimension of truth that can be revealed in their texts.

Lack and Virtue

In the final analysis, the dimension of truth in psychoanalytic experience points to a lack at the core of the subject and to the aporias that this implies for the subject's desire and love. This lack is also what makes the subject of the unconscious deviate from the dominating truth regime in Western civilization that Foucault connects to Christianity—and that has obedience as its goal:

> The Christian has the truth deep within himself and he is yoked to his deep secret, indefinitely bent over it and indefinitely constrained to show to the other the treasure that his work, thought, attention, conscience, and discourse ceaselessly draw out from it. And by this he shows that putting his own truth into discourse is not just an essential obligation; it is one of the basic forms of our obedience. (Foucault 2014: 313)

I would like to argue that psychoanalysis, instead of being a part of this truth regime and its modern vicissitudes, can offer a resistance to it, because it defines the dimension of truth not as one's true self hidden in the folds of the heart, but as a lack. And I think that this impediment to confession is also what can make it a counterdiscourse to neoliberal demands of self-realization, perfection, and performance, which result in increasing rates of anxiety and depression.

To wrap up, I would like to return to another of Lacan's aporetic formulas, namely, his famous maxim from *Seminar VII*: "From an analytic point of view, the only thing one can be guilty of is having given ground relative to one's desire" (Lacan 1992: 319). And I would like to understand it in the way Alain Badiou invites us to do when he says that it is about not giving up "on that part of yourself that you do not know" (Badiou 2001: 47).

However, unlike Badiou, Lacan connects desire and the dimension of truth that it indicates to discourse: "The fact that the symbolic is located outside of man is the very notion of the unconscious" (Lacan 2006: 392). That is also why psychoanalytic experience can lead, not to self-knowledge, but to transformation.

Thus, the aim of this reflection on truth, ignorance, and love in Lacan's theory of the subject—through some of his historical and literary references—was also to outline the shape of a virtue that can enable us to counteract actual neoliberal subject formations. In other words, the recognition of the subject of the unconscious as a way of not giving up the dimension of truth in love.

References

Augustine of Hippo. 2002. *The Confessions of St. Augustine*. Translated by A. C. Outler. New York: Dover Publications, Inc.

Bloch, R. H. 1991. *Medieval Misogyny and the Invention of Western Romantic Love*. Chicago: University of Chicago Press.

Badiou, A. 2001. *Ethics. An Essay on the Understanding of Evil*. Translated by P. Hallward. London: Verso.

Bloch, H. 1991. *Medieval Misogyny and the Invention of Western Romantic Love*. Chicago: University of Chicago Press.

Duras, M. 1997. *The Lover*. Translated by B. Bray. New York: Pantheon Books.

Febvre, L. 1944. *Autour de l'Heptaméron: Amour sacré, amour profane*. Paris: Gallimard.

Fink, B. 2016. *Lacan on Love. An Exploration of Lacan's Seminar VIII, Transference*. Cambridge: Polity Press.

Foucault, M. 2014. *On the Government of the Living: Lectures at the Collège de France 1979–1980*. Edited by Michel Senellart. Translated by Graham Burchell. Hampshire: Plagrave Macmillan.

Foucault, M. 1998. *The History of Sexuality: The Will to Power*. Translated by Robert Hurley. London: Penguin.

Klotz, J-P. 1995. "Passionate Dimension of Transference." In *Reading Seminar XI*, edited by R. Feldstein et al., 91–97. Albany: State University of New York Press.

Lacan, J. 1987. "Homage to Marguerite Duras, on 'Le ravissement de Lol V. Stein,'" translated by P. Connor. In *Marguerite Duras*. San Francisco: City Light Books: 122–129.

Lacan, J. 1992. *The Seminar VII: The Ethics of Psychoanalysis* Translated by Dennis Porter. London: Routledge.

Lacan, J. 1999. *Encore. Seminar XX*. Translated by B. Fink. New York: W. W: Norton & Company.

Lacan, J. 2006. Écrits. Translated by Bruce Fink. New York: W. W: Norton & Company.

Lacan, J. 2015. *Transference. Seminar VIII*. Translated by Bruce Fink. Cambridge: Polity Press.

de Navarre, M. 2004. *The Heptameron*. Translated by P. Chilton. London: Penguin Books.

Nichols, Stephen G. et al., eds. 1962. *The Songs of Bernart de Ventadorn*. Chapel Hill: University of North Carolina Press.

de Rougemont, D. 1983. *Love in the Western World*. Translated by M. Belgion. Princeton: Princeton University Press.

Verhaeghe, P. 2019. "The Function and the Field of Speech and Language in Psychoanalysis: A Commentary on Lacan's 'Discourse de Rome.'" *Contours Journal* 5. https://www.sfu.ca/humanities-institute/contours/LaConference/paper1/.

Žižek, S. 1994. *The Metastases of Enjoyment: Six Essays on Woman and Causality*. London: Verso.

Chapter 2

Where the Truth Lies in Psychoanalysis: The Role of Fictional Construction

Derek Humphreys

In his letter to Fliess addressed September 21, 1897, Freud affirms "that it was impossible to distinguish between truth and fiction invested with affect" (Freud in Masson 1985: 264–265). We can thus conclude that Freud's interest in the development of the notion of *Phantasie* in draft M (Freud in Masson 1985: 245–248) is not based on its possibility to grant access to a traumatic event or to any reality, but rather on its fictional character and the role of this "fictionality" in psychoanalysis. It is on this "constructed" truth that psychoanalysis can operate. Given the tension between truth and fiction as a keystone of the epistemological and praxeological revolution introduced by Freud, the aim of this paper is to discuss the concept of "phantasy" and the importance of its narrative effects.

Truth and Fiction in Constructions in Analysis

The problem of the relationship between truth and fiction is clearly posed in Freud's text *Constructions in Analysis*, which starts with the general question of what psychoanalytic work is all about. Freud contests the accusation that the psychoanalytic method is somehow arbitrary in treating its patients according to the motto "Heads I win. Tails you lose" (Freud 1937: 257): "That is to say, if the patient agrees with us, then the interpretation is right; but if he contradicts us, that is only a sign of resistance, which again shows that we are right." Freud takes this objection as an opportunity to reflect on the methods of the psychoanalytical cure and to question the importance of the truth of a hypothesis in psychoanalysis. To open up the conceptualization of psychoanalysis, Freud makes an appeal to metaphors derived from the fields of construction and archaeology. These metaphors shape the concept of truth in psychoanalysis throughout the article. Freud compares the methods of psychoanalysis with the procedures of archaeology—raising the image of a broken vase whose individual pieces are to be found and completely assembled following an original pattern. However, unlike the archaeologist who deals with "destroyed objects," the analyst's interest is centered on "something that is still alive" (Freud 1937: 257), which can take shape only in the dynamic relationship between the patient and the analyst. Freud affirms that the transferential relationship is the "raw material" (Freud 1937: 258) of the analysis from which we "have to put together what we are in search of [*das Gewünschte*]." The *Standard Edition* translates "*das Gewünschte*" in terms of a "searching," but, literally, Freud speaks here of something "desired." This desired thing, Freud continues, is "a picture of the patient`s forgotten years that shall be alike trustworthy and in all essential respects complete" (Freud 1937: 258). The task of the analyst in this relationship is "to make-out what has been forgotten from the traces which it has left behind or, more correctly, to *construct* it" (Freud 1937: 258–259).

The truth of psychoanalysis is thus not absolute, but rather a constructed or reconstructed one, which is always only a "preliminary work" in a dynamic process whose end is difficult, perhaps impossible, to determine. This idea is confirmed in *The Interpretation of Dreams* (Freud 1900) and the *Fragment of an Analysis of a Case of Hysteria*, which was published in 1905. Only a connected reading of both texts enables a full understanding of Freud's practice of interpretation. In fact, Dora's case can be read as a critique and an enhancement of the *Interpretation of Dreams* published five years earlier. In this text, Freud does not give up on the ambition of a complete deciphering of the dream narrative by means of free association, but he puts it into perspective by discovering a second element. In working with hysterical patients, Freud repeatedly came to a point at which analysis stagnated, even though the associative decoding was carried out to complete satisfaction. It occurs that the mere process of interpreting (*deuten*) is not enough to come to an end with the psychic processes underlying the dream formations. Freud names this second element, which had been missing up to this point, *erraten*, discerning. It is based solely on the analyst's intuition regarding the process of transference. In fact, the transferential experience, which intervenes when interpretation necessarily fails, cannot be interpreted within itself. This results in a paradox: every interpretation contains a constitutive part of something not interpreted, and that alone decides whether interpretation succeeds. "Transference," writes Freud, "which seems ordained to be the greatest obstacle to psychoanalysis, becomes its most powerful ally if its presence can be detected [*erraten*] each time and explained [übersetzt] to the patient" (Freud 1905: 117). The English translation of the *Standard Edition* is, on this point, not quite precise. Freud speaks in this sentence of *erraten* (making out) and übersetzen (translating) and thereby introduces a moment of contingency, affective concern, and necessary distortion into the seamless chain of logical arguments on which Freud's previous attempts to fully interpret dreams were based. It is therefore only coherent that the starting point and central issue of Freud's text is the discussion of the significance of the patient's "yes" or "no" in the analytical process. In the course of his claim, Freud opens the binary construction of affirmation and negation, of right and wrong, to a multifaceted game in which a "yes" can mean a "no" and a "no" can mean a "yes," and the rigid binary leads to a variety of interpretive options. This leeway opened up by the transferential experience is also the place of literary creativity, in which we can take "a carp of truth" by means of a "bait of falsehood." The "making out" begins when the surface of the discourse becomes pervious, the homogeneity of the narrative is broken through by a minor accident, an external, situation-related coincidence that finds its way into speaking. In this sense, the problem of interpretation, as Freud puts it, is fascinating because of the attempt to hold on to a concept of truth that, at the same time, opens up to contingency.

To return to *Constructions in Analysis*, the dynamics of poetry and truth, to quote the Goethean topos, which comes to a head in Freud's use of the metaphor of archaeology, is also reflected by the rhetorical structure of the text. The affirmation of comparisons, at this point, between archaeology and psychoanalysis, which are carried out in detail but implode in a final movement that simultaneously destroys the text and opens it to something else, is a typical way of proceeding for Freud in most of his writings. Freud ruins his own metaphor when he writes, at the end of his article, that the essential difference with the archaeologist is that "psychical objects are incomparably more complicated than the excavator's material ones and that we have insufficient knowledge of what we may expect to find, since their finer structure contains so much that is still mysterious" (Freud 1937: 260). A more resolute way to contradict his own initial metaphors is scarcely conceivable. The paragraph about the methods of archaeology presupposes an idea of completeness and achievement reached by following an interpretative process that systematically dives deeper into hidden layers. The object in psychoanalysis remains impenetrable and elusive. Freud's rhetorical turn suggests that the psychoanalytic method begins precisely where the metaphor of archaeology ends. Especially in *Constructions in Analysis*, but actually in all of Freud's writings, these two logics are at work—on the one hand, a progressive optimism aiming at complete enlightenment, and on the other hand, the idea of the absolute impenetrability and darkness of psychic processes—constantly working against and alongside each other.[1] In a way, the text performs the tension between *deuten* and *erraten* outlined in the previous paragraph. In this irreducible tension between logical and figurative elements, which compels the reader to repeatedly question the interpretation of what is being read, lies the literary quality of Freud's texts. It turns out that this interpretation is itself a figure of the text, a result of its specific rhetorical structure. In Freud, the contradictory meanings that exist within the text are at the same time dependent on each other and mutually exclusive. Following Paul de Man, this aporetic semantics, which always leads the text to the abyss of its own meaning and holds it there, is its literary core.

This deeply ambivalent description of the truth in interpretation can be related to Peter Szondi's reflections on the epistemological potential of philology. In his fundamental study *On Textual Understanding* (1978), Szondi explicitly turns against the idea of philology as a "science" dealing with a stable knowledge and clearly defined objects. He repeatedly insists that the subject of literary criticism is a specific one that is not given, but constantly recreated in the act of reading. Philology as the "art of interpretation" would thus be a knowledge that is constantly renewed in the concrete confrontation with the literary text: "The philological knowledge has a dynamic moment [...] because it exists only in the constant confrontation with the text, in the uninterrupted reduction of knowledge to understanding, to the comprehension of the poetic word" (Szondi 1978: 263). This definition of "knowledge as perpetuated understanding" (*Wissen als perpetuierte Erkenntnis*) seems to be close to Freud's concept of construction in its paradoxical claim to truth. According to Szondi, the interpretation of a poem is by no means intended to decipher the mystery of the poem and to expose it once and for all. Rather, the interpretation would be to point out its secret—to describe it, to go around it, to touch it without breaking it. The poem, writes Szondi, is a lock that springs open in a moment of successful reading and reveals something of its secret, but soon snaps again to only reopen in an upcoming and necessarily different reading. Nothing about this is arbitrary. Szondi's text revolves around a determination of the relationship between subjective interpretation and the objective, factual truth of the textual material. Szondi radically claims that the *trouvaille*, the concrete philological fact, must always be considered as a singularity. In this appreciation of a singularity emerging from the contingency of an encounter, Szondi's so-called "hermeneutical materialism" meets with Freud and applies the dynamic relationship of psychoanalytic interpretation to the reading situation. Of course, the philological fact exists as such, even without the reader—the poem is written, no matter who reads it. However, it becomes a proof, a component of an interpretation and an element of knowledge only in the ever-subjective encounter, in which it emerges as evident.

From a clinical point of view, the only truth of psychoanalysis is that of the symptom. It is by the act of enunciation in which the meaning and the intentionality of the conscious subject stumbles that the unconscious truth, usually called a symptom, emerges in the cure. As in the dream, the meaning of each representation is transformed when it can reintegrate a chaotic cluster without time or meaning, to bring out a new sense in a sort of *cadavre exquis*, an exquisite corps becoming a technical apparatus in its capacity to create new representations, pictures, words. This enunciation, in all its "non-sense," constitutes the truth on which the psychoanalyst's interventions operate.

The latter affirmation seems accurate when it comes to the well-established situation of the session. It seems less clear, though, when we are confronted with experiences not inscribed psychically or which manifest themselves only in transference. This type of situation seems especially interesting when it comes to the truth of psychoanalysis, insofar as it concerns situations in which the theoretical system and the technical apparatus on which the cure usually leans are pushed to its own limits, questioning in other fields the status of truth: that of the symptom that cannot be stated or that cannot yet be recognized as addressed to someone, the symptom that puts the experience of transference at risk. The development of the equivocal truths in the transfer situation require attention to detail.

Truth and the Transferential Experience

Psychoanalysis is, first and foremost, a position: it requires a distance from the certainties of all the instituted and immutable systems of knowledge to remain attentive to the transformations of society, bearing its eye on the singularity of subjective movements related to these phenomena. It thus follows the movements that the subject makes toward others, the cultural productions that the subject addresses to the social environment. It is in this context that we increasingly see the psychoanalytical situation beyond the technically stabilized space of the session, in an effort that responds to the transformations of society, culture, and subjective suffering. The material conditions of the setting—the asymmetry of the demand, the regularity of the sessions, a fixed time and space—are often destabilized, confronting the practitioner with different manifestations of the symptom. The mere reference to a knowledge, even supposed, is not a sufficient condition for the encounter in which the transferential experience can take place. The condition of tracing repetition as a "detorsion" of rhythm, of meaning, of content, requires a material point on which to rely, an *automaton* creating the conditions for the *tuchê*.

To install a psychoanalytic listening capable of resonating the textual dimension of what is said, opening to its unconscious multiple meanings, some basic elements must be identifiable in a fixed manner. In many clinical situations today, we can no longer rely on the "setting" as a guarantor of the context on which we would identify and trace the series of variables that make creative the encounter that we call transference. If this encounter takes place, in spite of everything, it is because another element can expose the heterogeneous series that perform a disjunctive synthesis in the transference when repetition becomes creation. It is on this element of current practice that I propose to focus our attention to think about the question of truth in the psychoanalytical situation.

The main interest of the so-called transference setting is its ability to help us establish a different kind of listening, in which we can follow the linearity of the story and, at the same time, have a surface listening in which we recognize the elements of harmony and disharmony, the poetic and musical aspects that constitute the substance of language. This latter allows us to identify the moments in which the discursive chain stops or jumps unexpectedly in a subtle manifestation of withdrawal, of breakdown, of regression. Thus, if narrativity makes it possible to establish the imaginary continuity of the ego, the materiality of language, on the other hand, allows us to access fragments of a pure present, without projection or perspective; a suspended instant of the present metonymically connected to an instant of the past that remains outside the temporality provided by imaginary continuity. These affectively flat passages without resonance can sometimes be captured in the space of the session and make us react (Botella 2001). However, it is always in the *Nachträglichkeit*—which characterizes the Freudian invention and which involves a fictional narrative, the narrative that makes experience an event—that the analyst's reactions make sense and produce a metaphorical (and therapeutic) effect (Pommier 2016).

This attention to the transferential manifestations associated with the textuality of language constitutes an element of elaboration of the temporality of the isolated enclaves of the narrative, when the experience does not seem to be part of the subject but remains enigmatic in its capacity to determine the present. In these situations, the narrativity, defined as the organization of a series of discontinuous experiences of reality in a fiction, loses its internal coherence, producing a frozen image. In the case of Lucy, this loss of consistency resulted in a blind adherence to a fiction, accompanied by a strong physical suffering.

Lucy, thirty years old, who had just started dating someone when I first received her, complained of unbearable pain during sex. She rapidly explained that she has been treated for a long time for recurrent and persistent gynecological infections that do not respond to medical treatment. She often looked for some relief in osteopathy, natural medicine, and a variety of exercises and massages. At the beginning of this work, I had to get used to this sharing of ills between several therapists. During the first session, she told the story of a rape, which she associated with the origin of her symptoms. Over time, I noticed that the narrative of rape was quickly presented in the encounter with her different therapists; as if, in her search for an answer to her symptoms, she had established a kind of causal linearity in which the somatic manifestation appeared to be the permanent painful effect of a traumatic event.

The account of the traumatic experience associated with the presentation and the origin of the symptoms was precise and detailed: at seventeen, when she was chatting with her boyfriend in a car parked in an uncrowded area, a man with pantyhose pulled over his head threatened the couple with a gun and sexually abused her. Finally, the man left, making fun of the young couple. Despite her shame and fear, Lucy decided to go to the police station, where she had to describe the traumatic scene several times, including in front of her father, then recognize the attacker among a group of men, causing her to feel like she was the victim of a sadistic and mocking trick that went on endlessly. Crisis psychotherapy was suggested to accompany her during the investigation, the confrontation with the aggressor, the trial, and even beyond. She seemed to have developed a strong attachment to this psychotherapist, who accompanied her for over a year. Even after the end of the psychotherapy, Lucy continued to visit her from time to time.

The narrative of the traumatic episode was probably constructed in this crisis therapy. It allowed her to organize a continuity from a series of scattered, discontinuous, and disorganized sensations experienced in the traumatic scene. With the construction, in crisis psychotherapy, of this "narrative knot," which served to give meaning to the traumatic experience—or at least an order and a continuity in relation to the ego—any new solicitation of the body becomes a symptom. This constructed narrative replaces the trauma, protecting Lucy from the repetition of an experience that she cannot control. If trauma, by definition, leaves no trace but breaks into the psychic apparatus, and thus, any repetition of the event is experienced with the same intensity as the first time, the story gives her the feeling of being able to locate and move away from the terrifying representation.

Freud defined the screen memory (*Deckerinnerung*) as a clear and apparently insignificant image that is used to cover up an unbearable and therefore repressed sexual experience. It is the result of a compromise in which the constructed (fictional) image works as *Decke* (cover, blanket, but also protection). The German word clearly suggests the idea of covering up, as well as secrecy, as when someone helps to cover up a crime, including that which occurs under the duvet: the repressed experience is replaced by this built image, which presents itself as a memory (a false memory). The French and English translations of this notion produce an interesting shift in meaning, in which the imaginary dimension prevails with the introduction of the screen: an invented image is projected on the screen to contain the excess drive. The Real continues to unfold, but the subject is as if captured by the image and therefore protected from the experience. As in a screen memory, the experience of aggression remains suspended, the gaze fixed on a surface on which another reality is organized—an "acceptable" one. The construction of a fictional narrative thus allows a certain management of the excess drive associated with the traumatic event. Lucy seemed to cling to this story, probably hoping to understand something of the elusive dimension of the traumatic experience. This fictitious construction somehow accompanies and also protects her to the point of making it a fixed image of herself with which she identifies.

In a visit to a new therapist during the third year of her analysis, in this case a masseur who first asked her to undress, Lucy said that she quickly decided to get dressed and leave. She said in session, immediately afterward, that she had not wanted to talk about the rape episode, the importance of which seemed to be questioned by this therapist, who was immediately interested in her bodily suffering. This had also introduced a feeling of disagreement with the narrative of the traumatic episode and the need to tell it differently, in a version in which she could recognize herself today.

The three years of analysis that preceded this episode, and which probably made this subjective movement possible, required an enormous amount of work on the reliability of the therapeutic relationship: the presence of a therapist who was always accessible, still alive despite her attacks, was fundamental. The reliability was tested in a context in which she did everything to find out the smallest details of the private life of her analyst and the other persons in therapy with the therapist. This tendency to question and to go beyond the limits of the clinical setting was persistent. In addition to her problems with her self-image, this tendency required face-to-face work. Therapy conducted with the patient on the couch became possible only later, when the sexual came out of the primary infantile dimension, opening up questions about femininity and relation to the other inscribed in the Oedipal context within the psychoanalytical situation. Questions about important infantile fears concerning the unknown interior of the female body and a certain form of masochism could then be raised.

This moment of "thaw," in which she abandoned the protective function of a construction intended to stop the excess drive, seemed possible only when a reliable environment allowed the questioning of the external "objective" reality. By exposing the body to the violence of the drives, Lucy took a step toward the unknown, where the only guarantor of a possible figuration was, indeed, the transferential setting. In the configuration of the transference—first, the presence of another, then the reliability of this presence, and finally its recognition as otherness—the Oedipal reorganization allowed this thaw and the consequent recovery, in the present, of a movement of subjective identity appropriation.

It would not be possible to examine in detail the evolution, step by step, of the new narrative construction of the event. This would require, at each stage, the precise analysis of the transferential aspects involved, the evolution in the content of the sessions, the changes in Lucy's position (the child, the young girl, the adult, the adult woman), and the disclosure of details that would undermine the anonymity of the case. Some important elements of this new construction, however, deserve to be discussed: Lucy remembered that her attacker had told her to masturbate, and that when he left, he had announced, mockingly, that he had used a fake pistol.

Even if the event was experienced psychologically as a rape, the removal of the narrative constructed in the crisis therapy exposed the victim's feeling of guilt, probably not yet worked through until that moment. In this regard, it is necessary to take into account aspects related to the identification with the aggressor as well as the feeling, often experienced by the victim, of having in some way created the conditions that led to the aggression. By questioning the reality of her story, the "false" arises—the fake pistol, the false criminal—and the truth seems shaken—the real culprit, the false victim—inaugurating a new feeling of guilt, important in the process of working through trauma.

Thus, Lucy's thoughts during the aggression began to take shape and could be verbalized: What did he want from us? What could I do to give him what he sought, so he would leave us alone? What scene was he asking me to play? For the first time in more than ten years, she returned to the traumatic scene, now exposed, to question it, and she began to unfold the experience she had lived, organizing it temporarily in language. By opening some discursive threads, knotted between sensorial inscriptions and unconscious thoughts, she recognized the disarray and confusion created by this enigmatic instruction in which, as in a set of mirrors, she had to "find her own pleasure" in front of her aggressor to excite him—she was a child lost in a confusion of tongues. Indeed, all of these questions pushed her to assume herself as the protagonist of a sexuality for which she was not prepared and which she could not yet recognize in herself.

These questions also actively involved her role in the aggression. This feeling of guilt is further intensified by the fake pistol, and probably the feeling that she could have known it, or even that she knew it and had done nothing about it.

After this episode, Lucy began to become wary of therapists and treatments as well as of the truth manifested by her body. This led to a change, first around the body: she began to suffer from an itch that no longer limited to the genital area but widened throughout her body and also affected her companion. Unable to find any biological substrate for the symptom, a team of medical specialists engaged the couple in repeated and varied prophylactic treatments—all useless. After several sessions spent talking about the insomnia produced by the itching, the therapeutic showers in the hospital, and the couple's arguments about which of the two could be responsible for the condition, she mentioned a consultation with a veterinarian. Then, reacting vehemently, I am surprised to hear myself say: "Stop this madness! You know there is nothing!"

Trauma confronts us with a void, an absence of representation. It can only be approached through the reactivation of a few sensory pathways. Lucy had established a transitory anchor to this absence of representation through the imaginary narrative that covered the traumatic "hole," but she was again exposed to the inability to organize fusion-defusion strategies around objects, to produce fantasies. When the body is solicited in this situation, it can only react by "burning"—producing an explosion of somatic manifestations. This bodily paroxysm, which calls upon the presence of another, leads me to leave my neutral place, that of the analyst, in a movement that surprises me and which I can only grasp in a differed (*nachträglich*) time. This brutal reaction, which seems to have succeeded here (the somatic manifestation disappeared, leading to a more metaphorical discourse and the verbalization of fundamental questions related to her sexuality) need to be situated and analyzed within the transference. "The analyst [...] has at his disposal material which can have no counterpart in excavations, such as the repetitions of reactions dating from infancy and all that is indicated by the transference in connection with these repetitions." (Freud 1937: 259)

As said earlier, the first two or three years of analysis were mainly focused on the reliability of both the analyst and the setting. During this period, Lucy evoked certain elements of her biography: she came from a religious family, and she often brought up the image of herself, still a child, playing with her body (she used the word "masturbating"), and the violent reactions of her mother, who seemed shocked and disgusted by her bodily explorations. She also spoke about a period during which she was totally fascinated by martyred virgins, such as Saint Barbara (who was locked up and later tortured by her own father, who "drew his sward upon her") and Saint Lucy (who met her death by "a sword thrust into her throat"). I had the impression of hearing a child when she spoke of these episodes of "masturbation," and her whole approach to the body and sexuality were from an infantile, primary level, without real eroticization. They only seemed to be that of the religious and hypereroticized representations of martyrization of the body.

It is in this context that it became possible for Lucy to question, for the first time, the notions of femininity and the Oedipal organization. First, thanks to the "thaw" of a story frozen by "crisis" therapy, which gave voice to a child subjected to strong repression and an exclusively religious representation of the body. After the itching stopped, the first metaphoric movement of this child came from her body, regarding the use of the toilets while in the consulting room. She was then able to say that, for years, since the beginning of her analysis, she had to urinate at least twice before each session, and run out at the end of each session to ask for the toilets at the cafe next door. For a year, the time and the content of the sessions was marked by this urgency of urinating and using the toilets, gradually leading to questions about the difference between the sexes. Many cloacal infantile fantasies arose, as well as the memory of some episodes of confusion in moments of intimacy with other adolescents in high school. These representations of herself as a teenager who could "get wet" in moments of confusion and excitement are thus acted over the sessions and then became narrative.

Conclusion

The medium with which the analyst works is language. Beyond its narrative dimension, its ability to communicate, language is in itself a substance capable of carrying affects. Thus, even if the session is part of an information exchange, the transfer is mainly organized on the musicality, the rhythm, and the texture of the language. Freud offers an approach to this materiality of language in the *Traumdeutung*: the dream condenses and displaces unconscious thoughts through blocks of images that must be deciphered to access the latent content they carry. Indeed, the raw material of the dream is, in itself, inconceivable—and unspeakable. The only thing we can do with the words a subject finds to organize a relatively orderly and sequential narration of a dream is to open, to unfold the multiple discursive chains associated with a representation. The narrative that is made of it is only one of the possible narrative choices, the truth of which lies in the declamatory strength, the poetic texture, the interpretative voice, determined by a given situation: its putting into singular words, with a rhythm, silences, cuts, associations linked to the contingency of this interpretation. This declaration becomes the medium by which the transfer acts and is represented.

In the clinical situation that is presented here, the subject needs to protect herself behind a protective construction when she is confronted with certain experiences that are incomprehensible or intolerable in intensity. This construction allows a continuity of the ego (in this case, the construction has allowed Lucy to create a professional and intellectual environment thanks to which she has been able to travel, get away from her family, and build herself autonomously), but the bodily experience remains deferred, manifesting somatically, particularly in the body-to-body encounter with the other. The removal of this protection and the consequent questioning of the conformity between the ego and the bodily experience are made possible by transference. The analytic situation thus allowed Lucy to subjectively regain possession of her body and her symptom, but the intensity with which the Real body was solicited produced an intense arousal, which resulted in a somatic "madness." It is within this transference context that I am taken by surprise by this madness in the form of a vehement reaction on my part, which takes me out of the analyst's neutral place. My own "madness" extinguishes the fire, and then the organization of a new construction becomes possible—one in which the experience, extremely condensed in the initial narrative, unfolds, giving the body and the language a metaphorical role. The third space that I inhabit when I leave my neutral place, and which allows me to register it in the transference to put it to work, to make it creative, is that which characterizes psychoanalysis and constitutes its truth. The narrative is here always a fiction, one of the many possible ways to carve up the experience as a whole, the elusive experience of the encounter. It was thanks to the first fiction that it was subsequently possible to reach the fantasy by which we understood the symptom in all its truth, in its actuality.

The narrative related to a traumatic event organizes an impenetrable and incomprehensible enclave, which preserves the imaginary continuity of the ego. This "foreign body" excludes everything that would not adapt to it. The imaginary here is the one that makes medium, substance, and material of language: when space and bodily experience organize a representation, become virtuality or an image of the image in the optical scheme with which Lacan associates the image to the experience of language. Indeed, the imaginary, narrative, or filmic continuity depends on the possibility of organizing space and bodily experience, as addressed to the other, in the quality of otherness, as a carrier of a third party, a carrier of the language. This desire for understanding, translation, creates words (*Fort/Da*) from a bodily experience of pure sound, *oooh, aaaah!* This otherness to which we address ourselves, to which we try to communicate something, to make it understandable, is a reminder of the norms of division and hierarchy that determine our relationship to the image, both in the visual organization of reality, following the norms of perspective, or in the grammatical and synoptic construction of the narrative. This results in the production of a certain number of condensed signifiers, whenever an element appears as missing in the process of fusion-defusion of drives. In trauma, this happens around a hole in the structure. This hole concentrates everything, which, in the integration of a representation of the body, remains excluded from the Oedipal adjustments and can only be approached by a fragmentary bodily experience. In Lucy, the absence of this Oedipal landmark had found a transitory solution in the construction of a narrative that covered this "hole." The creation of a reliable context, on which a law capable of guaranteeing that the other always remains in the same place, week after week, enabled her to find other benchmarks on which to expose herself to the violence of bodily experience in the construction of an image and a new narrative of herself. This is what allows Lacan to assert that "[…] the Oedipus complex is only a myth thanks to which they [the psychoanalysts] put in place the limits of their operations" (Lacan 1967–1968). Indeed, if the body manifests itself as fragmented in the contingent situation of the session, if I allow myself to come out of my neutral position to say a "stupidity" (Lacan 1967–1968), and if this stupidity ultimately makes sense, it is thanks to the establishment of a linearity, a ritualized organization of space and time, a representation of one's own body, limited by the law that governs the parental instances and is repeated in the encounter between the analyst and the analyzed. The space of the session thus becomes a linear space-time in which the indeterminable and the chaotic are inscribed and organized, a usual ritual that always returns to the same place, with a fixed and reliable law… a refrain that inscribes in a "LaLaLa" known a cry, which is, at its origin, pure body… the inaugural *Agh*, material and deep, of Faust, becomes an injunction and a sign, becomes a verb.

Access to the traumatic core is obtained by opening a breach in the narrative: when I am led, in the transference, to stop the surge of the somatic manifestation by emphasizing what Lucy thinks to be false without being able to say it, she detaches from the suspension created by the protective story-image. The mockery then becomes that of the subject facing herself; the symptom then speaks for itself. I insist here on the importance of the experience of transference, as a reminder of the Oedipal law, that is to say, of the symbolic and imaginary organization of the bodily experience of the body, of the Real, without which the moment of cessation of the story-image, instead of serving to construct a new symbolization in the contingent situation of the session, would only have made things worse. The truth of the analysis is neither that of the story nor that of the image; it is that of the construction that is made within the transference.

Notes

1 This becomes particularly striking in the chapter 7 of the *Interpretation of Dreams.*

References

Botella, C. 2001. "Figurabilité et régrédience." *Revue Française de Psychanalyse* 65(4): 1149–1239.

Freud, S. 1905. "Fragment of an Analysis of a Case of Hysteria." *The Standard Edition, volume 7 (1901–1905)*, 1–122. London: Hogarth.

Freud, S. 1937. "Constructions in Analysis." In *The Standard Edition, volume 23 (1937–1939)*, 256–269. London: Hogarth.

Lacan, J. 1967–1968. *The Seminar, Book XV: The Psychoanalytic Act.* https://www.tau.ac.il/~cohenron/ScanSeminar.pdf.

Masson, J. M. 1985. *The Complete Letters of Sigmund Freud to Wilhelm Fliess 1887–1904.* Translated and edited by J. M. Masson. Cambridge, MA: Harvard University Press.

Pommier, F. 2016. "Intimité et fantasme structurant. Penser l'intime." *Connexions* 105(1): 71–80.

Szondi, P. 1978. "Traktat über philologische Erkenntnis." In *Schriften*, Bd. 1, Frankfurt.

Chapter 3

Feminine Identification and Infinite Mourning

Christian Dunker

Problem Position

One problem left open by the Freudian theory of mourning concerns how we can verify whether the loss of the object was concluded: that is, whether its reconstruction is closed and if a new trace of it was integrated in the ego. Freud (1917) described the work of mourning, dividing it in three movements:

> (1) Reality-testing [*Realitätsprüfung*] has shown that the loved object no longer exists, and it proceeds to demand that all libido shall be withdrawn from its attachments to that object. The work of mourning [*Trauer Arbeit*] begins with a negative existence judgement, which examines the reality of the loss. (Freud 1917: 203)

The work of mourning (*die Arbeit die Trauer leistet*) begins with the libidinal withdrawal from the object and the evaluation of the reality of the loss to produce a judgment of existence.

> (2) This demand arouses understandable opposition—it is a matter of general observation that people never willingly abandon a libidinal position, not even, indeed, when a substitute is already beckoning to them. This opposition can be so intense that a turning away from reality takes place and a clinging to the object through the medium of a hallucinatory wishful psychosis. Normally, respect for reality gains the day. Nevertheless, its orders cannot be obeyed at once. They are carried out bit by bit, at great expense of time and libidinal energy, and in the meantime the existence of the lost object is psychically prolonged. (Freud 1917: 204)

Now we know that something lost has been lost, but we are unaware of what and which symbolic value has been lost with it. Self-esteem (*Ichgefühlt*) degrades and inhibitions are lost. The interest in work, love, and the world decreases. This diminishing of the self is interspersed by moments of exaltation or mania. An alternating identification emerges between feelings of repentance and self-criticism. Guilt and shame appear as an effect of not having loved the object enough, oscillating between rage and fear because of not having been sufficiently beloved.

> (3) Each single one of the memories and expectations in which the libido is bound to the object is brought up and hyper-cathected, and detachment of the libido is accomplished in respect of it. Why this compromise by which the command of reality is carried out piecemeal should be so extraordinarily painful is not at all easy to explain in terms of economics. It is remarkable that this painful is taken as a matter of course by us. The fact is, however, that when the work of mourning is completed the ego becomes free and uninhibited again. (Freud 1917: 204)

Here emerges a new trace of the object, a new identification, that rebuilds the loss in the ego. This third process is considered in order to think about the appearance of the superego and the acquisition of the ability to examine reality. The lost object becomes a part of the self, in which the subject loves, was loved, or would love, according to the subject's narcissism. This process inversely explains how the action of the superego becomes an obstacle to mourning and also how masochism operates as a pathological substitution of the object (narcissism).

To end the process of mourning, the process of comparison between an actual loss and a series of losses that happened before must be concluded. This is why a loss operates as a resignification (*Nachträglickeit*) of previous losses, turning castration into the center of convergence of such a process. In Freudian terms, mourning is a matter of phallic sacrifices. The end of mourning depends on a sacrifice, a moment of synthesis of being left by the other and of leaving the other, a synthesis that creates a new trace in the subject.

A biographical episode in the life of the psychoanalyst Donald Winnicott can be used as a paradigmatic example of an ending of mourning for clinical semiology (Kanter 2004: 203). After an unhappy marriage with sexual problems and without children, he separated from his wife and found a great love in Claire Britton, with whom he shared humor, poetry, and psychoanalysis. When Winnicott died in 1971, Britton entered a long mourning that ended as follows: she dreamed that they were again in one of those unforgettable situations, perhaps having an English tea. In the dream, he tells jokes as he usually did, and she experiences them as vivid and realistic. At this point, she states inside the dream, "*Everything is very good, but there is something wrong*," to which he responded, "*Of course there is something wrong. I am dead.*" She awakes laughing, and, since that dream, her mourning has been over. In psychoanalytic work, we often find this uncanny (*unheimliche*) trace as the sign of the end of a mourning process. Temporally speaking, this sacrifice could end in a ritual. In other words, the incorporation of the loss is complete once the ego is enriched through a cannibalistic process of acquisition.

Freud describes depressions and melancholy as the interruption or fixation in between one of those three moments. But we also observe a third pathological case of mourning, which we can call the *infinite mourning*. It is not a melancholy state, but a kind of incapacity to produce a new beginning, a loss to the openness of love, which opens a kind of a perpetual sacrifice. For example, in Portugal, Spain, and Brazil in the nineteenth century (Mehaffey 2003), once a widow loses her husband, she was obliged to dress in black and to maintain the appearance of grief for her entire life. If melancholy is incapable to start the work of mourning and some depressions are an effect of a bad or postponed work of mourning, there are also some cases of infinite mourning related to whenever a new psychic act is necessary to conclude the work of mourning, finally dissolving it in the general symbolic disposition to deal with the lack and the loss.

In this chapter, I argue that infinite mourning necessitates a supplement to the Freudian theory of loss. In such cases, I cannot insist on new comparisons and remembering work in relation to the object, but on the dissolution of the ego. The problem with the ordinary conception of mourning remains the theory of identification in psychoanalysis. Identification is based on cannibalistic incorporation, and the model of incorporation insists on introducing more and more traces of the object, according to the popular image that the process of acquisition involves "enrichment." My hypothesis is based on a parallel model of mourning, in which the end of mourning depends on a nonidentitarian concept of identification—an identification that suspends the unity of the ego, rather than incorporating a new trace of the object; an identification whose logical structure is nonpredicative.

Infinite mourning is classically associated with melancholy and psychosis. However, cases of infinite mourning are evident in depression, with no substantial mutation of the subject. In these cases, the division of the subject appears to need not only a symbolic and productive experience of *determination* of the loss, enriching the totemic self, but also infinite aspects and predicates concerning the loss of object. These cases do not need to live through mourning as an experience of *symbolic determination*, but as a productive experience of indetermination. In these cases, we should insist on the enrichment of self but as a change to the grammar of recognition.

If, in finite mourning, traces of the subject can be countable and exhaustively named and determined, for instance, as the alignment of natural numbers in a mathematical series (1, 2, 3… n), then in infinite mourning, what is lost is the rule of composition of this succession. The series of the traces of the object therefore looks uncountable, undetermined, and not commensurable to other losses, as in the irrational series of numbers between zero and one, for example (1/3, 0.666…, √2 … n). This brings us to some aspects of what Lacan (1973) pointed out with his theory of sexuation. One side of sexuation is based on the finite, countable, and determined relation to jouissance, while the other side is undeterminable and not countable. In the feminine side, *not-all* traces must be counted and *not-all* objects must be enveloped with narcissistic devourment, although *not-only* phallic traces are involved in a loss. To understand *infinite mourning*, we must oppose totemic, masculine, and identitarian mourning to animist, feminine, and nonidentitarian identification.

This chapter applies ideas previously developed in consideration of psychoanalytic anthropology (Dunker 2014) and the hypothesis of nonidentitarian theory of identification (Dunker 2017).

Self and Recognition

Let us return to the three premises of melancholia: objectal loss, ambivalence, and regression of the libido to the self. Objectal loss is a matter of reality, ambivalence considers the affects in relation to the other, and the regression of libido depends on a temporal move. In fact, Freud's text emphasizes the imaginary recognition of the other and the regressive move to symbolization much more than the reality of the loss itself.

The ambivalence of the imaginary self-other appears in the innumerable choice of words containing the term "self," *selbst* in German. Mourning, unlike melancholy, does not demote the self-feeling (*Selbstgefühlt*). The melancholic individual exhibits self-condemnation (*Selbstvorwurf*), self-reproach (*Selbstbeschimpfung*), self-criticism, (*Selbstkritik*), and self-depreciation (*Selbstherabsetzung*). The individual suffers from self-shame and finds satisfaction in self-denial, as Prince Hamlet did. The individual's attitude, as in depression, involves self-evaluation (*Selbsteinschätzung*). The subject is delighted by torment (*Selbstbestrafung*), which would ultimately lead to suicide (*Selbstmord*) (Freud 1917).

The struggle for recognition translates the symbolic value involved in how expectations and memories are focused (recognized), overinvested (Übersetzung), and turned off. Here, mourning is oriented toward the recognition of what has been lost. When this symbolic recognition fails, we are dealing with melancholy, which occurs when "the shadow of the object has fallen upon the ego, which can then be judged [recognized] by a given instance as an object, as an abandoned object" (Freud 1917: 115). The ego "would like to incorporate it, actually devour it, according to the cannibalistic oral phase" (Freud 1917: 115). This self-anthropophagic work kills oneself, recognizes and treats oneself as an object. There is no renouncement or sacrifice of the object; there is no "enjoying the satisfaction of being able to recognize itself as the best, as superior to the object" as price for remaining alive (Viveiros de Castro 2019: 215).

Freud's anthropological theories on cannibalistic incorporation revolve around the totemic fetishist animal, the origin of religiosity, the feeling of brotherhood, the hypothesis of a common ancestrality (*Urvater*), the function of the name in human exogamic cultures, the nature of myths, the horror of incest and its prohibition (Freud 1912–1913a). But before explaining how neurosis can be explained by the infantile return of totemism, he introduces a long chapter on animism (Freud 1912–1913b). The main point in this chapter stresses that animism is primarily a form of thinking that confuses reality with the symbolic order (Espina Barrio 2008). Freud therefore did not understand animism as a kind of primitive psychotic infantile style of thinking, but as a counterpart to the social theory of kinship. In particular, there is not only a minor idea at stake, but actually another way of dealing with symbolic bonds, which new anthropologists called perspectivism (Descola 2010).

Lacan's reincorporation of Lévi-Strauss's structural theory maintains the prevalence of totemic cannibalism (Zaffiropoulus 2003). That is why the concept of the name of the father is so important as the function that connects the law in the symbolic with the phallic signifier (Lacan 1998[1958]). In Lacan's interrupted seminar during 1963, the main issue seems to be a kind of revision of sacrifice theory (Lacan 2005[1963]). Lévi-Strauss's theory of totemism (Lévi-Strauss 182[1947]) reads the relation between culture and nature as connected to the law of incest. This law determines the social exchange in general and also explains the exogamic movement as a kind of reciprocity in which women have a place. This conception absorbs and generalizes the theory of sacrifice from Marcel Mauss (Mauss and Hubert 2017[1899]), which explains sacrifice as a kind of return of what someone has given. For Lévi-Strauss, societies in general are retributive symbolic systems, because their main law is deduced from an intrinsic connection between totemism and sacrifice.

Melancholy is a kind of self-sacrifice that happens when there is a failure in self-recognition. Freud said, "*Ihre Klagen sind Anklagen*," (Freud 1917: 202), meaning that "his complaints (*Klagen*) about himself are in fact quarrels against the other" (*Anklagen* is the beginning of a legal cause); in other words, their accusations are self-accusations (*Selbstanklagen*). This indetermination of who the author is and who the receiver of the action is, is called *transitivism* from a Lacanian point of view. Transitivism is a phenomenon first discovered by Charlotte Bühler (1928) as a special kind of identification often observed in the behavior of small children. For example, a child can hit another child of the same age on the left side of the face, and then touch the right side of his own face and cry by imagining the pain. For Lacan (1998[1949]), transitivism illustrates the confusion of the ego and the other, which is inherent in imaginary identification, in which an inversion (right to left) occurs, which is further evidence of the function of the mirror. Transitivism is also evident in paranoia, in which attack and counterattack are bound together "in an absolute equivalence." (Freeman 1976)

In searching for a model for the dissolution of transference and the end of the psychoanalytic process, Lacan argues that the process of traversing identifications, in general, has the structure of mourning. This experience of traversal elaborates the loss of all losses, separating the self from imaginary objects and interrupting transitivism between the object *a* and the symbolic ideals.

> In order to give you formulae-reference points, I will say—if the transference is that which separates demand from the drive, the analyst's desire is that which brings it back. And in this way, it isolates the a, places it at the greatest possible distance from the I that he, the analyst, is called upon by the subject to embody. It is from this idealization that the analyst has to fall in order to be the support of the separating a, in so far as his desire allows him, in an upside-down hypnosis, to embody the hypnotized patient. (Lacan 1988[1964]: 258)

Mourning transitivism oscillates between the loss of the once loved object and the maniacal exaltation in having survived it. This is the collusion between object *a* and ideal. This movement persists to the point when it has become possible to finish separating from the object. But Lacan added that the analyst has to embody this object in order to be left over. It is a strange embodiment, because, instead of introducing another trace in the self, it leaves something out; it separates and leaves out the analyst, the transference, and the identification. There is no introjection of the psychoanalyst here. There is not an incorporative, acquisitive, separating, limiting, and clarifying moment at the end of mourning. How, then, to delimit the termination of mourning between the two extremes: venting of anger and objectal indifference?

> Just as mourning moves the self to renounce the object by declaring it dead and offering as a reward, the permanence of life, so in each partial battle of ambivalence, the libido fixates on the object by devaluing it, lowering it. So to speak, also victimizing him. [...] We do not see, however, which of these two possibilities puts an end to melancholy regularly or more frequently, and the way in which this termination influences the later trajectory of the case. (Freud 1917: 212)

The classic bibliography of mourning has described typical phases of mourning, involving negation, rage, and depression, but even Klüber-Ross (1969) left relatively uncertain its final condition of acceptance. Allouch (1995) argued that mourning requires an effort of creation or sublimation, without which one can never surpass the alternating identifications. Leader (2008) emphasized that this poetic act needs a frame or a new language, often a writing experience, from which the object can be deposed. Kehl (2009) suggests that mourning termination involves a kind of reconciliation with time. Time, as a finite and infinite experience, seems to be a much more interesting criterion for consigning the end of mourning than the totemic substitution and the self-enrichment of the lost object. Devouring the dead father is a way to produce symbolic determination. Let us retain the resonance: *de-termination*, *the-termination*, *termination*.

The metapsychology of mourning involves transitivism of the agent of the act, ambivalence of affects, and alternativity of identification. In the totemistic paradigm, all these processes depend on the separation between "them" and "us," between death and survivors, between those who kill and those who were killed. Identification is the work of building a kind of "us." "Us" as a family, as a genealogical cultural belonging, as a common gender, as a specific, language-speaking being. *Selbst*, self, subject, or ego are different designations of the devouring or killing agent creating or extending unary traits of the object. Consequently, we only ever know who the enemies are, even when they appear inside of "us," as in the uncanny (*Unheimlich*) experience (Freud 1919). That is why melancholy occurs as a "shadow of the object fallen over the ego." Even when we work to recognize what was lost in the loss, there is an original, totemistic, and persistent distinction between *us* and *them*.

Animist Funerary Rite

The identification model of totemic sacrifice, described by Lévi-Strauss beginning with his initial observations of Indigenous populations in the south of Brazil (Lévi-Strauss 1973[1952]), is neither universal nor necessary to psychoanalysis, because it is no longer a consensual starting point for anthropology. New researchers, disciples of Lévi-Strauss, supplement the sovereignty of totemism with *animist perspectivism*. Gender difference (Strathern 2006[1987]) and theory of names and reciprocity (Wagner 2017[1975]) are supplementary facts to understand a nonacquisitionist model of cannibalism. Incidentally, the narrative mobilized to exemplify the perspectivism-animism identification is centered on the analysis of funerary rituals.

Arawetés are Tupi-Guarani people living in the eastern part of the Amazon, upstream from the Xingu river (Viveiros de Castro 2006). For Arawetés, human beings are abandoned by the gods (*Mais*), and the dead are evil people, because they are resentful and want to push the living people to the land of the dead. Shamans are killer warriors and occupy religious, political, and ideological positions of deep value, commanding funerary rites. Let's remember that shamans precede psychoanalysts (Lévi-Strauss 1988[1955]) in their social function, because they are polyglots, androgynous, diplomats between life and death, between friends and enemies. They not only deal with indeterminate and transitional experiences, as is the case in mourning, but they are also indeterminate people par excellence. They live between "us" and "them," marked by tattoos containing a mixture of traits of both the Arawetés and their enemies. In Arawetés mythology, gods are anthropophagous and are eager to eat the souls of the dead. Shamans are ambiguously responsible for bringing souls to the *Mais* banquets and to provide corpses to be eaten by mortals. "Eating" is both an alimentary and sexual experience, because, in return, they receive songs and words that are endowed with high spiritual value.

"*A recent corpse is an ugly, dirty, petty being, full of resentment for having died*" (Viveiros de Castro 2006: 459). The word for "us" (*bide*) in Araweté can be loosely translated into "humans" or "living people." *Tiwã*, on the other hand, designates foreigners in general, all those who are non-Araweté. While some foreigners are viewed as potential allies, others are considered enemies (*awin*). Gods are marked by a radical ambivalence, because they are simultaneously enemies and potential allies. They are part of the ideal of the ego and a mask of the object *a*, the evil corpse-eaters. The souls of true human enemies (*awin*) are not directly devoured by the *Mais*, because they have seen only their flesh. Like the "dummy god" of President Schreber, they cannot distinguish potential allies (*tiwã*) from proper enemies (*awin*). Enemies are ingested, in the anthropophagical sense, through the shamanic ritual, becoming a determined part of "us," and the shaman becomes undetermined flesh, composed of a contradictory substance, from both the enemies and the allies ("them"), as a potential food for the gods. Upon killing an enemy, a shaman enters a "death state," spending five days vomiting blood. The shaman's own soul merges with the victim's, and the shaman assumes an ambivalent position before the gods.

What we have here is a kind of reversal of mourning. Ambivalence must be solved from the point of view of the other, of the *Mais* gods, and not from the point of view of the *Selbst* or *self*. The shaman takes possession of the enemy spirit, but the enemy spirit also takes possession of the shaman, as in a Freudian ambivalence. But the concept of possession, crucial for totemic purposes, is not applicable here, so we have a problem in concluding mourning with the creation of a new trace in the self. Hence, instead of self-depression, the shaman creates a third position that neither pertains to the loss of "us" (family and Arawetés), nor to the loss of "them" (enemies and potential allies). Despite this, the end of the funerary traversal is marked with a new position. The shaman presents himself in a *feminine position* to be devoured by the gods' spirits, which is considered the reverse of the killer he once was while alive. In comparison with the Freudian totemic myth, the brothers are not eating the body of the dead father, but the animistic-perspectivism of someone (nor brother neither sister) offers himself to be eaten in a nontotemic sacrifice.

The other is in me, but the other is neither my rage enemy, the one I hate, nor the guilty narcissistic representative of "us." From the point of view of the gods, he is seen as feminine flesh for food. From the point of view of the living people, he is seen as a respectful phallic warrior. But the most important and different aspect of the animistic-perspectivism mourning appears in the fact that the point of view of himself has disappeared. Could we consider this as a new kind of identification or as an un-identarian identification?

Feminine Mourning

The counterexample presented in animistic funerary ritual unravels how the Freudian theory of mourning is, in some sense, a theory from a masculine perspective. Because totemism is at the center of the theory, it is susceptible to the critique that women are considered a mere possession for social exchange. The Lacanian amendment, through the concept of object *a*, introduces the crucial importance of some experience of indetermination in the process of mourning. However, this is not enough to deal with the precise moment of dissolution of identification. In Lacan's work, it seems that this moment is not only a matter of suspension of imaginary semblance, neither a point of assumption of desire in phallic positions, but that it could be connected to the emergence of feminine jouissance.

In his late work, Lacan ([1999]1972–1973) described feminine jouissance as "irrational," because it is not based in phallic proportionality. On the masculine side of sexuation, men are defined by an exception, those who are excluded from jouissance given the existence of the "one," the real mythical father who has access to all women. The phallic function divides people between us and them, the living and the death, men and women. Feminine jouissance is not complementary but supplementary to this, because in the field of women, there is no exception to castration. There is neither "us" not "them" in the feminine field, given that there is no consistent class of women (*the Woman does not exist*), and because there is no relation (rapport) between the one-as-exception and the not-all jouissance of women. We can clearly verify how the formulas of sexuation, presented and discussed between 1971 and 1973, are deduced from a rereading of Freud's *Totem and Taboo*. That is why there is the exception of the primitive father (*Urvater*) on the side of man, but the same exception does not exist on the side of the women. The incommensurability of the unit of jouissance in men, based on phallic function, and the unit of jouissance in women, based on not-all logic, is like the incommensurability between the series of natural numbers and the series of irrational numbers. In natural numbers, the rule of formation of the series is defined by the successor (+1). To be inscribed in the set of "men," someone has to incorporate this rule and its consequence, the existence of an interdiction (n-1) in the choice of desire. But the unit, and so the rule of composition in female jouissance, is not regular. The next irrational number is unpredictable, because there is an infinite number of irrational numbers between one irrational and the other. The structure of natural numbers exemplifies the naming process as an exogamic belonging to a common ancestor like the totem. Irrational numbers and real numbers do not reveal their rule of formation: they are deduced and recognized by methods as in perspectivism. The concept of difference is not the same on the masculine side and the feminine side, in accordance with the existence of two types of identification. For the second type, we must consider things that couldn't be written, without the inscription of a new trace. Lacan never gives us an anthropological reference for this supposition, even though this omission contradicts the Lévi-Straussian and Freudian totemic paradigms.

With this consideration in mind, the end of masculine mourning means to integrate that loss in a series of previous losses, until the original loss. The creation of a new trace is like a cannibalistic inclusion of a new number in the series. Feminine mourning involves an infinite and uncountable number of traces, in particular the trace that "never stops not being written" (i.e., one of the definitions of the Real in Lacan). This is why, in this identification, there is no self to say this is "us" and these are "them." There is a not-all set of beings that were lost.

The Arawetés assign two names for enemies; "sauce of *cauim*" (*cauim* is a kind of native beer) and "future song." "Sauce" represents what they once were, and "*song*" represents what they will be. The naming varies from past to future, indicating how time changes perspectives while changing the identity of the enemy. We have the same ambiguity in the Araweté word *tovajar*, which refers either to brother-in-law or to enemy. A brother-in-law is a potential ally, the opposite of an enemy. Enemies are the source of new words; they bring neologisms, words from an unknown, infinite language. Here, we have two examples of indetermination and a coincidence of oppositions between us and them, which requires a new system of recognition.

In a funeral rite, a shaman who has just killed an enemy refers to a certain woman as his wife. But from what point of view is he speaking? As a human being referring to "his" human wife, or the wife of the enemy, whose soul has been eaten by the gods? This is a linguistic example of the experience of dispossession necessary to solve infinite mourning. It is not only a question of appropriation and inheritance, but the maddening experience of getting rid of oneself.

Now let's remember the Freudian theory of mourning. I kill and devour the other (real). I must face the destiny of being devoured by another who is not the one I devoured (imaginary). I retain its traits (symbolic). Here, we have an ambivalent inversion (*Verkehrung*) of the action, from passivity to activity, but also transitivism return (*Wendlung*) to the other, as well as symbolic negation incorporation (*Verdrängung*) of the object. And now we can compare this operation with the feminine mourning based on the Arawetés narrative.

> The typical dead is thus a woman, as the ideal immortal is a warrior. Ideal but paradoxical [...] a killer dies when he kills his enemy, identifies himself with him, and only effectively takes advantage of these deaths when he dies: confronted with the gods, he is not treated as an enemy, because he is an enemy and so ultimately Mai. (Viveiros de Castro 2006: 210)

I died when I killed my enemy, as far as I've changed myself in this (symbolic) act. The shaman, who was once a killer, is in an ambivalent state of being alive and dead, being man and (imaginary) woman. The "feminization of the killer," his "fertilization" or "possession by the victim" is not a reversal of roles, inversive or transitive, creating a new trace in the self, but is solved by a "predicative condensation," which dissolves the self:

> The double negation, '*I am an enemy of my enemy*' does not restore an identity that would already be there as a principle and purpose, but, instead, it reaffirms the difference and makes it imminent, '*I have an enemy, and so I am, or the self is.*' (Viveiros de Castro 2006: 225)

A Clinical Case of Infinite Mourning

She had been living alone for more than twenty years since she had separated from her husband. Until then, she had a rich and busy life, full of travels and romantic encounters around the world, with an active participation in an intellectual life in diverse contexts. Five years ago, she lost her mother. Two years ago, she was fired from an important job. Until then, everything seemed sad but normal, but everything changed when her pet dog died six months ago. Suddenly, insomnia emerged; there was sadness, recurrent crying, and thoughts of emptiness. Her family, including brothers and cousins, seemed to be distant. She lost her taste for traveling and the joy for life.

As a young daughter, she had taken care of her mother after her mother had decided to separate from her father, when she was still a teenager. Her mother's separation from her father was concealed from her relatives. She, like her parents, was an immigrant, and returned to her country of origin once a year, as a kind of accountability. During these visits, her mother concealed the news of her separation from the family, which led to a brutal and shared denial of a loss, which she incorporated from her mother. The mourning of the separation of her parents was still alive, and it had been postponed since her adolescence. When her dog died, she resignified the death of her mother, the end of the marriage, and the loss of her job, but the process started an infinite mourning that had been latent since her adolescence.

When I insisted on the reasons for her divorce, she was intrigued, and we spent some sessions exploring why they slit up. Her work had something to do with it. He didn't want kids. But it took some time for her to remember that *she* had a lover at *work*. This forgotten lover operates as a self-reversing memory that inverted (*Verkehren*) the positions: from traitor to someone who had been cheated, from active to passive. She felt that her husband found her replacement in a younger woman, when, in fact, she had started a parallel relationship at work.

At this precise moment, one friend offered her another puppy, but she questioned whether she should accept it. Others might have been silent, but I replied that she could wait. When her mother got ill, she promised herself that she would never let her mother die alone, but she was absent when her mother died. She could not forgive herself. Though she knew of the ill health of her mother, she believed that if she were by her side, her mother would not have died. Her own presence would have saved her; love would have redeemed her. Thus, real loss can be covered up by a subject who offers herself as an object to make up for the lack of the other.

Supported by the striking fact that she had forgotten the real reasons for her separation from her husband, I insisted on knowing the context of her family's immigration to Brazil, but she could not explain it very accurately. She only said, "My father received an offer of employment" or "after the war, the work situation became difficult in Europe." These statements were true, but they were not the complete truth. Just as something was lacking in the history of her separation from her husband, something seemed to be lacking in the history of her family's immigration. Another reason for mourning was added here: the loss of a country of origin. This brought us to the signifier of the transference: "I came to look for you, because I was told that you understand politics, and I read some of your texts on the internet. After all, it was because of the 'lack' of politics that I got in this line of work."

But the signifier "politics" proved to be decisive in another context. On a trip to her home country, she consulted with some of her remaining family members about why her family came to Brazil, and the response was appalling: *politics*. She found out that her father's family might have been involved in some form of collaboration during the German occupation. After the war, her parents, who were married at that point, began to fear possible harassment. They decided to immigrate to Brazil, against the immediate will of her mother, who felt an infinite sense of regret about being separated from her family. Her mother never forgave her husband for that. Therefore, it is possible that this was the real reason for the separation of her parents. This was corroborated by the great fear that her father had shown during the Brazilian military dictatorship. He insisted that my analysand should never become involved in politics. When she started an analysis with an analyst known for his political action—and who was also incidentally of German descent—she was disobeying her father.

We took a long time in analysis, leaving many losses behind. The crucial point of the integration of series of losses was traversed through another mourning, the mourning of her mother, in the double sense: (1) the loss of her mother, who died alone, as did her dog; and (2) the infinite mourning of her mother, postponed by her divorce and forced immigration. The finite masculine mourning of herself was traversed by the infinite feminine mourning, as a heritage of the mother. In the first mourning, the task was to symbolically reappropriate her lost mother. In the second one, the question was how to be released from what she experienced as this mourning inherited from her mother's perspective. The lack she would have imposed on her mother, if she suspended her substitutive place and functioned as her mother's ally, is the lack of losing her own "self."

After three years of analysis, two things happened that closed this apparently interminable mourning. After a long time, counting losses from her point of view and comparing them from the point of view of her mother, she finally ended this process. She acquired a new pet dog and named it with a letter that represents her and her country of origin. She also announced that she would finally take a course abroad in a prestigious European university, which she had long desired to do but had inexplicably postponed.

The announcement changes her humor, and this was a permanent gain for the analytic process. She said she was accepted to the winter course. I responded, humorously, intercourse? She gets ashamed and laughs. But two sessions later, she said that, since my commentary, every time she pronounced the significant *winter course*, a strange musical resonance appeared in her mind. It wasn't only the remembrance of sexual life that she had strangely "forgotten," as so many other forgotten things we have seen in analysis. In a few months, she would turn "back" to this issue in an unprecedented way. Far away from the sexual, humor, and cognitive effects, the sound of *winter* as the sound of wind of her childhood came back to her, with all the political coldness and implicitness of her country of birth. This unpronounceable, poetic effect was the important event that ended her infinite mourning.

Conclusion

The case suggested that there are some mourning processes that take more time, because there is a certain kind of series of mourning's postponement at stake, the countability of negated or repressed losses explain a certain depressive orientation in life. Yet this was not the case. My analysand had a clinical presentation far from a depressive state, even though we could suppose she presented a manic defense. Affective inversions, identificatory reversions, and transitivism between activity and passivity occur in ordinary mourning.

But at some point, another process of mourning crossed her path, from which emerged the postponed mourning of her mother, in the double perspectival sense of it. "Her mother" was something like "my wife" or *tovajar* nouns for Araweté people. Her mother was the ally and the enemy. The separation from this identification is not a matter of erecting a new predicative trace into her ego, but a matter of disidentification, like the *sens-blanc* (semblant) of a meaning, as seen in the words *winter course*. The ritornello effect we have seen here is one of the aspects of the letter in contrast to the dimension of signifier, developed in Lacan's late work.

> [...] love is impossible and the sexual relationship drops into the abyss of nonsense, which doesn't in any way diminish the interest we must have in the Other. What we want to know—in what constitutes feminine jouissance insofar as it is not wholly occupied with man, and even insofar, I will say, as it is nor, as such, at all occupied with him—what we want to know in the status of the other knowledge [son savoir]. (Lacan 1999[1972–1973]: 87)

Her mourning was crossing this man as her father and as the "man" (husband) of her mother. As her father, he was part of her countable masculine mourning, but as the husband of the mother, it touches her feminine uncountable mourning. In the first process, he was, for her, the (-1) that makes the exception, being erected into the self by his issues linked to "German," "politics," and "winter," all marked by the letter with which she named her pet. The trace of the series, the (+1) is that which we gain in a mourning process. In the second process, her own self-experience as someone in a genealogic line was suspended, testifying to the infinite between zero and one, between sense and the nonsensical sound of winter.

References

Allouch, J. 1995. *Erotique du deuil au temps de la mort sèche*. Paris: EPEL.

Bühler, C. 1928. *Kindheit und Jugend: Genese des Bewußtseins*. Leipzig: Hirzel.

Descola, P. 2010. *Outras Naturezas, Outras Culturas*. São Paulo: Editora 34.

Dunker, C. I. L. 2014. "Discontent, Suffering and Symptom: Reading Lacanian Diagnostics through Amerindian Perspectivism." *Crisis and Critique* 1(2): 148.

Dunker, C. I. L. 2017. "Hegel Amerindian: For a non-Identitarian Concept of Identification in Psychoanalysis." *Crisis and Critique* 4(1): 103–120.

Espina Barrio, A. B. 2008. *Freud e Lévi-Strauss*. Recife: Joaquim Nabuco.

Freeman, T. (1976). On the Psychopathology of Transitivism and Appersonation. British Journal of Psychiatry, 129(5), 414–417. doi:10.1192/bjp.129.5.414

Freud, S. 1912–1913a. *Totem und Tabu (Einige Übereinstimmung im seeelenleben der Wilden und Neurotiker). Sigmund Freud Studienausgabe, vol. IX*, 387–444. Frankfurt: Fischer.

Freud, S. 1912–1913b. "Animismus, Magie und Allmacht der Gedanken." In *Totem und Tabu (Einige Übereinstimmung im seeelenleben der Wilden und Neurotiker). Sigmund Freud Studienausgabe, vol. IX*, 364–387. Frankfurt: Fischer.

Freud, S. 1917. "Trauer und Melancholie." In *Sigmund Freud Studienausgabe, vol. II*, 203. Frankfurt: Fischer.

Freud, S. 1919. "Das Unheimliche." In *Sigmund Freud Studienausgabe*, vol IV Frankfurt: Fischer: 242–274.

Kanter, J. 2004. *Face to Face with Children: The Life and Work of Clare Winnicott*. London: Routledge.

Kehl, M. R. 2009. *O Tempo e o Cão*. São Paulo: Boitempo.

Klüber-Ross, E. 1969. *On Death & Dying*. New York: Simon & Schuster/Touchstone.

Lacan, J. 1998[1949]. "O estádio do espelho como formador da função do eu [Je]." In *Escritos*, 96–104. Rio de Janeiro: Jorge Zahar.

Lacan, J. 1998[1958]. "Questão preliminar a todo tratamento possível das psicoses." In *Escritos*, 537–590. Rio de Janeiro: Jorge Zahar.

Lacan, J. 2005[1963]. "Introdução aos Nomes do Pai." In *Nomes do Pai*, 55–88. Rio de Janeiro: Jorge Zahar.

Lacan, J. 1998[1964]. *O Seminário livro XI "Os Quatro Conceitos Fundamentais da Psicanálise."* Rio de Janeiro: Jorge Zahar.

Lacan, J. 1999[1972–1973]. *On Feminine Sexuality – The Limits of Love and Knowledge. The Seminar of Jacques Lacan Book XX Encore*. New York: Norton.

Leader, Darian. 2008. *The New Black: Mourning, Melancholia and Depression*. London: Blackwell.

Lévi-Strauss, C. 1982[1947]. *As Estruturas Elementares de Parentesco*. Petrópolis: Vozes.

Lévi-Strauss, C. 1973[1952]. "As estruturas sociais no Brasil central e oriental." In *Antropologia Estrutural*, 141–154. Rio de Janeiro: Civilização Brasileira.

Lévi-Strauss, C. 1988[1955]. "O feiticeiro e sua magia." In *Antropologia Estrutural*, 193–215. Rio de Janeiro: Civilização Brasileira.

Mauss, M. and Hubert, H. 2017[1899]. *Sobre o Sacrifício*. São Paulo: Ubu.

Mehaffey, R. 2003. *Mourning in 19th Century America*. Philadelphia: University of Pennsylvania Press.

Strathern, M. 2006[1987]. *O Gênero da Dádiva*. Campinas: Unicamp.

Viveiros de Castro, E. 2006. A Inconstância da Alma Selvagem. São Paulo: Cossac Naiffy.

Viveiros de Castro, E. 2019 Metafísicas Canibais. São Paulo: Cossac Naiffy.

Wagner, R. 2017[1975]. *A Invenção da Cultura*. São Paulo: Ubu=.

Zafiropoulos, M. 2003. *Lacan y Lévi-Strauss o el Retorno a Freud (1951–1957)*. Buenos Aires: Manantial.

Chapter 4

The Truth of the Real

Peter Jansson

With the concept of the Real (*le réel*), Jacques Lacan opened the possibility for a new and radical understanding of truth in psychoanalysis. Based on the two other orders—the symbolic and the imaginary—truth can be defined as a cultural, social, and historical contract, or as what cannot be incorporated into the domain of fantasy and illusion. These forms of truth are not only found in other psychoanalytical schools but also in traditional epistemological systems. Throughout history, various objective truth concepts have been established to avoid relativism and keep the opportunity for making mistakes open: without truth, there is no difference between appearance and reality. Correspondence and representation theory, with roots in Thomas Aquinas and Aristotle, sees truth as the correspondence between statements and how they are related to reality. Ludwig Wittgenstein's *Tractatus* provides a model of truth: a claim is true if its factual relationship consists in reality. The coherence theory sees the truth (statement) of a claim as something that may be inserted into a coherent system of true statements.

These two forms of truth concepts can be reformulated in terms of Lacan's psychoanalytical theory and can be defined by the imaginary and symbolic order. Based on structuralist linguistics, the correspondence theory constitutes a naïve language view, in which the word/symbol is supposed to refer directly to an object in the external reality. By deepening and further developing Ferdinand de Saussure's structural linguistics, Lacan establishes a radical linguistic and epistemological theory, breaking up the historically and culturally determined sign's unity, separating the signifier (*signifiant*) from the signified (*signifié*), and introducing a barrier between them (Lacan 2006[1957]). The meaning never lies hidden in the individual sign, but exists instead in the relationship between the elements in the chain of signifying elements, which never create a manifest meaning, because it always slips away. The meaning will be elsewhere, under the horizon of the text, as a real rest we cannot access. Based on Roman Jakobson's language conception, Lacan states how the continuous metonymic movement of speech opens for a constant shift of meaning beyond the field of discourse that inscribes a lack (the Real) in which desire originates, and which can never be fully satisfied or symbolized. In this sense, Lacan's theory has radical epistemological implications and opens the possibility for a radically new concept of truth. Language does not refer the subject unmediated and immediately to the world, but can only be understood as a network of signifying elements that span the whole of an inaccessible reality, and as that which the symbol constantly seeks to capture, in an asymptotic movement. The meaning is not necessary the way it appears in the world; instead, the order of meaning and the truth of the Real are outside of the world (Lacan 1990 [1974a]).

With the real order, we enter into a new field of truth that cannot be integrated into the imaginary or symbolic order, and that thus takes a radically new position in relation to the classical philosophical understanding of knowledge and science. Lacan's radical concept of truth in terms of the Real also takes its point of departure from Martin Heidegger's break with correspondence theory—with truth as representation—which is insufficient in relation to a deeper truth, an original openness that must exist for a relationship to be established between the subject (the signifier) and the object (the signified). Heidegger finds an echo of it in the Greek term that he translates as "truth," *aletheia*, which is a structure of being itself, a truth that transcends us. No finite, human meaning can symbolize being's own openness, where the Real emanates. The truth is, at the same time, openness and closure. The experience of subjectivity is the fundamental way in which truth is covered, and truth through *aletheia* is linked to the disappearance of the being's original dimension, whose essence is to hide itself. It is according to such a paradoxical logic that Lacan, using a psychoanalytic rhetoric, can speak of "the truth's censorship"—and not a "censorship of the truth"—which points out that the truth itself is precisely this dual dynamic of hiding and showing, and which can take different expressions in the form of different modes (what Heidegger calls *existentials*). The truth of being can only be present as "trace," where Lacan's concept of the Real coincides with the categories of loss, absence, and disappearance (Wallenstein 1992). The Real establishes an incompleteness, a hole or a lack in the other orders, and we have a new concept of truth with consequences at both the theoretical and the clinical level. The Real is something that escapes symbolization—a residue that can never be incorporated into language or a meaningful structure—and it is on the border between the objective and the subjective dimensions. With the Real, truth is no longer something that relates to a positive object—whether it concerns a physical or an imagined reality—and it opens for lack and emptiness. Lacan says that psychoanalysis does not deal with the human being as such but with what the human being lacks, and this object is truth in the meaning of the Real, in the form of a lost object that underlies the dimension of desire and sublimation (Lacan 2006[1966]: 733; 1990[1974b]: 3).

But the Real as truth of being in the shape of pure lack, loss, and trace opens up an epistemological dilemma: there must be an ultimate guarantee that we do not end up in a philosophical arbitrariness, where the Real loses power and significance. A first affinity needs to be postulated for the truth not to be completely lost in a bottomless abyss. Throughout history, psychoanalysis has given its answer to this question by assuming, in the developmental psychological and temporal sense, a state of being of bodily unity between the child and the mother's body, and which Lacan defines as a real whole without deficiency, a presymbolic reality. It is in this sense that Lacan can speak of symbolization as a process that attacks, empties, or excavates the living body's real fullness. When the child leaves the real unity with the mother's body, the Real arises at the same time as a lost object, which Lacan calls the Thing, and which can be found only as a missing object. The real Thing is a mythical object, and the loss remains in the subject's history as a trace, an abyss that it will forever remain suspended over in the nostalgic attempt of desire to articulate, reconstruct, and re-establish unity with what has been lost. The child is forced to exceed its immanent immediacy and the real unity with the mother's body, and, in Lacan's sense—referring to Claude Lévi-Strauss's structuralist theory, in which the Oedipus complex assumes a strictly symbolic function—by subjugating the prohibition of the social and cultural order, the law, constitute a symbolically structured world based on what Lacan calls the "symbolic castration." A loss occurs that affects the subject's immediate reality and being. Herein lies the meaning of Lacan's fateful words that the symbol is "the murder of the thing" (Lacan 2006[1953]). In an original repression, a basic cleavage arises between the "signifier" (*the name of the father*)—which becomes a metaphor for the point of attachment for the chain of signifying elements and its infinite metonymic movement—the "signified" (*the mother's desire*) of the subject, and the *subject's desire becomes the (big) Other's desire* (Lacan 2006[1958]). A lack or a void is carved into the living body's real fullness, while, at the same time, the Real emerges as a residual of this process of symbolization, which escapes it. The real becomes a hard, impenetrable core, which resists symbolization and which has never been expressed in words, received a name or a linguistic form, and vice versa—from the horizon of the symbolic—it embodies a real hole in the heart of the symbolic order, a lack in the big other. The real thing is the impossible, and that which has been incomprehensible truth, the Real, will (afterward, through *Nachträglichkeit*) be hidden and forever disappear in the negative form of the trace. There is no awakening *from* the oblivion of the truth of being, but only an awakening *into* oblivion of the symbolic order.

With the concept of the truth of being—in relation to the imaginary and the symbolic order—the Real assumes different positions and shapes in the theoretical understanding of symptom formation and psychopathology or, as Lacan calls it—following Heidegger—clinical existential structures (Juranville 1984). Based on the real concept of lack—with the truth of being as a lost object—it is possible to define different forms of suffering that manifest themselves in human speech and in how they place themselves in the structure of desire and in the transference. Lacan talks about different "subjective positions," in which the subject creates a unique relationship with the world, being, and the Other (the symbolic order). Lacanian theory identifies four existential structures—the psychotic, perverted, neurotic, and sublimated—that testify to various possibilities to relate to the lost object of the Real and to different ways of living the deficiency and to be in the world. They basically differ from each other in what defense the subject uses in relation to the lack and the big other.

In the structure of psychosis, we encounter a rejection of the signifier of the Real that means that the lack and the loss do not receive recognition in the symbolic order. The original mother's desire is not under repression, there is no original affirmation of the basic signifying element (the name of the father), and the subject remains in the Real—identifies with the real mother—without access to the metaphorical meaning of language. *The words become things*. It is a form of negativity in the shape of anxiety or a violence against the symbolic order. There is a hole or a scratch in the symbolic tissue where the name of the father would have been attached (Lacan 2006[1958]). The rejection at the same time testifies to how a kind of ultimate truth arises within the psychotic subject, who lives a real truth that is inaccessible to other people, because it is not compatible with the oblivion and illusion of the symbolic order. In the psychotic structure, we have plunged into an unbearable crack, a real abyss in the big other, and Lacan—to describe the psychotic process (especially the phenomenon of hallucination)—articulates the following algorithm: "What has not come to light in the symbolic, emerges in the real." (Lacan 1993[1955–1956]: 13; 2006[1953b]: 324) In the case of the actual breakthrough of psychosis, the subject is called a situation or, more precisely, an appeal—it is placed in a symbolic contradiction to the name of the father previously rejected in its history—which it has no means of dealing with or responding to. In the place of the name of the father, there is only a gaping void. What we then perceive as a delusional system or paranoia is—as Freud already pointed out—a healing attempt, what Lacan calls a "stabilizing delusional metaphor," an attempt to (imaginatively) fill the real hole of the absence of the name of the father left behind in the symbolic order.

In the structure of perversion—which, in the French tradition after Lacan, is a clearly defined personality structure, not a vulgar designation or just a deviant sexual act, and in which one also places other problems, such as drug and gambling abuse, anorexia, bulimia, obesity problems, criminal behavior, and, in particular, borderline personality and narcissistic disorders—the signifier of the Real is denied. As a consequence of a denial of the truth and the law of castration, the perverted subject never fully enters into the symbolic order, but instead remains in a pre-Oedipal structure. The identification with the imaginary mother means that the subject fills her real lack. The structure of the perversion includes what Freud speaks of as a cleavage of the ego (*Ichspaltung*), where the deficiency is first recognized but then denied, and which Lacan formulates with an algorithm: "I know, but still…" A transgression of desire arises that removes the subject from the reality of the law and which, paradoxically, means that, due to the desire atrophy—a form of desirelessness—the perverted subject is someone "who does not want anything," because nothing is missing. In terms of *objet petit a*, the cause of desire—which is caused by the lack of the Thing and at the same time fills it out by means of imaginary objects—the perverted subject will become too close to the object, identify with it, and then the desire suffocates. By denying the lack, the perverted violates the big other (the name of the father), and, by self-enforcing the law—"committing" the law—the subject subordinates the law of jouissance (Lacan 2006[1963]: 652). It is a law that follows a compulsive logic, imposes an offense, disputes the legal nature of the law, and means that the perverted subject is transformed into what Lacan designates as an "instrument for the jouissance of the big Other" (Lacan 2006[1960]: 697). If the original object of the psychotic subject has not been lost, where the actual loss is rejected, the perverted subject denies the Real, because it has already found its object; no desire arises in relation to what was originally lost; in this way, the drive as a form of negativity will dominate the structure of perversion.

Like the previous structures, in the neurotic structure, the symbolic castration (e.g., lack, suffering, loss) is avoided, but it is here subject to repression (unlike rejection and denial), which means that the characteristic element of the real lack is repressed. The neurotic subject will forget a painful and unpleasant truth—it becomes unconscious—and what is displaced is not the lack in itself, but what denotes the loss, a symbolically signifying element (the name of the father) of desire that is transformed into a symptom, in the form of a "return of the repressed." In contrast to the previous structures, the neurotic subject enters into the symbolic order—in an Oedipal triangular structure—but where the mother's desire and then the law (the name of the father) are under repression (Lacan 2006[1960]: 698). In an identification with the imaginary father, a situation of conflict and rivalry arises, which makes it possible to avoid the truth of the castration in an imaginary way. In the neurotic's interpretation of the law, the prohibition is the deciding factor: "You shall not have a desire..." The neurotic subject introduces a relationship of hatred with the law, blaming the other for his suffering, thus avoiding imaginary castration and avoiding the grief work that it implies. The neurotic subject accepts a lack (the Real) that nothing can fill, but not that it in itself could have a deficiency. It cannot fully—as in the structure of the sublimation—identify itself with the symbolic order, the position of the law (only as a prohibition) and the dead father, and recognize the truth of castration, that human life is characterized by finiteness and death.

In the structure of sublimation, the Real is recognized in symbolic form. Is it an existential structure like the others? In structural terms, yes, but, in fact, no human being of flesh and blood can constantly live in sublimation. Theoretically, the structure of sublimation is also associated with difficulties. An identification with the basic symbolic element of the symbolic father is a possible assumption, but the castration, the real lack, can never be fully symbolized; there will always be a residue. Sublimation means an identification with the nonliving, which is the identity of the dead father. Scripture is such an act. Recognition of the law of castration can be achieved through Freud's concept of negation, when the truth, in Lacan's words, appears in lies or as fiction. To be in the structure of the sublimation is to assume the law and recognize a basic prohibition, but a prohibition that has a creative effect when it points out an object that cannot be included in the symbolic order. The law prohibits, but at the same time, it creates and constructs a real object from the emptiness of the Thing. Lacan arrives at the following algorithm: in the structure of the sublimation, the object is elevated to the "dignity of the Thing" (Lacan 1992[1959–1960]: 112, 130). All of the foregoing existential structures have access to the structure of the sublimation, and in all forms of sublimations, the category of emptiness is decisive, where the Thing occupies different positions—in the form of rejection, denial, repression, and recognition or negation—and is manifested in four different ways in the discourses of science, religion, art, and psychoanalysis (as a practice) (Lacan 2006[1966]).

Psychoanalysis as a practice can thus be attached to the structure of the sublimation—as theory, its fate is a form of negation—and, among the existential structures, it is what Lacan calls the "sublimation of sublimation." The practice of psychoanalysis experiences in the flesh the truth of sublimation, because it allows the castration, object *a*, to occupy the place of the Thing. The psychoanalyst is in this place but nothing can be created there. This applies to psychoanalysis as an act. The analyst listens, is silent, and talks—nothing more. How, then, is truth manifested in psychoanalysis as a practice? The sublimation and the work of grief are the goals of psychoanalysis. In the clinical reality, the object of the Real is a truth reference that appears in anxiety, which is, in Lacan's words, "that which does not deceive" (Lacan 2015[1962–1963]: 76). With the concept of the Real, Lacan laid the foundation of ethics in the psychoanalytical cure—to recognize and not compromise or sacrifice desire, in the sense of admitting the truth of the inevitability of the Real and the impossibility of fully symbolizing it. For the analysand's true desire to be manifested, the analyst cannot answer the analysand's demand for love, but only support the possibility of the desire to expose itself, merely letting the analysand "be" in loneliness, in the necessary work of grief, which is true love on the part of the analyst (Lacan 1992[1959–1960]: 303). The analyst becomes for the analysand, in terms of the object *a*, an irreplaceable and unique real treasure that must be acquired.

If the goal of the psychoanalytic treatment is grief and sublimation, it means that we can never fully reconcile the loss of the real truth. In grief, the sublimation's ability to symbolize the Real is in fact idealized and then hidden by a new veil. What happens in melancholy (not as a concept of depression), which is a structure that intersects the other structures, is that the subject, as opposed to grief, incorporates the loss in itself. In Freud's poetic formulation, the shadow of the lost object has fallen on the melancholy ego. If we in the melancholy structure can find an identification with the Real, as a lost object—the question is whether this subject's existence is more authentic in the sense that melancholy exposes a deeper truth than that of grief. If the grieving human being speaks and expresses a will to reconcile with suffering, the melancholic subject is immeasurably true in its silence in the light of the unshakable fact of death. In that way, melancholy testifies to a fundamental existential, silent, real truth—the impossibility of completely overcoming and coping with loss and lack in human life—with the *truth of the Real.*

References

Juranville, A. 1984. *Lacan et la philosophie*. Paris: Presses Universitaires de France.

Lacan, J. 2006[1953a]. "The Function and Field of Speech and Language in Psychoanalysis." In *Écrits*, translated by Bruce Fink. New York: W. W. Norton & Company.

Lacan, J. 2006[1953b]. "Response to Jean Hyppolite's Commentary on Freud's 'Verneinung.'" In *Écrits*, translated by Bruce Fink. New York: W. W. Norton & Company.

Lacan, J. 1988[1953–1954]. *The Seminar. Book I. Freud's Papers on Technique*. Translated by J Forrester. Cambridge: Cambridge University Press.

Lacan, J. 1993[1955–1956]. *The Psychoses. The Seminar of Jacques Lacan. Book III*. Translated by R. Grigg. London: Routledge.

Lacan, J. 2006[1957]. "The Instance of the Letter in the Unconscious or Reason since Freud." In *Écrits*, translated by Bruce Fink. New York: W. W. Norton & Company.

Lacan, J. 2006[1958]. "On a Question Prior to Any Possible Treatment of Psychosis." In *Écrits*, translated by Bruce Fink. New York: W. W. Norton & Company.

Lacan, J. 1992[1959–1960]. *The Ethics of Psychoanalysis. The Seminar of Jacques Lacan, Book VII*. Translated by D. Porter. London: Routledge.

Lacan, J. 2006[1960]. "The Subversion of the Subject and the Dialectic of Desire." In *Écrits*, translated by Bruce Fink. New York: W. W. Norton & Company.

Lacan, J. 2015[1962–1963]. *Anxiety. The Seminar of Jacques Lacan. Book X*. Translated by A. R. Price. Cambridge: Polity Press.

Lacan, J. 2006[1963]. "Kant with Sade." In *Écrits*, translated by Bruce Fink. New York: W. W. Norton & Company.

Lacan, J. 1977[1964]. *The Four Fundamental Concepts of Psychoanalysis*. Translated by A. Sheridan. London: The Hogarth Press and the Institute of Psychoanalysis.

Lacan, J. 2006[1966]. "Science and Truth." In *Écrits*, translated by Bruce Fink. New York: W. W. Norton & Company.

Lacan, J. 1990[1974a]. "Television." In *Television. A Challenge to the Psychoanalytic Establishment*, translated by D. Hollier et al. London: W. W. Norton & Company, 1990.

Lacan, J. 1990[1974b]. "Responses to Students of Philosophy concerning the Object of Psychoanalysis." In *Television. A Challenge to the Psychoanalytic Establishment*, translated by D. Hollier et al. London: W. W. Norton & Company.

Wallenstein, S.-O. 1992. "Lacan, Heidegger och det psykoanalytiska sanningsbegreppet" ("Lacan, Heidegger and the psychoanalytic concept of truth"). *Divan, Tidskrift för psykoanalys och kultur* (Divan., Journal of Psychoanalysis and Culture) 4 (April): 44–51.

CHAPTER 5

Truth and Sexuality
Foucault, the Genealogist of Psychoanalysis

Laurie Laufer

In his work, Michel Foucault analyzes the discursive deployment of sexuality, which historically establishes the link between sexuality, subjectivity, and the obligation of truth, a triad that he attributes to psychoanalysis as the descendant of a *Scientia Sexualis*. The latter seeks the truth in the heart of sex and is supposed to involve expression of the true sex and identity, accompanied by a practice of confession. In 1976, in *The Will to Knowledge*, Foucault demonstrated "how the history of the deployment of sexuality, as it has developed since the classical age, can be used as an archaeology of psychoanalysis" (1976: 12). Foucault's arguments put into perspective the reasons behind the articulation of truth, sexuality, and subjectivity. Why have truth games and veridiction regimens regarding sexuality been so rarely questioned? "What is the invention of truth? What is the adventure that has made it possible?" writes Foucault in the *Lessons on the Will to Knowledge* (1970: 199). In this chapter, I will explore the thread proposed by Foucault: "It seemed to me that the question that would serve as a guiding thread was thus: how, why and in what form did sexual activity constitute a moral domain?" (1984: 16).

"Confession Science"

In *The Emergence of Sexuality: Historical Epistemology and the Formation of Concepts*, Arnold Davidson (2001: 9) writes that "We are our sexuality, at least so we have been repeatedly told." He continues:

> In this sense, there is no doubt that it goes without saying that we cannot think of ourselves, of our most fundamental psychological identity, without thinking of our sexuality, of that deep secret layer of our desires that reveals the kind of individual we really are. And the 'triumph' of the humanities is precisely in highlighting, with all the strength of scientific

> concepts, the role played by sexuality in the formation of our personality, its privileged place at the heart of our psychic life. (Davidson 2001: 9)

Following Foucauldian thought, Davidson criticizes the emergence of truth games that articulate sexuality and subjectivity. The terms "sexuality," "homosexuality," and "perversion" no longer hold the same meaning as they did in Freud's time, because all notions should be considered in their contemporaneity. As Davidson writes:

> The concept of perversion or sexuality must not be identified with a self-sufficient object, the content of which could be discovered through a kind of intellectual intuition. These concepts should be identified according to the uses made of them, the connections that govern their use and allow people to participate in what Foucault considered to be specific 'truth games.' Since these uses, connections, and truth games are not analyzed in metaphysical or transcendental terms, as if they were fixed and non-revisable, it is not surprising that those who have been influenced by Foucault attach great importance to the 'history of the emergence of truth games'. (Davidson 1997: 56)

Notions and concepts are never immutable but subject to revision. It is therefore impossible to separate the concepts of practice from their usage. "The phrase 'dreams fulfil desires' can well be repeated over the centuries; notwithstanding, the statement is not the same for Plato and Freud," as Foucault (1969: 110) writes in the *Archaeology of Knowledge*. The conditions of use and the fields of experience are affected by theoretical events and shaken by their epistemological tremors. However, overlooking the modalities of their transformation widens the gap between a (Freudian) theory and the practice from which it originates. This is why Foucault criticizes in medicine—relayed by psychoanalysis in his view—all the violence of the power devices that tend to establish the truth of a body, or rather characterize the body in truth. For him, psychoanalysis and phenomenology are deployment of "veridiction" that aim to dominate and control bodies.

Foucault writes:

> And we must also admit that it is on the side of sex that the most secret and profound truths of the individual should be sought; only there can we best discover what they are and what determine them; and while for centuries we believed that sex things should be hidden because they were

> shameful, we now know that it is sex itself that hides the most secret parts of the individual: the structure of their fantasies, the roots of their Ego, the forms of their relationship to reality. At the intersection of these two ideas—notably, that we must not be mistaken by our sex and that our sex conceals the truest things in us—psychoanalysis has implanted its cultural vigor, promising us our sex, the true one, as well as this truth about ourselves that secretly watches over it. (Foucault 1980: 937)

In *The Will to Knowledge*, Foucault unravels and criticizes this entanglement between sex, truth, and subjectivity. In the nineteenth century, sex became an issue of truth and falsity. Compared to other societies, Western civilization especially stands out in the relationship between sexuality and truth: while some have established this relationship by founding an *Ars Erotica* to extract the truth from pleasure itself, Western civilization instituted a *Scientia Sexualis* in the form of a particular process: the practice of confession founded by the Catholic Church following the generalization of confession in 1215 (Fourth Lateran Council). This involves striving to express what is most difficult to say with the utmost accuracy: a form of truth about oneself and one's own desire. For Foucault, it is not only a question of analyzing how sexuality is caught in the matrix of power (Butler 1990) but also how it becomes a discursive deployment regulated by truth and confession.

Foucault writes:

> Theoretically, there are two main procedures for producing the truth of sex. On the one hand, there are the societies—and they are numerous: Chinese, Japanese, Indian, Roman, and Arab-Muslim societies—that have acquired an *Ars Erotica*. [...] Our civilization, at least at first sight, has no *Ars Erotica*. It is probably the only civilization to practice a *Scientia Sexualis*. Or rather, to have developed over the centuries procedures to tell the truth of sex, which are essentially ordered as a form of power/knowledge rigorously opposed to the art of initiations and masterful secrecy: this is the confession. (Foucault 1976: 76–78)

Westerners thus became the "beasts of confession" (Foucault 1976: 80). Subsequently, the confession of religion was substituted by science through the development of a science confession. The "apparatus of sexuality" is therefore situated in the historical dissemination of *Scientia Sexualis* between Christian confessional practices and the scientification of confession. This marks the birth of a "science confession," a scientification of the confession of sex, which progressed from the Catholic monastic tradition to the scientific instructions of the economic police authorities, courts, psychiatric hospitals, and psychoanalysts' couches… For Foucault, the object of this confession science is the "unconfessable-confessed," or the truth of sex. It is therefore necessary to find the truth of sex, because the truth is in the sex: in other words, the truth of individuals lies in their sexualities. "We ask sex to tell the truth and also to tell our truth."

Herculine Barbin: The True Sex

To put into perspective the stakes of truth and sexuality and the aforementioned science of confession, I will refer here to Foucault's reading of Herculine Barbin's memoirs from the mid-nineteenth century.

The memoirs of Herculine Barbin were discovered by Ambroise Tardieu, a forensic medical scientist well known at the time and already famous for his much acclaimed work *Les Attentats aux moeurs* (Offenses against Morality) (1857). In this true anatomical descriptive guide, Tardieu identifies, among other practices, the frequent practice of oral sex—a highly reprehensible practice at the time—based on the shape of an individual's mouth. Here, the doctor walks hand in hand with the judge. Sex is potentially the immediate vector of crime. "In any case, physical signs are excellent means to guide the search for justice" (Tardieu 1995[1857]: 389). Ambroise Tardieu invents a body according to the grammar of his era, and as Georges Vigarello writes in his preface to *Les Attentats aux mœurs*,

> We should stress this 'imagined' anatomy. It is underpinned by the desire to judge more than to show, but it poses a broader problem than simply identifying injuries or suspecting the victim. It is intended to *identify individuals* […]. A way to help unmask suspects […]. It is a social expectation, a precise concern that clearly goes beyond the effects of aggression alone, an obsession that developed as never before with 19th-century society and the abandonment of old orders: to better identify individuals rendered 'indistinct' by the supposed blurring of conditions, to better locate them, to better monitor them. The 'naked' body becomes an endlessly pried landmark, subject to the wisdom of the forensic doctor, since habits are no longer sufficient to reveal the social origin and condition of each person. (Vigarello 1995: 23-24)

This marks the beginning of the era of suspicion regarding sexual practices, which can henceforth be identified by the shapes and conformity of bodies.

In 1874, Ambroise Tardieu published a scientific book entitled *Question médico-légale de l'identité dans ses rapports avec les vices de conformation des organes sexuels* (The Forensic Issue of Identity and its Relationship with the Defects of Conformity of Sexual Organs), which included a manuscript discovered in 1868 in an attic in the Latin Quarter of Paris. Next to this manuscript was the corpse of twenty-eight-year-old Abel Barbin, who had just committed suicide. Abel was born Adelaid Herculine Barbin (nicknamed Alexina by his/her family) and renamed at the age of twenty-one after a court declared him/her male. This administrative decision took into account Barbin's "obvious male predominance" from a physiological point of view. In 1868, this "young man," who was working in a railway administration, died from carbonic asphyxiation. On the table, he left a letter addressed to his mother and a manuscript entitled *My Memoirs*, in which he recounted his lonely and miserable life.[1]

The civil status doctor in charge of recording the death examined the body and the genitals to see whether the deceased was suffering from a disease that could have explained his/her suicidal act. During this examination, Dr. Régnier noted with astonishment that "this is one of the most prominent cases of male hermaphroditism" (Barbin 1978[1868]: 141). Ambroise Tardieu (1874: 137; emphasis added) writes:

> The extraordinary fact that remains to be reported provides the most cruel and painful example of the fatal *consequences that can result from a* ***mistake*** *made from birth in the attribution of civil status.* As we shall see, the victim of this mistake, after spending 20 years dressed in the clothes of a sex that was not his own, struggling with a passion of which he was unaware, eventually warned by the explosion of his senses, then returned to his *true sex* and at the same time to the *real feeling of his physical infirmity*, taking life in disgust and ending it by suicide. [...] Certainly, in this case, the appearances of the female sex have been pushed too far, and yet science and justice have been forced to recognize the error and give back to this young man his true sex [...] I do not hesitate to publish almost all [of Herculine Barbin's memoirs] here, wishing not to lose the twofold precious teaching that it contains regarding the influence exerted by the malformation of sexual organs on emotional faculties and moral dispositions, and the gravity of the individual and social consequences that can result from an erroneous recognition of the sex of a newly born child.

Or, as Dr. Goujon writes:

> It is sometimes difficult and even impossible to recognize the true sex of an individual at birth, as it is not the same in later life and especially at the onset of puberty. It is indeed at this time, in people who have been the victims of such a mistake, that tendencies and habits emerge relating to those of their true sex. (Barbin 1978[1868]: 149)

The question asked by the doctors was: What is "real sex"? Consequently, Tardieu published *Mes Souvenirs d'Herculine Barbin* to scientifically demonstrate the tragic effects of a sexual assignment error and, foremostly, to establish a causal and truthful "rational" and "scientific" link between sexual affiliation and sexual attraction.

Barbin was raised in religious institutions among other girls. Regarding her gender reassignment, she writes: "What happened was not a revelation to me but yet another torment in my life" (Barbin 1978[1868]: 41). Accordingly, far from being a revelation that would deliver her from a "disastrous" identity, this new gender allocation caused her much more suffering than relief. Foucault comments: "Alexina wrote the memoir of his/her life after discovering and establishing his/her new identity: his/her 'true' and 'definitive' identity" (1980: 939). For Foucault, Barbin does not write as a man returned to "her true sex," to her "true identity."

> When Alexina writes his/her memoirs, he/she is not very far from suicide. *According to his/her perception, he/she is still without a certain sex*, but he/she is deprived of the delights felt when he/she was without one or when he/she had one that differed from those among whom he/she lived, and loved, and wanted so badly. (Foucault 1980: 939)

However, Barbin is not "without certain sex" when she loves and desires. Foucault probably skims over the modalities of the enunciation of Barbin's text. Even after her sex reassignment by the civil registry office, Barbin writes her memories in the female grammatical gender. Indeed, Barbin, in the language that supports her, in the body of her writing, loves as a woman and loves women:

> I was generally loved by my mistresses and my companions, and I returned this affection to them well. I was *born* to love. [...] I soon became a close friend with a charming young girl named Thécla, a year older than me. Certainly, nothing was more opposing on the outside

> than our physique. My friend was as fresh and graceful as I was not. We were called the inseparables, and indeed we did not lose sight of each other for a single moment. (Barbin 1978[1868]: 35).

It is this desire and erotic impulse that arouses the suspicions of the doctor and judge at the time. Because, as a woman, she wants a woman, Barbin is assigned to be a man by the medical profession. For Tardieu and the scientists of the time, a woman who loves and desires a woman can only be a man. The underlying issue here is the normalization of heterosexual desire. This heteronormativity is the rule according to which any alleged misassignment must be corrected.

Barbin has a passionate love and sexual relationship with the young Sara: "In our delightful intimate moments, she liked to give me the male qualification, which was later granted to me by the civil registry office" (Barbin 1978[1868]: 68). In the narrative of her erotic games—her partner calls her Camille in their love and sexual outbursts—and in her shared passion for her friend Sara, Barbin destabilizes the language, undoes and disrupts the gender hierarchy, moving from male to female gender, and does so in full consciousness. She is the one who stresses the grammatical gender changes:

> One evening, I asked my friend to share my bed. She accepted with pleasure. To describe the delightfulness that I felt with her presence by my side would be impossible! I was so *overwhelmed and happy*! We talked for a long time before falling asleep, me with both arms around her waist, she resting her face close to mine! […] Sara belonged to me now!!! She was mine!!! Whatever separated us in the natural order of things in this world now united us! Imagine what you want of our situation! (Barbin 1978[1868]: 61)

Raised and educated as a woman, a "socially constructed woman," living in a community of women, she narrates the devastating consequences of the "medical truth" of her undetermined sex on her life and body. Sexual practices here are based on the need to have a real sex and match sex to sexual attraction. Barbin is medically a hermaphrodite, although the findings of the medical expertise affirm the "clear predominance of the male sex." Let us quote Dr. Chesnet:

> From the above facts, what can we conclude? Is Alexina a woman? She has a vulva, *labia majora*, a female urethra. These are all feminine attributes: yes, but Alexina has never had her menses; the whole outside of the body is that of a man, and my examination did not reveal a uterus. *Her*

> *tastes, her inclinations, attract her to women. These are the* ***real witnesses of sex.*** We can now conclude and say that Alexina is a man, probably hermaphrodite, but with an obvious predominance of the male sex. (Barbin 1978[1868]: 142)

The real witnesses of sex are thus her attraction to women. But what happens when Barbin has been returned to "her real sex"? What should have allowed Barbin to love her/his friend Sara after the name and sex change in her/his civil status, without hiding and without feeling shame and anxiety, became the tipping point to suicide. Barbin's "true sex," established by the social scientific discourse, with her/his sexual identity returned to its "truth," rather pushed her/him to suicide. Barbin writes:

> So it was done. The civil status called me to join this half called the strong sex. I, raised until the age of 21 in religious houses and in the midst of my companions, was going to leave a whole delicious past far behind me, like Achilles, and enter the race, armed with my sole weakness and my profound inexperience of men and things! (Barbin 1978[1868]: 102).

It is precisely these passages of suffering that Tardieu tries to censor, leaving just a few pages to avoid breaking the momentum of this writing style that Foucault (1980: 938) considers to be a "lifestyle," a tone of writing that also expresses ways of being in the world. This is why Barbin can write that "[t]his incessant struggle of nature against reason exhausts me with each passing day and leads me in great strides to the grave" (Barbin 1978[1868]: 116-117). Barbin was thus correct in writing that she would become the object of gaze and scientific language, the object of these "princes of science," but not, as she says, to "analyze all the pains that have burned, devoured this heart down to its last fibers," but rather to open, dissect, expertly assess the reality of a body, and to become intoxicated by the fantasy of their science so as to discover the truth of sex.

Medicine corrected the harm done to the subject, while Tardieu and his learned colleagues never challenged the validity of Barbin's act of sex rectification. Canguilhem writes:

> The characteristic of a false science is to never encounter the false, to never renounce anything, to never to change language. For false science, there is no pre-scientific state. The discourse of false science cannot be denied. In short, false science has no history. (1977: 46)

More precisely, what Tardieu censors is the story of Barbin's suffering, ex-Alexina, as he silently passes over the written account after the change of her/his civil status.

In this context, sexuality and sexual practices become the focus of a scientific discourse that determines the identity of a subject: everything happens as if the truth of a subject were reducible to their sexual identity. According to Foucault, with modern sexuality and its discursive deployment, the subject becomes a "psychological man." "Do we really need a real sex?": this is the question asked by the philosopher in his presentation of the Herculine Barbin's memoir known as Alexina B (Foucault 1980: 935).

Is truth not at the service of a categorization of the ego, which the subject interiorizes so as to be identified and recognized in the other's gaze? Sexuality is one of the fields subjected to this regime of veridiction in order to constitute the identity and personality of a subject, while modern medicine enters this field of veridiction that claims to be "the truth of sex."

Foucault (1980: 935) writes: "It took a long time to postulate that a hermaphrodite should have only one true sex." In the Middle Ages, he argues, it was the role of the father or godfather (i.e., those who "named" the child) to determine the sex that would be retained at the time of baptism. Then, from the eighteenth century onward, biological theories of sexuality gradually led to the rejection of the idea of mixing the two sexes in a single body and thus restricting the free choice of uncertain individuals. "From now on, to each one a sex, and only one. Everyone has their first profound determined and determining sexual identity" (Foucault, 1980: 935). From a medical point of view, this involves deciphering the real sex hidden behind appearances. Foucault comments:

> I am well aware that 19th- and 20th-century medicine has corrected many things in this simplistic and reductive logic [...]. However, the idea that we must have a real sex is far from being completely dispelled. Regardless of the opinion of biologists on this matter, in psychiatry, psychoanalysis, and psychology, as well as in popular opinion, there lurks the notion, at least in a diffuse way, that there are complex, obscure, and essential relationships between sex and truth. We are certainly more tolerant of practices that violate the law. But we still believe that some of them insult 'the truth' [...]. Perhaps we are willing to admit that they are not in serious breach of the established order. But we continue to believe that there is a 'mistake' [...] Sexual irregularity is more or less perceived as belonging to the world of chimeras. (1980: 935)

It is therefore a matter of "telling the truth" about sexuality, and as Foucault writes, "sexuality, much more than an element of the individual that would be rejected outside of him, constitutes this link that people are forced to establish with their identity in the form of subjectivity" (1978: 528). Yet Freud and Lacan have consistently shown that, in the experience of human sexuality, there are multiple differences and genders, diverse sexual behaviors and practices: in short, complex and subtle differentiations in sexual diversity that are subjected to a variety of norms according to time and place, which are themselves more or less necessary. Freud claimed that norms are arbitrary and conventional, stemming from a fiction and therefore the social imagination. Adopting this idea, Lacan said during an interview on *France Culture* in 1973, later published in the journal *Le Coq Héron* in 1974, that "[t]here are social norms because there is no sexual norm, that's what Freud says." A variety, a variation, a verity that is therefore fiction, a discursive chimera, in short.

Variation, Verity, Varity

Lacan, quite differently from Foucault, operates a relativization of truth. Lacan states that truth has a fictional structure: it is therefore manufactured, ultimately relating to the semblant. Lacan eventually created the neologism of *varity* (variable verity). Language as such, the symbolic, has a fictional structure. Lacan noted the impact of this variability. He did so by inventing a neologism that subverted his own concepts of truth and already put a serious dampener on the truth (understood as "half saying"). Thus, with "varity," the variability no longer only affects the truth of statements but rather the truth itself, as Lacan says. "We should see the openness to the dimension of truth as a variable. In other words, by condensing two words like that, I will call varity with a small swallowed *e*, variety" (Lacan 1977: 116).

Truth as metaphor becomes an invention of oneself or the "aesthetics of existence" according to Foucault's expression, a "lifestyle" as he wrote about Herculine Barbin. Multiplicity, variation, variability, possibilities, experiences, and events therefore lie at the heart of Foucauldian epistemology, thus reversing the classical patterns of identity, fixed and defined categories, and transcendence. In his inaugural lecture at the Collège de France in 1971, Foucault announced his working method:

> The fundamental notions that are now required are no longer those of consciousness and continuity (with the associated problems of freedom and causality), or sign and structure. They are rather event and series,

> with the interplay of the related notions of regularity, randomness, discontinuity, dependence, transformation. (Foucault 1970-1971: 58-59)

For Foucault, the category of *desire* recalls that of a psychological unconscious and sex that bears the subject's identity as its truth. By contrast, the notion of *pleasure* is depsychologized, because it refers to no meaning and no explanation. That is why Foucault appreciated the *aphrodisia* of the ancient world. The acquisition of these techniques does not refer to any identity of the subject (Foucault 1984: 213). Truth is driven out by the notion of the Real and therefore meaning. In *Television*, Lacan writes: "I always tell the not all truth, because it is not possible to tell all of it. To tell all of it is impossible, as words are materially absent. Yet it is even through this impossible that truth holds to the Real" (1973: 509). This way of looking at multiplicities and the scope of possibilities contravenes any attempt to categorize, whether it be along identity, practices, or disciplinary lines, for example. Considering flows and multiplicities, considering the genealogy of the event, considering displacements and series: these are the epistemological issues according to the Foucauldian method.

By way of illustration and inspired by the Foucauldian method, I would like to compare three lists that undo the principle of fixed and rigidified sexual categories and show, by means of their multiplicity and variation, the fluidity, play, and irony relating to the invention of the sexual, which no longer occurs in the context of the games of veridiction but rather in the games of variation. The three proposed series relate to Freud, Kosofsky Sedgwick, and what can currently be found on Facebook. Would Freud have smiled if he had known that his twentieth lecture on human sexual life would have given rise to such multiple variations?

In this lecture, Freud lists (without categorizing) all kinds of sexual practices, only to conclude that they all form part of "normal sexuality" (this is in 1916, and Freud gives this lecture to Viennese doctors):

> The first group includes those who have renounced the union of the two genitals and who replace the genitals of one of the couple engaged in the sexual act by some other part or region of the body; in this they disregard the lack of stable organic arrangements as well as any impediment offered by feelings of disgust. (They replace the vulva, for instance, by the mouth or anus.) Others follow, who, it is true, still retain the genitals as an object—not however, on account of their sexual function but of other functions in which the genital plays a part either for anatomical reasons or because of its propinquity.

The Freudian list is long and avoids the psychiatric terms of its time as much as possible: the fascination with excreta, clothing, breasts, shoes, and hair braids; the appetite for corpses; the enjoyment of seeing and being seen, beating or being beaten, and so on. Freud concludes:

> Well, Ladies and Gentlemen, what attitude are we to adopt to these unusual kinds of sexual satisfaction? Indignation, an expression of our personal repugnance and an assurance that we ourselves do not share these lusts will obviously be of no help. Indeed, that is not what we have been asked for. When all is said and done, what we have here is a field of phenomena like any other. A denial in the form of an evasive suggestion that after all these are only rarities and curiosities would be easy to refute. On the contrary, we are dealing with quite common and widespread phenomena. If, however, it is argued that we need not allow our views of sexual life to be misled by them because they are one and all aberrations and deviations of the sexual instinct, a serious answer is called for. Unless we can understand these pathological forms of sexuality and can co-ordinate them with normal sexual life, we cannot understand normal sexuality either. (Freud 1916: 346-348)

Eighty years later, in 1998, following the gender studies of Butler, Rubin, and others on inventiveness in gender and sexuality, Eve Kosofsky Sedgwick (1998: 115) wrote about the term "queer":

> The open matrix has possibilities, gaps, intersections, dissonances, resonances, failures, or excesses of meaning when the constituent elements of someone's gender and sexuality are not (or cannot be) constrained to monolithic meanings. These are the political, linguistic, epistemological, and figurative adventures and experiences of those of us who like to define ourselves (among many other possibilities) as female and aggressive lesbians, mystical faggots, fantasizers, drag queens and drag kings, clones, leathers, women in suits, feminist women or feminist men, masturbators, madwomen, divas, snap!, manly submissive guys, mythomaniacs, transsexuals, wannabes, poofs, truckers, men who define themselves as lesbians sleeping with men […], and all those who are able to love them, learn from them, and identify with them.

The possibilities are endless, and twenty years later, in 2018, Facebook offers the possibility to choose one's gender or genders from more than seventy-five items:

> Agender, androgynous, other, none, refuses to conform to gender stereotypes, nonconforming gender, variable gender, variant gender, fluid gender, pangender, atypical gender, questioning gender, neutral gender, queer, allosexual, altersexual, non-binary, two-spirited, bigender, cis, cisgender, cisgender girl, trans girl, woman, cis woman, trans woman, FTM, trans boy, cis boy, cisgender boy, transgender boy, transsexual boy, man, cis man, cisgender man, transgender man, transsexual man, male-to-female, female-to-male, inter-sexual, intergender, intersex, MTF, neutron, two-spirit, trans person, transgender person, transgender, transsexual, transvestite, trans, trans'.

If there is an irreducible part of the psychoanalytical subject, it is the subject that does not fit into any normative discourse. Analytical practice must deal with a subject who is confronted with a reality that surpasses them, a reality that goes beyond the normative and biological order. The unconscious and the drive break with the "normal" and "natural" course of things. Psychoanalysis proliferates on the excess, on the irreducible remains of the norm. What is at stake here is an attempt to deconstruct nosographic, sexual, racial, and communitarian categories, not to produce a "universalizing" whole but to establish a relationship with knowledge. This approach finds a meeting point with what Jean Allouch says about the possible practice of psychoanalysis:

> In fact, the restricted definition of the subject by the signifier [...] is enough to require the psychoanalyst, in their fraternity with the analysand, to welcome them by excluding any sort of categorization: nosographic, sexist, racial, communitarian. What do I know about the person who enters my consulting room seeking psychoanalysis? Will I judge them by their appearance like a phenomenologist, claiming that they are male, female, homosexual, religious, poor, intelligent, black, young, or whatever? Precisely not. An analytical cure, from the perspective of the psychoanalyst, can only occur with this abstention. If Freud, in a gesture as foundational as Descartes's methodical doubt, had not known how to cast his knowledge aside, to step away from Charcot's pseudo-mastery, a Freudian movement would simply never have occurred. (Allouch 2007: 77)

What kind of psychoanalyst thinks in categories? What sort of a psychoanalyst is fortified behind demarcation lines? During his seminar Crucial Problems to Psychoanalysis on May 5, 1965, Lacan made the following analysis:

> A subject is a psychoanalyst, not a scientist barricaded behind categories in the middle of which they try to sort things into drawers to store the recorded symptoms of their psychotic, neurotic, or other patients, but inasmuch as they enter the signifying game. (Lacan 1964-1965: unpublished)

The signifier cannot fix any absolute truth; it carries a fundamental instability and cannot fix any definitive meaning.

Analytical practice emphasizes that any identity construction, any gender truth, and any identity truth can become a problem for the subject. The young White, active, cisgender, and heterosexual man, and the White heterosexual, passive, and maternal woman: these supposed representatives of imaginary health are deconstructed by and on the psychoanalytic couch. The normative discourses that can fool them are undone, and their identities are lost in a "shop of accessories," as Lacan said. During his seminar on the theory of the ego, Lacan points out

> that the Ego is the sum of the identifications of the subject, with all that this can entail in a radically contingent manner. If you allow me to imagine it, the Ego is like the superposition of the different coats borrowed from what I will call the junk of its accessory shop. (Lacan 1954-1955: 187)

The contingency and bricolage of identifications are exactly what the ego is. And if "the sexual being is authorized by themselves and by others," to borrow Lacan's expression, it is from this perspective of contingent bricolage. Nothing more, but nothing less, because in a way, the experience of analysis also involves becoming aware of this contingency and discarding the frictions that we create for ourselves, not to mention their pathological and extravagant effects. This is why we can say that the so-called identity proliferation supposed in the LGBTQIA+ movement targets the impossibility of the sexual by instituting a horizon of *contingency*, given that new letters are forever ready to emerge and rearrange themselves in a movement that exceeds symbolic laws and imaginary fixations. This idea is supported, on the one hand, by the proposal that the Real emerges historically and, on the other hand, by the exposure of the contingent character in a few, which opens all the others to infinity (cf. Lacan 1973–1974: 190; Ambra 2018).

Psychoanalysis thus consists of two stages: first, constructing a fiction and producing identifications, and second, undoing a fiction and disposing with identifications with the other for the analysis. Therefore, because there is relativization of the truth, nothing prevents us from thinking that this fictionality can vary according to historical periods. There are only fictional effects of truth. To experience the invention of oneself or the aesthetics of existence in all the variations of its truth, would this not be one form of knowledge of analysis?

Translated from French by Nicolas Evzonas

Notes

1 Tardieu included this manuscript in *Question médico-légale dans ses rapports avec les vices de conformation des organes sexuels* (1874). Note that he did not publish the entire manuscript. "First and foremost, he missed some of Barbin's memoirs. Tardieu seems to have received the complete manuscript from Dr Régnier who established the death certificate and performed the autopsy. He kept it, publishing only the part that seemed important to him. He neglected the memories of Barbin's final years, all that he considered to be complaints, recriminations, and inconsistencies. Despite extensive research, it was not possible to find the manuscript that Tardieu had in his hands" (Foucault, in Barbin 1978: 131).

References

Allouch, J. 2007. *La Psychanalyse est-elle un exercice spirituel? Réponse á Michel Foucault.* Paris: EPEL.

Ambra, P. 2018. "Das fórmulas ao nome: bases para uma teoria da sexuação em Lacan." PhD supervised by Nelson da Silva Junior and Laurie Laufer. São Paulo: Paris.

Barbin, H. 1978[1868]. *Mes Souvenirs* [My Memoirs]. Edited by M. Foucault. Paris: Gallimard.

Butler, J. 1990. *Gender Trouble: Feminism and the Subversion of Identity.* London: Routledge.

Canguilhem, G. 2009[1977]. "Qu'est qu'une idéologie scientifique?" In *Idéologie et Rationalité dans l'Histoire des sciences de la vie*, 39–55. Paris: Vrin.

Chesnet, H. 1978. "Question d'identité; Vice de conformation des organes génitaux externes; Hypospadias; Erreur sur le sexe." In Herculine Barbin, *Mes Souvenirs.* Paris: Gallimard.

Davidson, A. 1997. *Au risque de Foucault.* Paris: Éditions du Centre Georges Pompidou.

Davidson, A. 2005[2001]. *L'Émergence de la sexualité. Epistémologie historique et formation des concepts.* Paris: Albin Michel.

Goujon, E. 1869. "*Étude d'un cas d'hermaphrodisme imparfait chez l'homme.*" *Journal de l'anatomie et de la physiologie de l'homme*: 609–639. Also in Herculine Barbin, *Mes Souvenirs*, 141–154. Paris: Gallimard, 1978.

Facebook, s.v. Gender.
Foucault, M. 2015[1969]. *Archéologie du savoir*. Paris: Gallimard.
Foucault, M. 2011[1970-1971]. *Leçons sur la volonté de savoir: Cours au Collège de France*. Paris: Seuil.
Foucault, M. 1971. *L'ordre du discours*. Paris: Gallimard
Foucault, M. 1976. *Histoire de la sexualité*, tome 1, *La Volonté de savoir*. Paris: Gallimard.
Foucault, M. 2001[1978]. "Sexualité et pouvoir." In *Dits et Écrits*, tome II. Paris: Gallimard.
Foucault, M. 2001[1980]. "Le vrai sexe." In *Dits et Écrits*, tome II. Paris: Gallimard.
Foucault, M. 1984. *Histoire de la sexualité*, tome 2, *L'Usage des plaisirs*. Paris: Gallimard.
Freud, S. 1999[1916–1917]. *Conférences d'introduction à la* psychanalyse. Paris: Gallimard.
Kosofsky Sedgwick, E. 1998. *Construire des significations queer. Les Études gays et lesbiennes*. Paris: Éditions du Centre G. Pompidou.
Lacan, J. 1978[1954–1955]. *Séminaire II: Le Moi dans la théorie de Freud*. Paris: Seuil.
Lacan, J. 1964-1965. *Séminaire XII: Problèmes cruciaux pour la psychanalyse*. Unpublished.
Lacan, J. 1973. "Télévision." In *Autres Écrits*, 509-545. Paris: Seuil.
Lacan, J. 1973-1974. *Séminaire XXI: Les Non-Dupes Errent*. Unpublished.
Lacan, J. 1976-1977. *Séminaire XXIV: L'Insu que sait de l'Une-bévue s'aile à mourre*. Unpublished. Séance du 19 avril 1977, in *L'Unebévue*, n°21, L'unebévue éd.
Laplanche, J. 2007. *Sexual: La Sexualité élargie au sens freudien 2000-2006*. Paris: PUF.
Tardieu, A. 1995[1857]. *Les Attentats aux mœurs*. Grenoble: Jérôme Millon.
Tardieu, A. 1874. *Question médico-légale de l'identité dans ses rapports avec les vices de conformation des organes sexuels*. In H. Barbin, *Mes Souvenirs*. Paris: Gallimard.
Vigarello, G. 1995. "La violence sexuelle et l'œil du savant." In A. Tardieu, *Les Attentats aux mœurs*. Grenoble: Éditions Jérome Millon.

Chapter 6

Yearning to Be
Authenticity and Truth in Clinical Psychoanalytic Practice

Patricia Gherovici

"Imagine denying your core and soul" (3). "If I become a woman I will be my real self" (182). "I think it's much easier for a trans woman or a trans man who authentically kind of looks and plays the role" (197). The preceding quotes from Caitlyn Jenner's *The Secrets of My Life* (2017), a memoir "written during the pivotal first years of becoming her authentic self" (front flap), exhibit a typical reference to truth and authenticity. We can thus ask what is "true" and what is "authentic" in the realm of gender transition. In this domain, can we follow Martin Heidegger, who criticizes the concept of "truth" defined as an adequation between thought and reality in order to promote a concept of authenticity as unconcealment? It looks like this has been the itinerary of Judith Butler's *Gender Trouble* (1990), her first book appealing to a notion of authenticity and reducing gender to performance, to an imitation for which there is no original. The trans response to these conflicting positions would consist in pursuing an undeniable truth, which is all the more powerful because it contradicts the appearance of the body. I will explore the concept of "realness" as pointing to the convergence of these problematic ideas. In doing so, I will rely on Janet Mock's groundbreaking memoir *Redefining Realness* (2014), and I will compare it with what we learn to be the truth revealed by some clinical vignettes that I will soon discuss.

In *Television*, Jacques Lacan famously affirms that he always speaks the truth. "Not the whole truth, because there's no way to say it all. Saying it all is literally impossible: words fail. Yet it's through this very impossibility that the truth holds onto the real" (1990[1974]: 3). What is this "real," a real to which the truth can attach itself?

Lacan's Real is a notoriously complex concept. The Real is defined in opposition to the categories of the Symbolic and the Imaginary. It is what escapes the Symbolic, in other words, what can be neither spoken nor written. Thus, it cannot be reduced to a meaning. The Real is an impossibility, a limit to the speakable and thinkable, a breach in comprehension and sense; it resists symbolization as much as it does a univocal imaginary representation.

As Lacan surveyed his career in 1970, he listed these three well-known categories: "I began with the Imaginary, I then had to chew on the story of the Symbolic [...] and I finished by putting out for you this famous Real" (*S XXII*, quoted in Mellard 2006: 49). Lacan had begun approaching the Real by situating it in relation to the death drive and the repetition compulsion. For him, the Real had nothing to do with Freud's reality (*Wirklichkeit*) or with the reality principle. Instead, the Real resists incorporation into our ordinary experience of reality.

In *The Interpretation of Dreams* (1900), Freud anticipated Lacan's Real as the dream's navel, as a tangle that cannot be unraveled, as the point that delineates the boundary with the unknown. The dream's navel is the place where Lacan located the Real encroaching upon the Symbolic. Lacan also approached the Real via hallucinations when he examined Freud's Wolf Man case and Schreber's memoirs. The Real reappears "like a punctuation without a text" (Lacan 2006: 324) when the name-of-the-father is not operative (foreclosed) and the symbolic function of castration is refused by the subject. There, the signifiers of the name of the father and of castration reappear as Real in the form of hallucinations. More exactly, the concept of foreclosure entails that "*what did not come to light in the Symbolic appears in the Real*" (Lacan 2006, italics in the original: 324). In *The Four Fundamental Concepts of Psychoanalysis* (1998), Lacan approached the Real in terms of compulsion and of repetition. Generated in the Real of trauma, repetition perpetuates the failure of symbolization. Finally, the Real became "that which always returns to the same place" (Lacan 1998: 49). Trauma was conceptualized as the impossible-to-symbolize Real.

Lacan's later seminars of the 1970s introduce the Borromean knot, with its three interlocking rings of the Real (R), the Symbolic (S), and the Imaginary (I). A new symbolism linked the Real with writing, because even when the Real resists symbolization, writing may be considered as somehow Real too. The Borromean knot provided both a material object that could be manipulated and a metaphor for the structure of the subject. In the final years of his teaching, Lacan saw the symptom as "the most real thing" that subjects possess (1976: 41). To reach the end of analysis, analysands must modify their relationship to the Real, which is the irreducible hole in the Symbolic from which the subject's fantasy and desire derive.

For Lacan, the Real is connected with the notion of sexual drive and also means the absence of complementarity and completion in sexual relations, because "there is no such a thing as a sexual relation." Of course, he did not mean that people do not engage in sex, fall in love, or assume a more or less precarious sexual identity, but rather that there is something constitutively out of sync and inherently incommensurable, even incompatible, in human sexuality. Between men and woman, and between men and men, and between women and women, between neither men nor women, there is nothing but difference. All combinations are possible but there is no symmetry.

This disparity seems to confirm a mismatch that resides in the unconscious, an unconscious we can call homosexual, meaning that there is one single (or same) sexual option: the unconscious seems to know only one way to signify sexual difference—the phallus, which apparently has no feminine equivalent. Thus, a fundamental asymmetry emerges: whereas, in Freud, the phallus and penis can at times be confused, for Lacan, the phallus is not the anatomical organ but a symbol, a conceptual tool thanks to which sexual difference is introduced. While men can pretend to have it, and while women can act as if they are it, there is only the phallus to define two different sexual identities. The phallus might exalt difference, but it does not resolve it.

Let us explore a little further one of the most controversial, envied, and contested psychoanalytic notions. Tim Dean writes that for Lacan it is clear that the phallus is not the penis—or in Judith Butler's interpretation, a "synecdochal reduction" (Butler 1993: 139) or a dildo—but "a red giant herring" (Dean 2000: 14). I would argue that the phallus is as Dean says, a misleading clue comparable to the use of smoked herrings to mislead hounds following a trail. To pun somewhat on the phrase, I would like to suggest that the phallus is less a red herring than a "read" herring—it is subject to interpretation, and it will always be read like a text. Sexual difference is Real and resists symbolization—it is truth half said and it needs to be decoded, or better said, recoded.

To test these claims, I will now turn to my first example, Janet Mock's memoirs. Mock is a television presenter, journalist, trans activist, and author of *Redefining Realness: My Path to Womanhood, Identity, Love, and So Much More* (2014), a memoir of her transition as an impoverished multicultural person of color, and of *Surpassing Certainty* (2017), a *Bildungsroman* predicated on the idea of following one's truth to the end.

Mock's books are well received and have become *New York Times* bestsellers. When Mock dedicated her first autobiographical text to her partner, she invoked truth: "For Aaron who loved me because of myself, held me accountable to my truth and became home" (Mock 2014). In *Redefining Realness*, Mock works with a notion of "realness" that takes inspiration from Dorian Corey's definition in the 1990s classic documentary *Paris is Burning*.[1]

The film *Paris is Burning* chronicles the African American and Latino, gay and transgender communities involved in the drag ball culture of New York City. It documents the complex structure of the ball competitions in which the contestants join specific "categories" or themes. Ball participants compete walking in a runway and are judged according to several criteria: dance talent, beauty of their attires, and "realness" in their drag. "Realness" in this context is their ability to "pass" and not be "read" when they embody stereotypes. "Realness" is not a competition category but a standard to judge the credibility of the performance. For example, in the category "banjee realness," "banjee boys" are judged by their ability to pass as their straight counterparts. The most convincing macho men from the hood, those with an urban, tough swagger, get the trophy. In the case of trans women, realness concerns not just winning the ball competition but their survival in the outside world. When trans women assume society's cis norms of gender embodiment, as Corey explains in the film, "they can walk out of that ballroom into the sunlight and onto the subway and get home and still have all their clothes and no blood running off their bodies." In the film, Corey calls them "*femme* realness queens." Mock emphasizes that the issue is not just about performing or competing but that "realness" quickly becomes a matter of life and death because it "enables trans women to enter spaces with a lower risk of being rebutted or questioned, policed or attacked. 'Realness' is a pathway to survival." Mock explains further:

> I am aware that identifying with what people see versus what's authentic, meaning who I actually am, involves erasure of parts of myself, my history, my people, my experiences. Living by other people's definitions and perceptions shrinks us to shells of ourselves, rather than complex people embodying multiple identities. I am a trans woman of color, and that identity has enabled me to be truer to myself, offering me an anchor from which I can uplift my visible blackness, my often invisible trans womanhood, my little-talked-about native Hawaiian heritage, and the many iterations of womanhood they combine. (Mock 2014: 249)

Thus we see that realness goes beyond merely "passing" and "conforming," it is an expression of an inner truth that can only be half said and that plays a key role in survival.

While Mock acknowledges that her appearance has granted her advantages in life, being able to navigate the world rarely exposed as trans, "unchecked, seen as my true self without being clocked or spooked, as the girls would say colloquially" (Mock 2014: 154), she challenges the use of the word "passing."

"Passing" is based on the assumption that "trans people are passing as something they are not," which would imply that trans people are untruthful, pretend to be what they are not, "that they are 'fake' and live 'false lives'" (Mock 2014: 155). Mock questions the idea that trans people are deceivers who will at some point be exposed when their true identity is uncovered. Mock argues that a trans woman who "knows herself and operates in the world as a woman, is seen, perceived, treated and viewed as a woman" is just being herself, she "isn't *passing*, she is merely *being*" (Mock 2014: 155). The quest for realism in realness becomes an ontological demand.

In her more recent memoir *Surpassing Certainty* (2017), Mock goes even further in discussing the intersection of truth and being, when she tells about how her gender story can make her vulnerable to exposure: "Privacy wasn't even granted to a girl like me who had spent years standing out by merely *being*. It was the price I paid for living my truth." (Mock 2017: 16) Mock's emphasis on *being* confirms my clinical experience with psychoanalytic patients who identify as trans. Quite often, those who undergo gender transition do so, because they deal less with the problems of sexuality than with questions of life and death. When someone says, as I often have heard, "If I hadn't transitioned, I'd be dead, I would have committed suicide," what is at stake is less gender fluidity than finding a livable embodiment, which means a new way of being. Let us keep in mind that gender transition is more about mortality, the limit between life and death, than about sexuality, the border between male and female.

The wish to cross the frontier between the sexes is often experienced as the desire to traverse a mortal threshold, a passage from an impending doom to a possible renaissance; above all, what is at stake is the crossing of an ultimate frontier. Quite often, the predicament of analysands identified as transgender hinges around existential issues. I will reiterate my contention: behind gender trouble are issues of life and death. This ontological issue is an insight shared by Paul B. Preciado who, in a recent interview (EL MUNDO, Spain, April 19, 2019), defined himself as a dissident of the sexual system. Preciado wishes to dismantle identification while demanding the abolition of gender assignment at birth. Preciado argues that our societies are pathologically obsessed with identity: we only see race, nationality, and sex. Challenging the prevailing imperative to become your authentic self, he rejects any self-definition in terms of gender or race; he instead moves on to emphasize the status of the body as a living body in a state of precariousness.[2]

What is the truth that can only be (half) said by realness? Let us take a look at some examples from clinical practice. The first example is of a cis patient, who asked for help while on the brink of suicide. He had broken up with a girlfriend who left him after getting pregnant with his child and having an abortion, because, even though he wished to have a family someday, he expressed that he could not see himself as a father and asked her to end the pregnancy. While recounting his history, he shared with his analyst an amazing ability to intuitively figure out a creative solution to compensate at a moment when he could not fully rely on the phallus. Earlier in his life, as a young man, while dating a woman he liked a lot (she became his first love), he had found himself at a loss in situations that could lead to a sexual act. He did not know what to do with her; he would feel at a loss in sex, unable to know what to do with his penis, because his organ felt perfunctory. He would hold hands with her, lie down in bed embracing her for hours, all the time aware that he was expected to do something else that he could not bring himself to accomplish.

Feeling compelled to do something, he figured out an ingenious solution. Aware that he lacked a knowledge he was supposed to have, he consulted an expert. He made an appointment with a doctor and made up a lie: he told him that he had pain during sex and needed help. The doctor suggested a circumcision. After the medical intervention, while his penis was healing, looking at the bloody stitches under the bandages, horrified at the bruises and the swelling, a change took place. He was able to have sex with the woman he loved. With this creative ruse, this man managed to make up for the inadequacies he experienced in his relationship to his virile organ and became able to perform sexually. The loss of a little flap of skin created a hole that granted access to sexual enjoyment. A strange sort of supplement, the cut in the Real of flesh resulted in something of the phallus being inscribed.

Like in ancient comedy, the phallus also takes center stage in my second clinical example. This is a young cis woman who identified as a lesbian and consulted me for depression. I will call her Miranda. She contacted me when she was a twenty-four-year-old emerging artist in a relationship with an older woman. They lived together, and she described her girlfriend as something of a doting mother, someone whom she did not find particularly attractive but who would take care of all her needs—she would pack her lunch, wash and fold her laundry, clean the house, remind her of her appointments, take care of the cats, and also push her beyond her limits sexually in ways she seemed to resent. Miranda would accept engaging in sexual practices that caused her pain and exhausted her. Sex with her partner was something she did not enjoy but instead accepted as what was expected from her. In their sexual explorations, Miranda seemed not to know exactly what she liked, only what displeased her, but she was curious and her search for an answer found an outlet. At the time of the consultation, she was already working a nightshift job at a sleep lab for men with erectile problems. Her job as a lab technician consisted of "prep," that is, putting sensors on the patients' penises and then waking them up during the study to measure their penises when they reached REM sleep to verify whether they had nocturnal erections. Her encounter with the male sexual organ in various states of tumescence had some effect. The image of the penis that she measured and tested, albeit a substitute for the imaginary phallus, paved the way for her search of a more stable object to cause her desire. Miranda eventually got tired of the sleep lab job and devoted all her energy to her art, in search of a more abstract, unique phallus. She also broke up with her girlfriend and started dating a man, another artist, with whom she fell in love, and she eventually moved in with him. But this is not the area where the most dramatic change took place.

Miranda made sculptures. The evolution of the materials she used had the function of introducing phallic signification; they helped her open the way to confirm the other's lack and extract the remainder of phallic signification—the object *a*. As an artist, she first worked with sculptures in wax only. The wax sculptures were fragile and would occasionally melt during the summer. The seduction of the appearance and disappearance of the object, a *fort-da* of sorts, losing the spool on purpose to retrieve it in order to lose it again, led her to work on bronze sculptures. Miranda derived great pleasure from the creation and breaking of the clay mold and, above all, from the loss of the first wax positive model, suggestively called "lost wax." This mode of satisfaction found its limits. The work on bronze sculptures was challenging, the material was expensive, and she needed someone's help to pour the metal. Once the sculptures were completed, they were heavy and hard to move and store. She kept a few of her works in a friend's garden, and they got stolen, most likely for the value of the metal and not for the artwork. An interesting change took place, Miranda was taken with enthusiasm when she found a material to use for her artwork that she claimed was not only beautiful, translucent, and great to draw on but also indestructible. Thus, Miranda found her art form, drawing, and by way of her material, Mylar, a sinthome with transformational properties. By sinthome, I mean a symptom that does not need to be eliminated or cured; it functioned as a singular, creative solution. Using this plastic drafting paper allowed Miranda to finally claim her artworks in Mylar as "truly… My… mine."

In "Science and Truth," Lacan says that "there is something in the status of the object of science that seems to me to have remained unelucidated since the birth of science." Lacan argues that science is governed by a particular kind of object that, he claims, can only be articulated and comprehended by psychoanalysis. For Lacan, this "object" is the mighty, unattainable object that is the cause of desire, the object petit *a*. The object petit *a* emerges as something "inserted [...] into the division of the subject by which the psychoanalytic field is quite specifically structured" (Lacan 2006: 864). In the ensuing paragraphs, Lacan identifies a causal function for this object that makes it stand apart from "knowledge" as it is usually understood. When subjects refuse knowledge, because they are bound to a truth that knowledge cannot fully grasp, psychoanalysis helps by reconstructing the truth behind the objects of desire that determine subjectivity.

For Janet Mock, and many of the analysands I have worked with who identify as trans, realness is a move away from the Real, a truth about themselves that, once realized, allows them to find a more livable embodiment. This is a creative solution that follows Lacan's logic of the sinthome. Mock evokes painful experiences of feeling afraid of being exposed as a trans woman when meeting a stranger (2017: xviii). She is dancing in a nightclub and meets a handsome man named Branden. Janet notices a woman in the nightclub—a former high school classmate whose name she cannot recall, who is looking at her. "I had grown familiar with this particular look—knowing, intense and direct. *She knows me*" (2017: xiv). Eventually, this woman finds a moment alone with Branden and warns him that Mock used to be "a dude" (2017: xvi). But Branden finds it absurd and laughs it off as a jealous comment. Mock wonders about what motivated this woman to make this revelation, pondering the relationship between truth and knowledge:

> Was it a commitment to truth? Did she believe that he deserved to know? Did she think how he would react? And how was she certain that he did not himself know, or that I did not tell him? I still do not have answers. (Mock 2017: xvii)

That night, Mock, still shaken and feeling that she has something to prove, goes swimming in the nude with Branden. She writes:

> I was nude but not naked, wrapped in an enigma that Branden would never figure out. Forced disclosure always shook me, leaving me in a frightened space where my body served as proof of my realness. The need to prove myself was never ending in its plea to affirm, connect, deny and erase. I aspired to be like Toni Morrison's Sula, a woman who shuns the demands placed on her by her watchful community, a woman who lacks an ego, a woman OK in her otherness. Her only aim is to be consistent, not in the world or those around her, but with herself. (Mock 2017: xviii)

She continues: “I vacillated between revealing and concealing myself [...] I trusted no one. I disappeared into myself. This left me alone with untruths” (2017: xix).

Initially, Mock chose to keep to herself the fact that she is a trans woman. All along, she vacillated between flaunting and concealing herself; for many years, she avoided her truth. Finally, Mock reaches a place where she no longer denies or hides herself:

> I chose to wear the cloak of normality as part of my own survival. I wanted to accept myself, without rebuttals, without denials, without exile. I followed a recipe handed down to me by women I knew also benefited from blending and passing. [...] Now I’ve finally reached a place where silence is no longer an option for me. My survival depends on my ability to speak truth to power, not just about myself, but for *us*. I’m committed to getting *ours*. It requires me to relay how I struggled with living, dreaming, loving, fucking, being seen, and simply *being* in my body, in this world. This is a universal experience. (Mock 2017: 20)

Mock took the title of this second memoir from an essay by Audre Lorde, “Sister Outsider,” in which Lorde talks about the sacrifices that come when speaking up: “And at last you’ll know with surpassing certainty that only one thing is more frightening than speaking your truth. And that is not speaking.” And yet, Mock’s truth, like that of psychoanalysis, even when spoken, can only be half said.

Indeed, like Lacan says in *Television*, truth in psychoanalysis is one the side of the Real. This is illustrated by the story of a patient who revealed the truth of his suffering with the bluntness of someone who had become a martyr of the Real. While having great fun playing soccer, the surge in pleasure would create an invasion of jouissance that he experienced as coming from the exterior: he would hear a voice saying “fuck me.” His analyst suggested that in those instances he could try saying “fuck you.” Hopefully, their analytic work would lead to a place where he could say to the voices that were stealing his jouissance, making him an object of enjoyment, “what the fuck?” The analysand gave himself a precise diagnosis, “split minded,” which was much better than “schizophrenia” or “paranoia,” and much closer to the truth of his situation.

Conclusion

These clinical examples read alongside Mock's testimony suggest that one should take into account the function of realness that cannot be reduced to either Lacan's Real or to reality. The patient who measured the erections of anonymous penises was not touching the Real of the phallus but what I would call its realness: never given fully, but instead always tested in the context of a medical probing that nevertheless could exert a huge impact on her choice of love object, and more importantly, start a productive metonymic displacement of objects that cause desire, of objects *a*. The analysand who needed an unnecessary circumcision was not just approaching the Real of castration, as one might hastily conclude, but also learning to come to terms with the realness of an organ that felt foreign to him. The other patient, the soccer player with a split mind, did not have the realness of the phallus at hand, and thus no effect of realness that could regulate the big other from inflicting a boundless jouissance that reduces him to being fucked. By examining the trans experience of realness, psychoanalysis can learn to formulate a more hospitable interpretation of the arc that connects the principle of reality to an unapproachable fullness of being.

Notes

1 Judith Butler's *Bodies that Matter* (1993) also followed Corey's definition quite closely.

2 https://www.elmundo.es/cultura/literatura/2019/04/19/5cb079a321efa0041c8b4664.html.

References

Butler, Judith. 1993. *Bodies that Matter: On the Discursive Limits of "Sex."* New York: Routledge.

Butler, J. 1990. *Gender Trouble*. London: Routledge.

Dean, T. 2000. *Beyond Sexuality*. Chicago: University of Chicago Press.

Jenner, C. 2017. *The Secrets of My Life*. New York: Grand Central.

Freud, S. 1900. *The Interpretation of Dreams*.

Lacan, J. 1990[1974]. *Television*. New York: W. W. Norton.

Lacan, J. 1998. *Seminar XI: The Four Fundamental Concepts of Psychoanalysis*. New York: W. W. Norton.

Lacan, J. 2006. Écrits: The First Complete Edition in English. Translated by Bruce Fink. New York: W. W. Norton.

Mellard, J. 2006. *Beyond Lacan*. Albany: State University of New York Press.

Mock, J. 2014. *Redefining Realness: My Path to Womanhood, Identity, Love, and So Much More*. New York: Atria Books.

Mock, J. 2017. *Surpassing Certainty: What My Twenties Taught Me*. New York: Atria Books.

CHAPTER 7

The Truth of Gender
Psychoanalysis's Unthinkable Trauma[1]

Nicolas Evzonas

In the preface to Herculine Barbin's autobiographical account, Michel Foucault (1980) describes the nineteenth-century obsession of the medical and judicial systems with defining the sexual identity of people with atypical genitalia. The ruthless determination of experts to reveal the "true sex" of Herculine Barbin led him/her to commit suicide, because the sex assigned to him/her was incompatible with his/her subjective perception and inner truth, which would nowadays be called the gender experience.

It is particularly intriguing that psychoanalysis, which marked an epistemological turning point by drawing attention to the complex psychic reality of the human subject, tends to regress to a univocal and linear conception of material truth when it comes to gender. What makes analysts cling so fervently to the uncompromising concreteness and transparency of binary sexual difference? How can we understand the unexpressed aggressiveness and "anxiety of regulation" (Corbett 2009) that transpire in numerous psychoanalytic studies on gender-variant subjects (Faure-Oppenheimer 1980; Millot 1983; Czermak and Frignet 1996; Castel 2003; Chiland 2003)? Violent interpretations and pathologizing diagnostic labels, applied thoughtlessly by numerous practitioners contaminated by the collective biases of the psychoanalytic field, border on transphobia.

Let me mention the broadening of this term by Alessandro Alessandrin and Karine Espineira (2015): transphobia involves not only the conscious rejection of trans people but also "cisgender presumptions" or, to paraphrase Eve Kosofsky Sedgwick (1990), the unquestioned "epistemological privileges" of cis identity. In this case, we could speak of a cisgender psychoanalytic solipsism, which often goes hand in hand with White, male, bourgeois, heterosexual ipso-centrism. This narcissistic enclosure, which is resistant to mixing and difference, often reinforces the exclusion frequently endured by trans individuals and augments their distress. Griffin Hansbury (2017) discusses the colonization of nonbinary populations through coercive metapsychological interpretations that destroy rather than recreate their psychic space. Should we confine ourselves to the metaphorical meaning of this colonization? Do analysts, who express themselves in public and conflate the authority conferred by transference with a cultural mission to prescribe good and bad gender, not adopt an oppressive approach by dooming the minority subject to social ostracism?

In this contribution, I will illustrate the overdetermination of psychoanalytic prejudices toward trans individuals and the related obsession of a "true" gender. First, I will focus on the social and cultural infiltration of metapsychological concepts by showing how popular opinion—the doxa—contaminates scientific neutrality. Second, I will argue in favor of generalized trauma and universal gender uncertainty. From this perspective, the amplification of an immutable, coherent, and authentic identity will be understood as a defense against the primitive anxieties related to otherness and existential precariousness. I will thus consider the reductive metapsychological construction based on the perceptive reality of the genitals to be a trauma specific to psychoanalysis. By analyzing the mechanisms underlying the decomplexification of gender and its fetishist equation with a literal truth, my aim is to contribute to the mentalization of this transgenerational trauma of psychoanalysis with clinical, epistemological, and political consequences.

Metapsychology and Doxa

While Freud (1912) maintained that psychoanalysts wield flammable tools, alluding to the moments in treatment when transference flares because of instinctual effervescence, Adrienne Harris (2009) asserted that analysts work with culturally contaminated tools. Long before the feminist discourse and gender studies, Karen Horney (1926; 1935) argued that metapsychology was oriented by a male gaze and contaminated by the social environment. Michel Neyraut (1974), however, described the existence of transference prior to the analytic situation, which is inseparable from the historical situatedness of psychoanalytic thought and the sociocultural norms that frame this historicity. In other words, there is pretransference knowledge that is ideologically laden and capable of orienting and disorienting the analyst's listening. Piera Aulagnier (1984) delves deeper into the contradiction inherent in the analyst's "impossible profession," namely, the requirement to assume two paradoxical roles when listening to the analysand: the "subject-supposed-to-know" and the "subject supposed to be ignorant." These arguments all point to the transferential challenges and, more precisely, to the difficulty in reconciling metapsychology as historically and culturally "situated knowledge" with the free-floating attention required during analytical sessions, which is supposed to put the known on hold to let the unknown emerge.

This complexity reaches a pinnacle in the case of gender-variant people, because analytical listening often tends to become deaf to the subject's singular speech and parasitized by the most common prejudices. For example, the systematic equation of trans identities with psychoses, borderline pathologies, or perverse structures; the amalgamation of trans and homosexual subjectivities; the idealization of sexual difference to safeguard mental health; and the "misgendering" and intentional "deadnaming" of patients—all these facets should be questioned in light of the gender binary, which is deeply rooted in our culture. In other words, we should historicize the metapsychological emphasis placed on anatomical sexual difference, which has resulted in an array of normative assumptions about the process of becoming a subject.

In his groundbreaking work *Making Sex*, Thomas Laqueur (1990) postulated that the definitions of sex and gender are historically variable and changeable. He showed that Western thought was initially built around a one-sex model founded by Aristotle and Galen in Greek antiquity. Men and women were thus arranged according to their degree of metaphysical perfection along an axis, with the summit of perfection being represented by man. From an anatomical perspective, the only difference between men and women was the position of their genitalia: inside the body for women and outside for men. Gender was therefore an immutable fact of nature dictated by the perfect hierarchy of the cosmos, whereas sex was an effect of convention and a minor anatomical distinction.

In the eighteenth century, a two-sex model superseded the one-sex version. Women and men were henceforth considered to be immeasurably different in terms of anatomy and physiology, with gender used to define "biologically" determined qualities, virtues, and roles. Sex was an immutable fact of nature, while gender was an effect of biological determinism in the universe of cultural conventions.

In this context of radical male/female opposition, not to mention the Western world's penchant for binary thinking, various metapsychological theorizations emerged relating to castration, the taboo of incest—only its heterosexual version as Gay Rubin (1975) posits—the biological bedrock of gender difference, and the developmental failure attributed to subjectivities, which question the vital complementarity between men and women. In the United States, almost no psychoanalyst challenged these assumptions until the 1980s. In France, even creative revisionist theorists such as Janine Chasseguet-Smirgel and Joyce McDougall believed that eliminating sexual differences would lead to psychosis

(Goldner 1991). Let us recall the fatal prediction of Chasseguet-Smirgel (1976: 149): "Too much access to femininity for a boy may constitute an irreparable trauma and lead to his psychic death." But Ken Corbett (2009) asks: A trauma for whom? For the boy or for the normative order? He also comments on an excerpt in which Robert Stoller (1968: 127) describes how feminine boys have an early aptitude for painting, not only in their flamboyant use of color but also in their utilization of imaginative objects. Without adequate explanation, Stoller then denounces this creativity and flamboyance as a beautiful sign of psychopathology that will be eradicated with time or analytical treatment. In Stoller's abrupt shift, Corbett reads the anxiety of regulation concealed as diagnosis.

To illustrate how the social norm penetrates the psychoanalytical corpus, let me cite the French psychiatrist Georges Lantéri-Laura who conceives science as a form of ideological knowledge resulting from the introjection of cultural prejudices. In his 1979 book *Lecture des perversions: Histoire de leur appropriation médicale* (Reading Perversion: A History of Its Medical Appropriation), he writes:

> Scientific discourse is both the (true or presumably true) knowledge of phenomena and the knowledge of social opinions about them [...] Regarding perversion, we cannot forget that it is the doxa that delimits the field of phenomena treated by the episteme: social opinion indicates the field of perverse behavior, and scientific knowledge depends on this opinion, even if it modifies the extent of this field along the way. (Lantéri-Laura 1979: 15)

Let us not forget that the chosen explanatory model—to whatever register it belongs—was developed by applying an extrinsic pathogenic process to a set of pre-identified behaviors, for reasons unrelated to this process, and in any case, for reasons of social ethics. Even if the knowledge seemed perfect to us, we cannot forget that it was acquired from the observation of multiple cases identified as perversions, for reasons that have nothing to do with this knowledge and that prove to be cultural. We thus see that the psychiatric discourse always takes second place and that it is never in agreement with it (i.e., popular opinion). It presupposes a social sampling of behaviors but masks the sampling process itself as well as the underlying socioethical motivation. (Lantéri-Laura 1979: 138)

Lantéri-Laura shows that the medicine of perversions does not make the epistemological rupture that it claims to undertake in relation to the religious field and popular opinion. He thus dismantles the mechanism of medicopsychiatric thinking from the presuppositions dictated by social ethics and good morals.

Lantéri-Laura's analysis could be applied to the psychoanalytic conception of trans identities as psychotic or pervert structures. I thus argue along with Thamy Ayouch that:

> popular opinion circumscribes the trans pathology within the framework of culturally bound gender dimorphism, while the production of psychoanalytic knowledge remains dependent on this opinion […]. The discourse that claims to express a truth about trans and proceed from science is only one opinion among others. (Ayouch 2015: 307)

The heart of the problem remains Foucauldian: the maladaptive becomes the unnatural, which in turn becomes the abnormal, the ill, the bad, and the insane.

I will give yet another example to show the incorporation of the doxa in metapsychological theory. In a recent article, French analyst Lionel Le Lorre (2018) demonstrates that, in a footnote dated to 1909 in his *Three Essays on the Theory of Sexuality*, Freud's hesitation between a curable homosexuality represented by the figure of the "presumed homosexual" and a treatment-resistant homosexuality represented by the "true homosexual" was influenced by Ferenczi's distinction between subjective and objective homoeroticism. This corresponded to the unequal differentiation between the socially "recoverable" masculine homosexual and the effeminate homosexual irremediably in breach of dominant norms:

> Freud renews one of the best shared topoi, situating this first group of inverts in a logic that aims at their essentialisation. Even if Freud pleads against the well-established conception of homosexuality as a degeneration, the caricature of the 'poof' busy with needlework is not far off. With regard to the second group of homosexuals, the 'presumed inverts' (hapax), whose name is anything but psychoanalytical, the material once again allows us to easily identify the other socially attested topos whose ideal of virile camaraderie is to be grasped as a counterpoint to the previously isolated figure of the 'poof.' In short, Freud's theoretical elaborations can be deduced from a social prejudice imported into psychoanalytical doctrine, which structures the long note of the Three Essays and reproduces the same gender division referring to the specific sexual role of partners (active versus passive) based on an interpretation that isolates the purpose of the drive rather than its object. (Le Corre 2018: 85)

The Freudian designations of "presumed homosexual" and "true homosexual" foreshadow Robert Stoller's distinction from the late 1960s between "primary transsexual" and "secondary transsexual" based on the early or late rejection of the male organ and, implicitly, on the extent and depth of this rejection (cf. Person and Ovesey 1974). Once again, this is a socially colored phallocentric dichotomy between the "real" and the "fake" trans, between the curable and the incurable. Stoller (1968) also differentiates between the "core gender identity," a kind of real self, and "gender role," a sort of social masquerade. This new opposition points to the hidden existence of a gender truth that must be unveiled, which recalls the ordeals inflicted on Barbin by experts seeking to reveal his/her "true sex" (Foucault 1980). The quest for truth survives to this day in what the French-Chilean sociologist Karine Espineira (2011: 200) calls "the therapeutic shield" to designate the official protocol of hormone and surgical gender transitions, which she describes as "a corrective enterprise" that refuses to acknowledge itself, because it "treats docile and socially useful transsexuals" who reaffirm the established gender binarity.

This association between transgender and homosexual subjectivities is important insofar as psychoanalysts systematically reduce trans identities to a defense against homosexuality in a seemingly normative fashion, a possible consequence of the idealization of Freud's analysis of the Schreber case (cf. Castel 2003). This systematization, often without clinical support, does not fundamentally differ from certain social representations of trans women as gay men and trans men as lesbians. Here, I will call on the Foucauldian philosopher Arnold Davidson who analyzes the "conceptually unthinkable":

> Before the mid-19th century, persons of a given anatomical sex could not be considered to psychologically belong to the opposite sex, since, at that time, anatomical sex subsumed a person's identity [...]. Sex surgeries were not only technically impossible in previous centuries, but they were also conceptually impossible. (Davidson 1987: 22)

According to this logic, early psychoanalysis could only have understood transgenderism in reference to the conceptual categories available at the time. Does this not indicate why Freud (1911) overlooked the issue of gender identity in his interpretation of Schreber's memoirs, instead proposing a theoretical construction about repressed homosexuality?

It is impossible to omit a tribute to Jean Laplanche, the only mainstream French psychoanalyst to defend the primary existence of gender diversity by drawing parallels with the history of languages. The reference to linguistics is paramount, because it shows that gender attribution is different in each language. From this perspective, gender assignment is arbitrary and depends on the cultural and linguistic context. Laplanche further argues that gender plurality is secondarily reorganized by the perception of anatomical sexual difference, which is structured by the rigid code of the excluded third party, namely, the presence or absence of the male genital organ. More precisely, he maintains that the binary law of castration like the Oedipus complex—two cornerstones of classical psychoanalysis that are undermined by certain transgender experiences—constitute mytho-symbolic entities as historically contingent patterns or cultural codes that serve to restrain the anarchy of primitive partial drives (oral, anal, and paragenital):

> Contrary to Freud's view according to which the very core of the unconscious resides in the Oedipal relationship, we should not situate such structures on the side of the repressed but rather on that of the repressing; not on the side of the primary drives but on that of the forces that create order and desexualize it in the name of laws of alliance, procreation, etc. (Laplanche 2003b: 212)

Metapsychology and Primitive Anxieties

It would be reductive to consider normative metapsychological theory founded on the perceptive reality of genitalia to be a mere cultural byproduct. Let us try to understand what Ken Corbett (2009) calls "the anxiety of regulation" in light of the extreme complexity of gender and identity construction, which psychoanalysis can help to clarify—despite being a prisoner of the very complexity that it seeks to elucidate.

Freud's (1917) great insight was to show that "the Ego is not Master in its own house" and that subjective stability is relentlessly compromised. Slips of the tongue, dreams, symptoms, and other manifestations of the unconscious reveal the inability to consolidate a coherent identity. Lacan (1954–1955) notes that subjectivity is the sum of an individual's identifications with all that this entails in terms of the radically contingent. The ego, whether imagining itself to be cis, trans, or otherwise, lacks a hard core of truth; it is a scaffold (bricolage) of identifications that gives the illusion of a solidly built identity. While activists strive to show that trans identities are normal expressions of subjectivity and not illnesses, psychoanalysis stresses the contrary, namely, that any identity construction is pathogenic.

André Green (quoted in Perelberg 2008: xvi) specifies that identification, as a way of thinking in the unconscious, is linked to the fantasy of the primary scene where one oscillates between masculinity and femininity with fluid positions and representations. By contrast, identity, which is defined by the conscious self-image, constitutes an illusion of unity that contrasts with the fluidity of the masculine and feminine. From this perspective, we can better grasp the aphorism of Adrienne Harris (1991): gender is a "necessary fiction" and a contradiction between a socially ineluctable conscious identity and a chaotic multiplicity of unconscious identifications. Viewed from this perspective, the distinction between gender congruence and incongruence becomes obsolete. Gender is intrinsically dysphoric, and the putative cisgender euphoria is a deception induced by the confusion between social consensus and well-being.

Virginia Goldner, known for her work in the field of domestic violence, writes:

> I am still very struck by how hypernormative genders seem to hold so much early trauma history. Scratch the surface of normotic genders, they bleed. For man, it is the knee jerk phallic masculinity that is instituted and maintained by shaming. (Corbett et al. 2014: 301).

Let me also mention Claude Ballier's (1999) work, which reveals an unprecedented gender discomfort among cis sex criminals.

So as not to confine myself to sheer psychopathology, I will mention the example of cisgender male athletes who use narratives to prove their masculinity such as tennis champion Andre Agassi, haunted by the specter of a domineering father whom he sought to ward off through a quest for sporting excellence. By the same token, some cis women, such as tennis player Amélie Mauresmo, struggle to prove their femininity; Mauresmo's opponents reproached her for playing like a man, thus insinuating that she was not a "real" woman. These stories bear similarities with some trans biographies, such as that of American athlete Renée Richards, and thus plead in favor of a generalized gender dysphoria (cf. Hughes 2018).

Let me now turn to the field of plastic surgery: Are transgender subjects alone in their desire to confirm their sense of masculinity or femininity by means of the scalpel? Psychoanalysts who perceive this request as "transsexual madness" (Chiland 2003) seem to forget that this presumed madness is rooted in the difficulty shared by all to juggle what Françoise Dolto (1984) calls "the unconscious image of the body." In this regard, Winnicott (1970: 270) points out that we are all forced to negotiate a fundamental challenge and find compromising solutions, namely, "how to transform the body one has into the body one is." The clinical experience of Andrea Linhares (2004; 2005) in reconstructive surgery enabled her to identify similar specular issues in trans and cisgender patients, thus de-exceptionalizing trans surgeries that many analysts consider to be a mutilation of symbolic representation.

If the universal uncertainty of gender is conveniently projected onto subjects who deviate from the norm, can we not imagine a similar mechanism regarding the copious musings about the alleged trauma of trans subjectivities? A detour through metapsychology is still necessary to point out the pitfalls of metapsychology itself. Lacan (1938) makes the birth of the ego coincide with the intrusion complex, thus highlighting the fundamentally exterior and traumatic dimension of the ego that is born in the Other. In a Lacanian vein, Patricia Gherovici focuses precisely on gender:

> Within the unconscious the proclamation 'I am a man,' 'I am a woman,' exemplifies the inherent alienation in subjectivity that is derived from the very fact of language. We are split on the choice of meaning (that is the signifier that comes from the Other) or being of the subject. This impossible position is a terrific conflict, one in which choosing meaning comes at the cost of disappearance under the Other's signifiers, while choosing being risks losing meaning, which comes from the Other. (Gherovici 2010: 197)

The primacy of an alienating other also lies at the heart of Jean Laplanche's (2003a; 2003b) conception of gender. In his view, the child is bombarded with gender assignments impregnated with unconscious meanings. These enigmatic external messages are traumatic insofar as they surpass the child's means of understanding and lead to a forced identification by the other. While Laplanche introduces the notion of the "intimate socius" to designate the socially inserted and culturally bound caregivers who implant gender signifiers in the child's body ego, it is notably American psychoanalysts who made extensive advances on gender trauma induced by the norms and power relations mediated by the parental unconscious. Thus, Adrienne Harris (1991; 2009), Virginia Goldner (1991; 2003; 2011), and Lane Layton (2004), to quote just a few eminent examples of North American practitioners who are also inspired by the social sciences, describe a generalized gender pathogeny following a paradoxical situation: on the one hand, the subject is supposed to forge a unique subjectivity based on plural messages and singular identifications; on the other, they must submit to binary norms and choose to be either male or female, with these signifiers also being full of connotations of superiority and inferiority. This double bind is therefore at the origin of repression, splitting, isolation, and multiple other defenses that distort the ego. The subject is forced to perform gender ideals for fear of losing the affection of loved ones, mourn what they are not allowed to be or have, accept the subordinate position if they tick the "woman" box, or play the charade of phallic aggressiveness if they tick the "man" box. Gender appears to be both a trauma and a solution to that very trauma.

From this perspective, trans identities shed light on a burning question with which we all struggle: How can we choose and shape our gender—and at the expense of what violence? Is this fundamental violence rekindled on both sides of the psychoanalytic couch? Do normalizing interpretations not ward off unthinkable anxieties revived by traumatic gender narratives? Does the reduction of trans identities to chaotic constructions not amount to a disavowal of the chaos and inchoateness inherent in any identity? In a similar way, we can understand the theorizing of the confusion between the signifier and the organ in trans subjects to reflect the confusion of psychoanalysis, which literalizes gender identity through the scotomization of its internal complexity. We could thus speak of a fetishist conception of gender based on the concreteness of external markers and the perception of visible differences such as the presence or absence of the penis (cf. Gozlan, 2008; 2011). The fetish solution would help to deny the anguish of the other, which designates a primitive engulfing object rather than a secondarily represented sexual object.

Let me finish by recalling that Freud (1937: 250) closes his testamentary paper "Analysis Terminable and Interminable" by evoking the "biological bedrock" of rejecting femininity in both male and female patients. Does the sudden transformation of a psychic reality into an innate and inalterable fact not point to Freud's self-admitted countertransferential unease regarding the feminizing maternal other? I thus maintain that when analysts demetaphorize gender identities and regress to literal, linear, and material verities, they refuse to think in the sense of Bion, that is, they fail to transform unbearable experiences into alpha elements of dream, phantasy, and emotional truth.

Conclusion

My contribution would be incomplete if it did not include a few suggestions about how analysts can work through transphobia and deepen their truthful connection with patients who are likely to arouse cultural biases and primitive anxieties.

I would like to insist on the need for analysts to constantly question their position in order to guard against potentially deleterious countertransference.

Indeed, the anxieties associated with gender trauma are inescapable. It is therefore paramount to name these unthinkable emergences and make them thinkable. Pierre Fedida (1992) reminds us that countertransference primarily relates to the economic dimension of the psychic apparatus: if there is an overflowing unbound tension, there is a risk of a discharge on the analysand. When Melanie Suchet (2011) wonders, in her treatment of a trans boy, whether her patient's transition will undermine her own gender stability, she binds through her language and thinking an anxiety that usually remains unnamed and unthinkable in the psychoanalytic literature (cf. Hansbury 2017).

It also vital to systematically analyze the unconsciously overdetermined choice to work with a specific population of patients or clients. When Colette Chiland (2003) boasts about seeing three hundred transgender people in consultation, while repeating that she ended up in the field of trans identities by chance, one can easily detect the defensive aspect of her statements, which are impossible to dissociate from her ambivalence toward her patients.

I would further like to stress the importance of thirdness when the transferential relationship becomes too complicated. The setting of supervision proves to be crucial, especially when dealing with psychic structures that are resistant to spontaneous triangulation. In view of the major hesitations in France to extensively speak about countertransference, including within the context of supervision—hesitations that often stem from overly focusing on the patients' internal objects or overemphasizing the analyst's neutrality—I argue that it's necessity to simultaneously work through one's countertransference unease in a variety of settings. Several Anglo-Saxon models of psychoanalytical training are based on the concomitant investment of personal analysis and a separate space for supervision.

Clinical research is another means of sharpening one's critical reflexivity and elaborating complex countertransferential challenges. As Winnicott (1947: 69) writes, "psychoanalytic research is perhaps always, to some extent, an attempt by an analyst to take the work of his or her own analysis beyond the point to which his or her own analyst might take it." Writing can be a valuable means of self-analysis and self-supervision, although the choice of patients about whom to write may occasionally conceal unprocessed aggressiveness regarding the transference.

We may also follow the example of Freud, who advised against being confined to the insular space of the consulting room and instead gleaning information from elsewhere. To abandon the arrogant enclosure of disciplinary knowledge is to accept being destabilized by the emergence of the unexpected, which is the basic requirement of conducting scientific research and exploring the unconscious. Sharing our work in conferences and peer-reviewed journals also allows us to re-examine our clinical, theoretical, and ethical stances. A final route may be the sort of colloquy permitted by this anthology.

Notes

1 This chapter was originally published in the bilingual French-English journal *Research in Psychoanalysis*. Nicolas Evzonas (2020) "Psychoanalytic Transphobia or a Generalized Gender Trauma" 30(2): 103A–112A.

References

Alessandrin, A. and K. Espineira. 2016. *Sociologie de la transphobie Sociology of Transphobia.* Bordeaux: MSHA.

Aulagnier, P. 1984. *L'Apprenti-Historien et le Maître-Sorcier: Du discours identifiant au discours délirant*. Paris: PUF.

Ayouch, T. 2015. "Psychanalyse et transidentités: hétérotopies." *L'Évolution psyhiatrique* 80(2): 303–316.

Ballier, C. 1999. *Psychanalyse des comportements sexuels violents*. Paris: PUF.

Chasseguet-Smirgel, J. 1976. "Some Thoughts on the Ego Ideal." *Psychoanalytic Quarterly* 45: 345–373.

Castel, P. 2003. *La Métamorphose impensable*. Paris: Gallimard.

Chiland, C. 2003. *Transsexualism: Illusion and Reality*. Middletown, CT: Wesleyan University Press.

Civitarese, G. 2013. "The Grid and the Truth Drive." *The Italian Psychoanalytic Annual* 7: 91–114.

Corbett, K. 2009. "Boyhood Femininity, Gender Identity Disorder, Masculine Presuppositions and the Anxiety of Regulation." *Psychoanalytic Dialogues* 19(4): 353–370.

Corbett, K. et al. 2014. "Talking Sex, Talking Gender - A Roundtable." *Studies in Gender and Sexuality* 15(4): 295–317.

Czermak, M. and H. Frignet, eds. 1996. *Sur l'identité sexuelle*. Paris: Association Freudienne Internationale.

Davidson, A. I. 1987. "Sex and the Emergence of Sexuality." *Critical Inquiry* 14(1): 16–48.

Dolto, F. 1984. *L'Image inconsciente du corps*. Paris: Seuil.

Espineira, K. 2011. "Le bouclier thérapeutique." *Le Sujet dans la cité* 1(2): 189–201.

Faure-Oppenheimer, A. 1980. *Le Choix du sexe*. Paris: PUF.

Fedida, P. 1992. *Crise et Contretransfert*. Paris: PUF.

Foucault, M. 1980. *Herculine Barbin: Being the Recently Discovered Memoirs of a Nineteenth-Century French Hermaphrodite*. New York: Pantheon Books.

Freud, S. 1912. "The Dynamics of Transference." *The Standard Edition* 12: 97–108.

Freud, S. 1917. "From a Difficulty in the Path of Psychoanalysis." *The Standard Edition* 17: 135–144.
Freud, S. 1937. "Analysis Terminable and Interminable." *The Standard Edition* 23: 209–254.
Gherovici, P. 2010. *Please Select your Gender*. New York: Routledge.
Goldner, V. 1991. "Toward a Critical Theory of Gender." *Psychoanalytic Dialogues* 1(3): 249–272.
Goldner, G. 2003. "Ironic Gender/Authentic Sex." *Studies in Gender and Sexuality* 4(2): 113–139.
Goldner, G. 2011. "Trans: Gender in Free Fall." *Psychoanalytic Dialogues* 21(2): 159–171.
Gozlan, O. 2008. "The Accident of Gender." *The Psychoanalytic Review* 95(4): 541–570.
Gozlan, O. 2011. "Transsexual Surgery: A Novel Reminder and a Navel Remainder." *International Forum of Psychoanalysis* 20(1): 45–52.
Hansbury, G. 2017. "Unthinkable Anxieties." *Transgender Studies Quarterly* 4(3–4): 384–404.
Harris, A. 1991. "Gender as Contradiction." *Psychoanalytic Dialogues* 1(2): 197–224.
Harris, A. 2009. *Gender as Soft Assembly*. New York: Routledge.
Horney, K. 1926. "The Flight from Womanhood: The Masculinity-Complex in Women, as Viewed by Men and by Women." *The International Journal of Psychoanalysis* 7: 324–339.
Horney, K. 1935. "The Problem of Feminine Masochism." *The Psychoanalytic Review* 22(3): 241–257.
Hughes, L. 2018. "Wronging the Right-Body Narrative: On the Universality of Gender Uncertainty." In *Current Critical Debates in the Filed of Transsexual Studies: In Transition*, edited by O. Gozlan. London: Routledge.
Lacan, J. 2001[1938]. "Les complexes familiaux dans la formation de l'inconscient." In *Autres Écrits*, 23–84. Paris: Seuil.
Lacan, J. 1978[1954–1955]. *Séminaire I: Le Moi dans la théorie de Freud*. Paris: Seuil.
Lantéri-Laura, G. 1979. *Lecture des perversions: Histoire de leur appropriation médicale*. Paris: Masson.
Laqueur, T. 1990. *Making Sex: Body and Gender from the Greeks to Freud*. Cambridge: Harvard University Press.
Layton, L. 2004. "A Fork in the Royal Road." *Psychoanalysis, Culture and Society* 9(1): 33–51.
Linhares, A. 2004. "Quand le sexe fait visage: l'identité sexuelle au regard de la clinique du dévisagement." *Champ psychosomatique* 34(2): 67–87.
Linhares A. 2005. "Le sexe et l'informe." *Recherches en psychanalyse* 3(1): 43–52.
Le Corre, L. 2018. "Guérir l'homosexualité masculine?" *Figures de la psychanalyse* 36(2): 79–91.
Laplanche, J. 2007[2003a]. "Le genre, le sexe, le sexual." In *Sexual: La Sexualité élargie au sens freudien*, 153–194. Paris: PUF.

Laplanche, J. 2007[2003b]. "Trois acceptions du mot « inconscient » dans la cadre de la théorie de la séduction généralisée." In *Sexual: La Sexualité élargie au sens freudien*, 195–214. Paris: PUF.

Millot, C. 1983. *Horsexe*. Paris: Seuil.

Neyraut, M. 1974. *Le Transfert*. Paris: PUF.

Perelberg, J. 2008. *Time, Space and Phantasy*. New York: Routledge.

Person, E. and L. Ovesey. 1974. "The Transsexual Syndrome in Males. I. Primary Transsexualism." *American Journal of Psychotherapy* 28(1): 4–20.

Rubin, G. 1975. "The Traffic in Women: Notes on the Political Economy of Sex." In *Toward an Anthropology of Women*, edited by R. Reiter. New York: Monthly Review Press.

Sedwick, E. K. 1990. *Epistemology of the Closet*. Oakland: University of California Press.

Stoller, R. 196. *Sex and Gender: On the Development of Masculinity and Femininity*. New York: Science House.

Suchet, M. 2011. "Crossing Over." *Psychoanalytic Dialogues* 21(2): 172–191.

Winnicott, D. W. 2010[1970]. "On the Basis for Self in Body." In *Psychoanalytic Explorations*, 261–283. London: Karnac.

Winnicott, D. W. 1949. "Hate in the Countertransference." *The International Journal of Psychoanalysis* 30: 69–74.

PART 2

Psychoanalysis and the Philosophy of Truth

Chapter 8

Sophist's Choice[1]

Mladen Dolar

> The psychoanalyst is the presence of sophist in our epoch,
> but with another stature.
> Jacques Lacan[2]

There is a choice to be made about sophistry; the very appearance of the sophist always entails the call for a choice, a decision, and the decision concerns the status of truth. Of course the first obvious choice that comes to mind is the one launched by Plato, and then by Aristotle: there is a choice to be emphatically made between the true philosophy and its counterfeit, between the philosopher and the impostor that is the sophist, the one who is going through the motions of philosophy without espousing its essential tenets, first and foremost the quest for truth, and the make-believe philosopher. The fake philosopher is the greatest danger to philosophy, so the whole Platonic and Aristotelian enterprise can be seen as sturdy fortification that philosophy must erect against this threat. What should be applied when facing the sophist is the famous Marx brothers' joke,[3] though without its twist: "This man looks like a philosopher and talks like a philosopher, but don't let that fool you, he is not really a philosopher."

The condemnation of sophistry as the inner perversion of philosophy was indeed the founding gesture of philosophy, and because sophistry, in different shapes and sizes, kept haunting philosophy as its shadow, the history of philosophy also in many ways coincides with the history of reiteration and recurrence of this condemnation. Philosophy and its double. There was a quasi unanimity in harsh condemnation, yet the condemned vice nevertheless kept springing up, like jack-in-the-box, tenaciously reiterating the threat. It is as if Plato's *Sophist*, the paradigmatic instance and the origin of this struggle, already staged this predicament, because in that dialogue, there is curiously no sophist who would defend the cause of sophistry, the titular hero is conspicuously absent, yet he seems to be nevertheless unbeatable, he defies all the attempts to classify him, to pin him down, and even seems to take an ambiguous victory in the end.

The centuries-long battle concerned the epistemological grounds—safeguarding the true knowledge against its semblance, the proper argument against the faulty one, the discourse aiming at truth vs. rhetoric aiming at efficacy—and this shook hands with moral outrage and indignation—safeguarding the true social values against relativism and degeneration, to which one can add the questionable economic interest of selling knowledge for money.[4] The sophist looks like a modern entrepreneur, selling his quasi-philosophical skills on the market and caring only about their efficiency, not the truth.

Barbara Cassin's work is largely and passionately devoted to taking a different view of sophistry, and what an impressive oeuvre it is. If, through the whole tradition, the choice was to be made between philosophy and sophistry, and there was no doubt as to what one should choose in this alternative, she now courageously and undauntedly presents another choice to be made. She doesn't shy away from taking the Marx brothers' joke with its twist and all: "This man looks like a philosopher and talks like a philosopher, but don't let the appearance deceive you, he really is a philosopher, a philosopher actually more interesting and subversive than The Philosopher." The sophist is, quite literally, a philosopher "with a vengeance," representing the revenge of discourse on philosophy, the price philosophy has to pay for the disavowal of its own discursive and performative gesture, for its blindness as to its own embeddedness in discursivity, its disowning the power and the effects of language it is using. So the choice between true philosophy and sophistry that philosophy since Plato has been imposing on us is actually a nonchoice. It is a choice whose terms would have to be dismantled: what is presented as a perversion of the true discourse is rather a structural effect of this discourse itself, indeed its necessary "sophistic effect," as the title of her book goes, her magnum opus (Cassin 1995). Thus philosophy, in its crusade against sophistry, which has raged for millennia, was actually combating its own shadow, the shadow that it necessarily and unwittingly produced by its own discursive devices. There is a fateful disavowal, on the part of philosophy, of the powers of rhetoric, of its own rhetoricity, which it mistook for a mere tool in the deployment of its proper concepts. Conceptuality vs. rhetoricity—such was the choice made by philosophy, unaware that there is no concept without rhetoric and that conceptuality can never be disentangled from its discursive underpinnings. But showing that the choice between philosophy and sophistry is actually a false choice still implies that there is a choice to be made. Choosing not to choose between philosophy and sophistry is a choice of another stance, because what follows is not an ecumenical reconciliation between the two archenemies, or a division of labor between the former foes. A new battlefield presents itself, the battlefield of language and its incalculable effects, implying a structural subversion of philosophical propositions, where the new tenets have to displace the old ones. This is where, in her view, sophistry joins forces with psychoanalysis.

Psychoanalysis looms large in this new battlefield. Barbara Cassin takes it as an ally in these new struggles to be fought, as a kind of new embodiment of sophistry and its revenge on philosophy. In her reading, psychoanalysis essentially takes sides with the powers of discursivity—let's say, to make it short, with the capacity of language for homonymy rather than its capacity for synonymy. Sophistry was traditionally accused precisely of using homonymy—this was one of the essential bases of sophistic reasoning and its contended fallacy, the linguistic ground of faulty reasoning.[5] Words contingently and erratically sound alike; they reverberate beyond their capacity to make sense; they produce effects that blur the lines of all attempts to clearly delineate concepts and keep them well defined. The unconscious always appears as a glitch, a pun that uses the haphazard materials of homonymy, permitting a slide, a short circuit, where a chance encounter brings together the unexpected distant meanings and plays tricks on them.[6] This is clearly at the opposite end from the logic of synonymy, where one and the same meaning can be expressed by a number of different terms, keeping its unity of sense and the identity of a concept despite the divergence of means. The fact of homonymy, at its simplest, is a precondition for the unconscious (whereas synonymy conditions the realm of philosophy and its quest for meaning—this is what the principle salva veritate meant: one can use various means and vehicles, provided that truth be salvaged and remain intact). Sophistry always thrived on puns and double entendre, equivocations and faulty arguments, homonymy and short circuits, rather than on conceptual unity, clear definitions, and classifications. On the one hand, the claim to truth, universality, unity, and idea; on the other hand, mere punning, playing tricks with words, contingency. But psychoanalysis presents a new and particularly revealing stage in this eternal struggle, even its culmination and a reversal: Aren't the formations of the unconscious constantly using precisely the sophistic means—bad puns, wordplay, the faulty argument, the homonymy?[7] And don't they use this as a vehicle to produce the crack of sense, the gap in the production of meaning—a crack where truth can arise? Couldn't one say that the unconscious is structured like sophistry, yet nevertheless producing truth? If Lacan claimed that the unconscious is structured like a language, then it is certainly not like the language of Plato, but rather like the language of Gorgias and company. Yet it is only in this sophistic element and with its haphazard means that truth emerges and doesn't cease to surface. Lacan famously proposed the prosopopoeia of the unconscious: "I, truth, speak" (*Moi, la vérité, je parle*)

(Lacan 2006: 340). One can perhaps propose another one: "I am the sophist who always speaks the truth."

Psychoanalysis, in this view, aims at the locus of truth precisely in the erratic logic of homonymy rather than through concepts in their sensemaking capacity. There is a fateful "decision of sense" made by philosophy, to evoke the title of another of Cassin's books (Cassin and Narcy 1998), the decision to be debunked in its most telling birthplace (among others), the Book Gamma of Aristotle's *Metaphysics*, with its emphatic choice of the principle of noncontradiction and the excluded third. Psychoanalysis, the last avatar of the sophistic underside and underdog, stands at the opposite end; it consistently treats language through the ways that counteract the Aristotelian ban. Most conspicuously, there is no contradiction in the unconscious, as Freud adamantly maintained, nor the excluded middle, yet it is the very locus of an errant truth.

Lacan, with his knack for simplicity, invented a concept to cover this side of language, *lalangue*. If the signifier, based on differentiality and distinction, can give rise to linguistics and to science, even to the high scientific ambitions of a new epistemology of humanities (this was the epistemological program of structuralism), then the contingent nature of signifiers, based on chance encounters and overlaps, can only give rise to what Lacan called *linguisterie*, linguistery as opposed to linguistics. If the first part can be summed up by *la langue*, then this second part can be aptly rendered by *lalangue*, a self-referential pun, which itself displays in its name what it was supposed to demonstrate. *Lalangue* is but a homonym, a minimalistic one, guided not by salva veritate, but *salva voce* (or *salvo sono*), rescuing the sound, the voice, rather than truth, and yet pointing to another kind of truth through this—can we say "fidelity to the sound"? If the work of the unconscious can be epitomized by two basic mechanisms, condensation and displacement, *Verdichtung* and *Verschiebung*, metaphor and metonymy, then both are based on this second contingent flip side of the signifier.

Still, one is not easily done with philosophy and its elaborate procedures, and the symptom of this, for Cassin, is Lacan's insistence on matheme. The insistence on matheme goes back not to sophistry, but precisely to Plato's and Aristotle's crusade against sophistry: on the one hand, to Plato's extolling mathematics as the ultimate science,[8] and on the other hand and in particular, Aristotle's invention of logic. What is logic if not the formidable tool to cure language of punning, equivocations, ambiguities, slippages of sense? To be rid of precisely what makes the unconscious possible at all. Logic has always figured as a language doctor, with its proposal of constructing an ideal formal language that would be rid of trials and tribulations of ordinary language and would secure formal means for salvaging the unity of sense. The paradox of this enterprise was that one could eventually only do this by formal means, in other words, by relying on form devoid of content, ultimately by entrusting the rescue of sense and logos to the senseless letter. Logic always isolated the form as opposed to content, and the invention of mathematical logic, with matheme proper, only brought this to the gist. Curing the language of equivocation and proliferation of meanings came at a price, that of maintaining univocity by something that jettisons meaning. Logic is a philosophical endeavor of long and venerable standing, at the end of which one can find Lacan's infatuation with matheme. (The most prominent example of this, his notorious formulas of sexuation, is entirely based on a certain reading of Aristotle's logical quadrangle.)

A cursory look at *Encore* (*Seminar XX* 1972–1973) reveals the striking fact that Lacan introduces two concepts (not quite introduces—they were long in the making) that go in completely opposite directions, *lalangue* and matheme, without ever quite explaining their conceptual relation, their complicity or opposition. For Cassin, there is a choice to be made. Indeed, her book *Jacques le sophiste* (2012), with its ambition to spell out the relations between logos, sophistry, and psychoanalysis, ends on the note of an emphatic choice. Let me quote the last sentence of the book,[9] first in her elegant French and then in my clumsy and glossing English translation:

> Lacan de rester les bras ballants entre l'amour du mathème aux relents de philosophie et l'effectivité, au moins aussi joyeuse qu'angoissante, d'un blabla de parlêtre—que, et pas seulement en tant que femme, je choisis. (Cassin 2012: 238)

> Lacan stays balancing [oscillating, but this can also mean undecided, or idly, helplessly] between [on the one hand] the love for matheme with philosophical residues [where philosophy is still lingering] and [on the other hand] the efficacy, equally joyful and anguishing [at least just as joyful as anguishing], of a blah-blah of a speaking being—which, and not only as a woman, I choose.

The final word is thus "I choose," *je choisis*, the choice that Barbara Cassin emphatically assumes as her own with this parting shot. There is a choice to be made between *Jacques le philosophe* and *Jacques le sophiste*, and it appears that there are two souls residing in Lacan's breast, just as in Faust's: the soul of a lingering philosopher and that of a joyful (and anguished) sophist. They are at odds, at least in the way she presents her case, and it's the latter that would have to be chosen.

This choice subtends Cassin's entire argument, and the final sentence takes a stand on something that kept presenting itself as a choice throughout the book. For example, the passage in which she briefly comments on a quote from Lacan's ... *ou pire*:

> 'The real affirms itself, through an effect which is not the least, by affirming itself in the impasses of the logic [...]. There we can touch by the finger, in a domain which appears to be the most certain [namely, arithmetic], that which opposes the entire sway of discourse [*la prise du discours*], the logical exhaustion, that which introduces an irreducible gap [*béance*]. It is there that we designate the real.' [Lacan 2011: 41] Hence my question, which persists since the prologue: are there [would there be] two distinct ways to touch the real, the enjoyment of discourse [*la jouissance du discours*] and the matheme? (Cassin 2012: 153)

The discourse vs. the matheme—such are the terms of a choice, posited midway through the book as a question, to be decisively resolved in the last sentence. (But was there ever really an unresolved question? Wasn't there rather a decision already taken at the beginning, defining the standpoint from which the book could be written at all? A script subtending already its title?) The choice furthermore involves a choice in favor of enjoyment (*la jouissance du discours*), enjoyment which pertains to the discourse as such, to the blah-blah, to speaking for the pleasure of speaking—which was what the sophists were constantly accused of. Whereas it seems that there can be no question of the enjoyment of matheme—is matheme thus singularly devoid of enjoyment, the killjoy?[10] It seems that discourse, with its *lalangue*, is endowed with an endless and limitless proliferation of enjoyment, whereas the matheme looks like an attempt to cut it short.

If the sophist is to be rehabilitated and put on a par with the analyst, there are indeed some statements by Lacan that clearly point to the support of the sophist. Apart from the one put up as the motto (the psychoanalyst as the presence of the sophist in our age), for example, "I was wrestling with [Plato's] *Sophist* during these pseudo-holidays. Probably I must be too much of a sophist myself for this to interest me."[11] He seems to be unimpressed by Plato's condemnation, and he seems to be rather taking the side of the absent sophist under attack. Furthermore, part of Lacan's constant and ample engagement with philosophy can be put, in a wide sense, under the heading of what Cassin proposes as "sophistic listening to the history of philosophy" (Cassin 2012: 63), listening with an analytic ear to the embeddedness of philosophical concepts in *lalangue*, their slippages, the unwitting discursive consequences of philosophical propositions. Moreover, as an aside, there is the striking similarity in the fact that analysts, like the sophists, take money for what they are doing, thus entering into the suspicious realm of being paid for "delivering [the alleged] knowledge/truth." "There is like a black-out concerning what people were getting from the oracle of the sophists. No doubt there was something efficient/effective, for we know that they were paying them very dearly, like the psychoanalysts."[12] Furthermore, Socrates "was practicing a sort prefiguration of analysis. Had he demanded money for it [...] he would have been an analyst, before the Freudian letter" (Lacan 2001: 569). But I can't pursue this line here any further.

In this choice, such as it is set up by Cassin, it is not merely the enjoyment that is at stake, but in the same breath, the question of sexual difference. Barbara Cassin chooses "*pas seulement en tant que femme*," not "just like a woman" (*pace* Bob Dylan), not only in the capacity of a woman (one can perhaps surmise the structure of "this is not my mother"), thereby implying that there is indeed the feminine side of enjoyment at stake in discourse, in the blah-blah, which then entails that the other side, the side of matheme pertaining to philosophy (*aux relents de philosophie*), is to be taken as masculine. There is a choice of femininity vs. masculinity, in line with sophistry vs. philosophy, and one has to opt for the feminine part, but not merely on the grounds of being a woman—the implication is that there would have to be grounds independent of sexual position for making the choice of the feminine side as the viable one, rather than the matheme in its alleged masculinity.[13]

There is a subplot to the sexual part of this story, because the particular proponent of the matheme, who is secretly and openly the target all along, is obviously Alain Badiou. One only needs to peruse his books, filled with formulas, to see the absolute centrality of the matheme, at the simplest as something that is not the effect of discourse and cannot be reduced to the properties of language (cf. his stance against the linguistic turn, etc.). Thus Cassin would find in Badiou, who is her closest friend-foe (they wrote a couple of books together as a very odd couple), a worthy representative of masculinity. So we are bemused to learn that Badiou is a man and Cassin is a woman, and that this bears important theoretical consequences, if obliquely, because of course there can be no question of biological sex—but nevertheless... As they state themselves in the introduction to their joint book:

> What is at stake in these two studies, or readings, or openings, one by a woman and the other by a man (an important point), is indeed knowledge, considered by one of us in terms of its intimate connection

> with matters of language and by the other in terms of what philosophy purports to say about truth. So, with regard to Lacan's 'L'Étourdit,' to the modern theory of sexuation, and to the paradoxes of language and the unconscious, the (male) philosopher, at any rate, can say that what we are dealing with here is a new confrontation between, or a new distribution of, the masculinity of Plato and the femininity of sophistics. (Badiou and Cassin 2017: 2)

So here we have it, in full view, and oddly, Badiou and Cassin both subscribe to this division themselves. For Cassin, the danger that lurks in matheme is not so much that of reinserting psychoanalysis into philosophy (that too), but rather that of inserting philosophy into Lacan, to make him espouse the philosophical agenda through the matheme, and generally through the concern about logic and formalization, the dimension cut of a radically different stuff than the punning of discourse and its jouissance. The Lacanian adage "there is no sexual relationship" can acquire a new sense here—not only quite literally and trivially that there is no sexual relation between this odd couple, as far as I know, but empathically that there is no relation, sexual or other, between the philosopher and the sophist.

Badiou, for his part, also always adamantly insisted, throughout his career, that there is a choice to be made: first of all, the emphatic choice between philosophy and sophistry. The mission of philosophy is ultimately to repeat, to reassert, in each epoch and under different circumstances, the Platonic gesture against the ever-new varieties of sophists. The battle of/for philosophy is always the same, up to the recent avatars of sophistry under the guise of the linguistic turn, deconstruction, and various postmodern brands of antiphilosophy. But the aim of Badiou's philosophical project is not to rescue meaning against sophistry, as in the tradition, anything but; the crucial point is the insistence on the fundamental status of matheme, obvious in his notorious stance that "mathematics is ontology," his heavy reliance on set theory ("the pure doctrine of the multiple"), the operation of One, etc.[14] Matheme is *hors-sens*, outside of sense, and even more, *ab-sens*, ab-sense. There is again the question of choice. In his book on Parmenides, he proposes a choice when confronting this beginning of philosophy, to oppose the fickleness of discursivity by the stringency of matheme: "Poetry and predominant language, or matheme and formalism? The readers are called upon to choose" (Badiou 2014: 12). He, too, subscribes, if implicitly, that there is a choice to be made—ultimately, between what Lacan called matheme and what he called *lalangue*. (Of course, there is no choice to be made, for Badiou. On the level of truth procedures between mathematics and poetics, philosophy has to do justice to both, yet the basic ontological structure cannot be grasped without mathematics: there is no ontology without set theory.) Matheme may seem to be a better candidate for a conveyor of philosophy in its quest for truth, because it is not entangled in the "linguistic turn" and the endless quirks of language. No division into *langue* and *parole*, no puns and slides, and furthermore no voice, because the mathematical-logical terms can only be written. If speech is duplicitous and masks as much as it reveals, then the matheme purports to wear no mask—or does it?

Now for Lacan—as opposed to Lacan's occasional identification with the sophist, one can invoke his resolute insistence on mathemes as what can be integrally transmitted and insistence on mathematical formalization as "our goal, our ideal."[15] How does this coexist with the other side? One apparent way to understand it is that the endless poetics, effusiveness, proliferation of *lalangue* has to be brought to the austerity and asceticism of the matheme. And one can invoke Lacan's mechanism of *la passe*, the end of analysis, as the necessary trajectory from the one to the other, because analysis always starts with the proliferation of *lalangue*, and its end, *la passe*, ultimately involves the production of transmissible knowledge epitomized by matheme.

Is there indeed a matter of choice? We seem to be confronting a strange situation in which Badiou and Cassin have made a different choice on the basis of the "same" Lacanian tenets: one opting ultimately for the matheme and standing up for philosophy, and the other opting for *lalangue* with all its homonymy and puns, opting for the sophistry inscribed into language as its structural effect, both maintaining and proclaiming fidelity to Lacan.[16] It is as if each of the two, Badiou and Cassin, would take one part of Lacan (and both things are definitely part of the Lacanian doctrine), make their choice, and ultimately play the one against the other.

I would rather like to argue that one should refuse or circumvent or rework the terms of this choice. There is no choice to be made between the two. Both point into a radical direction of the Real that is at the core of psychoanalysis, and it is precisely in their mutual codependence and co-implication that one can get to this real. Lacan's insistence on both has to be taken seriously. The centrality of reflections on language made his early fame: "The Function and Field of Language and Speech in Psychoanalysis" was the title of his essential manifesto, the notorious "Rome discourse" in 1953; "the unconscious structured as a language" was the canonical formula, and this all seemed to entail the prevalence of the symbolic, massively present in his teaching in the fifties. But "language" was then pushed into two opposite directions, that of *lalangue*, the capacity of language for homophony and punning, and that of matheme, the formalization and the letter. Both presented language under the auspices of something that internally exceeds its anchorage in the symbolic, two ways in which the symbolic cannot be considered in its separation and autonomy, sustained merely by the signifier. Two ways in which the signifier cannot be considered in its "purity and independence," which was the great dream, the fundamental fantasy of structuralism.

At the risk of simplification, language was traditionally considered through its two manifestations, the vocal and the written, the voice and the letter. The Saussurean revolution, the introduction of the logic of the signifier, sidestepped this division altogether and proposed a completely abstract logic of differentiality as the key to language, an immaterial logic disregarding its two material manifestations, or regarding them as secondary and derivative. Considering our problem in this light, it is as if *lalangue* reintroduced the dimension of "the voice in the signifier" (homonymy, echoes, sound similarities, etc.) and the matheme reintroduced the dimension of "the letter in the signifier" (voiceless, senseless, something that can only be written, etc.). But this "reintroduction" didn't involve a return to the traditional division: it operated on the basis of the symbolic, presenting its own internal twists, "excrescences" of their inherent materialization—and there is no pure signifier without its "excrescences" (or one could say "becoming object of the signifier"). What they have in common is that they don't abide by the pure differentiality that defined the symbolic order in its autonomy, yet they are not introduced as heterogeneous or alien to the symbolic; they inhere in it and inhabit it as its own inner "slides." But this "deviation" of the symbolic may then put into question the stark division into the three dimensions of the symbolic, the imaginary, and the Real, which was the foundation of Lacan's teaching throughout, the three dimension to be knotted together on the basis of their irreducibility to each other (indeed, the introduction of sinthome in later Lacan can well be seen as a symptom/ sinthome of it—not without a pun). *Lalangue* and matheme lead to *sinthome*.

There is a radical difference in envisaging language via the symbolic or through the lens of *lalangue*. Jean-Claude Milner lucidly presented the difference between the two in these terms:

> *La langue* [language] is entirely reducible to negative relations; each linguistic sign exists only as opposed to another; its elements have no positivity by themselves; their sensorial qualities are of no consequence. [...] Homophony, on the contrary, depends on the *qualia*. *Lalangue* is integrally positive and affirmative. (Milner 2017: 88)

But if they are cut from different cloth, does this then raise the question of precedence? Which comes first? The positivity of *lalangue*, which is then molded and restricted, regulated (repressed) by the intervention of the signifier? This is the thesis proposed by Milner, but I don't think that the question can be resolved in these terms. It is ultimately essential that the preceding "positivity" (like the infants' babbling, repetition, experimenting with sounds)[17] can only appear as such on the basis of the "negative" cut of the symbolic (just as the alleged "positivity" of drives can only be deployed on the basis of the cut of castration.)[18] (But this is a matter of another discussion.) In a nutshell: the cut ultimately precedes what it cuts into. This is what Slavoj Žižek also points to in his most recent book:

> It seems much more appropriate to focus on the very gap that separates language from *lalangue*, and to conceive this gap ('symbolic castration') as preceding both terms of the opposition. More precisely, the two terms—language and *lalangue*—do not move at the same level: the basic opposition is that between language and what lacks in language (the lack of which is constitutive of language), and *lalangue* comes second, it fills in the gap of this lack. (Žižek 2020: 436)

The "positivity" of matheme presents a different problem and temporality. It is based on an intricate "artificial" invention and construction designed to counteract the insufficiencies of the symbolic, its impasses and slides, most prominently its constant contamination with *lalangue*. Matheme is the anti-*lalangue*. It should purge the language of contingency. Its weapon is the sturdiness of the letter, but a letter that is divorced from the phonematic nature of language, from its function to literalize the phonemes, the apparent first purpose of alphabetical writing.[19] It is the dimension of the letter precisely irreducible to the symbolic. If, in the whole tradition of what Derrida has called phonocentrism, writing was seen as secondary, derivative, supplementary, accessory in relation to the primacy of the pure self-presence of the voice (the notorious "metaphysics of presence"), hence dangerous and disruptive, then with the matheme and the whole enterprise of formalization, it is precisely this secondary auxiliary addition that gains the stature of the savior, the steadfast weapon against the vagaries of chance encounters of voices and sounds. It purports to be the rampart of necessity against the tides of linguistic chance—but the point of its Lacanian use is to counteract this understanding and rather to pinpoint its utter ambiguity.

I will limit myself to two points. Lacan doesn't address the relation between the two strands directly, but nevertheless gives some cursory indications. The mathemes, he says, "are integrally transmitted. We haven't the slightest idea what they mean, but they are transmitted" (Lacan 1998: 110). They are capable of integral transmission at the price of meaning and understanding. But this comes with a warning: "Nevertheless, they are not transmitted without the help of language, and that's what makes the whole thing shaky." (Lacan 1998: 110) And more pointedly:

> Mathematical formalization is our goal, our ideal. Why? Because it alone is matheme, in other words, it alone is capable of being integrally transmitted. Mathematical formalization consists of what is written, but it only subsists if I employ, in presenting it, the language I make use of. Therein lies the objection: no formalization of language is transmissible without the use of language itself. It is in the very act of speaking that I make this formalization, this ideal metalanguage, ex-sist. (Lacan 1998: 119)

Furthermore, there is the famous "The analytical thing will not be mathematical [*Le truc analytique ne sera pas mathématique*]. This is why the discourse of analysis differs from the scientific discourse" (Lacan 1998: 117). The first important point is that the formalization of matheme is not to be conceived as a metalanguage in relation to the ordinary language and its *lalangue*—not only because we always have to use language as a vehicle and the framing of formalization, and thus formalization itself depends on being framed by *lalangue*, but also because there is no metalanguage in relation to the Real, and this holds for both *lalangue* and matheme. There is no metarelation between the two, because they both touch upon a real, rather than designating it or trying to spell it out as something external to them. The real is not some dimension out there that they would try to pin down by different means; the Real emerges precisely in the paradoxes and impasses of their deployment (in both strands), and there is no other way of getting to it. Regarding the relation between the two, the point is not that the matheme has the capacity to be rid of equivocity, ambiguities, and slides of language (epitomized by *lalangue*), so that we could then hold on to the letter and formalization in its univocity as the best way to tackle the Real. The point is rather that formalization, in its effort to cure the impasses of language, itself runs into its own impasses. Both sides in their seeming opposition are rather held together by their shared impasse, although it may appear under different guises in the one and the other, and it is by their shared impasse that they pertain to the Real.

Thus, formalization is not a way out of the trickery, ambiguity, and homonymy of language, but rather a way of formalizing it, seizing it, yet not through the neutrality and stability of logical form: the history of logic is the history of tackling paradoxes produced by its initial gesture itself, the impasses that formalization itself has always entailed. Just as "a language [...] is nothing else but the sum total of equivocations that its history has allowed to persist there" (Lacan 2001: 490), so the logic is nothing but the sum total of paradoxes it had to tackle since its inception (starting with the liar paradox, which extended its long shadow to Russell's critique of Frege): "I will just recall that no logical elaboration, starting from before Socrates [and also elsewhere than in our tradition], has ever proceeded but through a kernel of paradoxes—to use the term that is acceptable everywhere." (Lacan 2001: 492) Logic may not be a matter of punning and slides, it was invented precisely to thwart them, yet this invention itself cannot escape the reinscription of the very impasse it was trying to avoid and to cure. But this is not to be seen as its failure and deficiency: the fact that it necessarily leads to impasses is the way that it holds to the Real. The logic, the matheme, is not a happy way of how to disentangle oneself from a mess, but how to run into another mess by trying to avoid the first one. The formalization always turns out to be the formalization of the impasse of formalization.[20]

This is also why proposing matheme as masculine and the jouissance of *lalangue* as feminine is a questionable way of conceiving it, because, first, the paradoxes of the impossibility of inscribing or defining the sexual difference pertain to both sides, and the logical way of circumscribing the feminine position is the point of the formulas of sexuation—they inscribe precisely the impossibility of its inscription. Inscribing the impossibility of writing what "doesn't stop not being written" (Lacan 1998: 94)—matheme as such is not a "male" way of inscribing the exceeding feminine impossibility and thus bringing it to the letter, an attempt to bound the unbounded. To make it quick, "Gödel," at its simplest, may be taken as an index of the nonwhole, nontotalizable nature of logic itself, the impossibility of its simple placement on the masculine side. In other words, the speaking errant truth of sophistry—"I am the sophist who always speaks the truth"—and the matheme don't relate to each other as truth and knowledge: matheme is precisely not the knowledge spelling out the errant truth in no uncertain logical-mathematical terms, it is itself another way of presenting the errant truth and its impasses, not in any metaposition in relation to it.[21]

If the aim of analysis is the production of transmissible knowledge, hence the procedure of *la passe*, this entails a reduction of the proliferation of sense (propelled by free associations, interpretation, etc.), cutting it short, producing a break, a cut not merely of non-sense, but of ab-sense.[22] As Lacan put it:

> [Interpretation] is directed not so much at the meaning as toward reducing it to the non-meaning of the signifiers, so that we may rediscover the determinants of the subject's entire behavior [...] not in its significatory dependence, but precisely in its irreducible and senseless character *qua* chain of signifiers. (Lacan 1979: 212)

So there is a fundamental imperative of formalization, the reduction of the signifiers to the senseless letter, yet this shouldn't be too quickly translated into a choice between *lalangue* and matheme. To put it bluntly and most economically: "All Lacanian word plays are mathemes." (Milner 2017: 88) They condense the endless punning into formulas that, despite their seeming demeanor of witticisms, present the radical direction of ab-sense, a break. The proliferation of punning can be cut short by a pun—if it's a proper one, in other words, if it can function as a matheme. This is what makes the difference of "Lacanian puns," with their capacity to become formulas, in relation to the vast propensity to punning at large.

There is another way of approaching the problem, already started above, and this is my second point. One can say that there are two conditions for the unconscious: first, no unconscious without homonymy, the contingent encounter of sounds, the echoes, the re-con-sonances, the realm of chance beyond the differential logic of the signifier and its necessity; and second, no unconscious without the letter, and one can sense this already in Freud's constant use of "metaphors" of cipher, deciphering, of rebus and hieroglyphs when speaking of the unconscious, based on the implicit analogy with writing. This becomes explicit with Lacan: one of his most famous texts bears the title "The Instance of the Letter in the Unconscious" (1957), in which the implied difference between the signifier and the letter looms large.[23] Not just the instance of the signifier, but the letter and its inscription. It was only much later that he could fully spell this out with his theory of the matheme. We have, on the one hand, the voice value of sound encounters in homophony, and, on the other, the senseless letter deprived of voice value, both based on "materialization" rather than on the purely negative nature of the symbolic, on "becoming voice" and "becoming letter" of the signifier. Both the voice and the letter are that in the signifier that doesn't contribute to making sense. But they seem to be opposed and unrelated, with no common measure, the volatility of the passing voice vs. the fixity of the letter.

There is a long tradition that imposed a "spontaneous" view that, in this opposition, the voice is conceived as feminine, evoking the boundless feminine jouissance, whereas the letter is regarded as masculine (the letter of the law, logos, logic, etc.). In my book on the voice, I spent a long time scrutinizing the long and inveterate "metaphysical" tradition of combating the seductive, intoxicating, and threatening powers of the feminine voice (the emblematic instance are the Sirens), the constant source of danger and decay, by the means of logos, the anchorage in the word, the letter, the unity of sense, the submission to the law (Dolar 2006: 42–52). The Lacanian point is simply that one shouldn't give in to this spontaneous hang, this quasi-natural tendency: one should insist not simply on their co-belonging, but on their speculative unity, as it were. This is where the Hegelian infinite judgment is perhaps the conceptual device that needs to be put to its full use: that the voice can ultimately be epitomized by the letter of the matheme, and that the letter in its seeming fixity "equals" the vacillation and fleetingness of the voice. As in Hegel, the infinite judgment acknowledges the full discordance and incommensurability, the cleft, the nontotalizable nature of the two entities, yet posits their identity through this very cleft. The spirit is a bone—the spirit of *lalangue* (pertaining to what is in French most appropriately called *mot d'esprit*), the bone of the letter? *Même combat*. Shall one say philosophy-sophistry—*même combat*? This then completely displaces the traditional notion of truth that the one held in awe and the other scorned, but the errant truth of psychoanalysis sidesteps that choice.

If there is no choice to be made between the two, this then opens up the field of many stark and arduous choices and decisions concerning the truth, the knowledge, and the Real.

Notes

1 This chapter was originally published in *Crisis and Critique* (2019) 6(1): 67–84. This is a revised version.
2 *Problèmes cruciaux de la psychanalyse*, May 12, 1965, quoted in Cassin (2012): 52.
3 "Gentlemen, Chicolini here may talk like an idiot, and look like an idiot, but don't let that fool you: he really is an idiot." (*Duck Soup*, dir. Leo McCarey 1933)
4 For a good account of this last point, cf. Marcel Hénaff (2002) *Le prix de la vérité: Le don, l'argent, la philosophie* (Paris: Seuil).
5 For the homonymy as the clue to sophistic reasoning, cf. Cassin (1996): 342–357, with her close reading of Aristotle's "Sophistical Refutations."
6 To take just one example that is close to my heart: Freud's patient, in describing her family, says: "they all possess *Geiz* [avarice]—I meant to say *Geist* [spirit]." (Freud 1975: 106) There is the contingency in German of *Geiz* and *Geist* sounding alike,

almost a homonymy, bringing together in a short circuit two entities that are starkly opposed: spirit as the elevation beyond the worldly concerns, striving for the ideal, the transcendence; avarice as the selfishness and greed, accumulating only for one's self-interest. The patient could say what she really thought of her family by the contingency of homonymy, the short circuit of sound similarity. It is tempting to elevate this particular pun to a parable: avarice is the symptom of spirit, its dark secret, its hidden clause, its sinister flip side—something that calls for writing a history of their intertwinement, for which one could propose the most apposite German title *Die Phänomenologie des Geizes*. It so happens that I attempted to write one (*O skoposti*, Ljubljana: Analecta 2002, available only in Slovene).

7 In his later teaching, Lacan rather used the term homophony than homonymy. Is there a difference? Milner argued that homonymy is rather the way that linguistics acknowledges the facts of homophony and neutralizes them to salvage their object, *la langue*. "By invoking homonymy, the linguist relies on the external world and the practical use of language. In order to save *la langue*, he puts his trust in *le langage*." (Milner 2017: 91) Homonymy appears as a nuisance to be rid of to salvage sense and communication, while homophony envisages it in its senselessness. I continue to loosely use "homonymy," but this distinction should be kept in mind.

8 The inscription on the entry into Academy allegedly ran: "Let no-one ignorant of geometry enter here." Plato's particular predilection for geometry stems from the Pythagorean tradition.

9 This is the last sentence before the epilogue, which is written in another tenor and gives an account of an autobiographical event.

10 Cassin opposes Badiou's coupling of matheme and anxiety (anxiety being a telltale sign of touching upon truth, *index veri*) with the coupling of discourse and enjoyment. But surely anxiety is also an index of enjoyment (of its too-muchness)? In the last sentence, she quite rightly bypasses this distinction ("just as joyful as anguishing"). But there is no word of the "affect of matheme."

11 "La troisième," quoted in Cassin (2012): 56. "*Efficace*," says Lacan—but what is the relation between efficiency and truth? Is truth efficient? "The fact that the sense of their interpretation had effects doesn't entail that the analysts are in the truth, its effects are incalculable. It doesn't bear witness to knowledge since in its classical definition knowledge is ascertained by a possible prediction." (Lacan 2001: 558) So both knowledge and truth are divorced from efficiency, and the analyst's knowledge cannot predict what is essentially contingent.

12 "Mon enseignement, sa nature et ses fins" (1968), quoted in Cassin (2012): 80.

13 This could be strangely in line with Nietzsche's exclamation that truth is a woman (in the opening line of *Beyond Good and Evil*), so that, in this new avatar, the nonwhole nature of *lalangue* would present the part of the speaking truth, while matheme would represent the "masculine" knowledge trying to capture it, with

no more success than the caricature philosophers and clumsy seducers that Nietzsche depicted and derided.

14 For the present purpose, we can set aside the differences between mathematics, set theory, traditional, and mathematical logic.

15 For Badiou, the sophist's choice, the choice of antiphilosophy, can be ultimately reduced to the thesis that "there is no truth." Thus, for him, Lacan represents a paradoxical antiphilosopher who resolutely insists on truth, an antisophist antiphilosopher. For Cassin, the sophist "doesn't aim at truth, but at discourse: being, and truth if you wish [!], is an effect of saying" (2012: 76). Thus, not the abandonment of truth, but truth that has the makings of another "sophistic effect," among many.

16 Cassin, sidestepping the issue somewhat, says at some point: "Why not matheme, among other things?—would I gladly say, just as the sophist says apropos of truth." (Cassin, 2012: 184) So why not truth, among other things, but not as the ultimate issue, focusing philosophy on the (fateful?) path of the absolute. She seems to be saying "I gladly [*volontiers*] concede truth, and matheme, but only among other things, *entre autres*." Badiou, for his part, can only be horrified by this kind of offhand talk, he adamantly insists on holding on to truth in its eternity and invariance (beyond the temporal dialectic that psychoanalysis is bound with, cf. Badiou 2017: 61), and holding on to truth that is not constituted by the act of saying (beyond any kind of linguistic turn—and matheme is the best vehicle to oppose the linguistic turn).

17 This would account for the privilege of the mother tongue: it is the only language in which *lalangue* precedes the acquisition of *la langue*. With all other languages one learns later, the sequence is reversed.

18 This is a matter for another discussion. I guess this is the point that, at its simplest, opposes Lacan and Deleuze, whose starting point is the positivity of desiring production (which follows the logic of the drives).

19 Freud frequently uses the analogy with hieroglyphs and rebuses when speaking of the language of the unconscious. Couldn't one see there, in analogy with the repression of *lalangue*, the "return of the repressed" in the realm of writing, of what was repressed and relegated to a mythical past by the invention of the alphabet?

20 For all this, cf. the striking analysis of Alenka Zupančič (2017): 66–70.

21 Badiou argues quite rightly and at length that there is a Lacanian triad truth-knowledge-real where none of the terms can be put in metarelation to others. Cf. Badiou and Cassin (2017): 49 ff.

22 Cassin argues that Freud's enterprise could be largely put under the heading of looking for "sense in the nonsense," as the general thrust of his interpretations, which, for Cassin, qualifies "the entire Freudian project as submitted to Aristotelianism" (Cassin 2012: 135–136), an expanded salvaging of sense, reaching even the remotest corners of nonsense. Whereas Lacan's endeavor ultimately

aims at “nonsense in the sense” (Cassin 2012: 138), abandoning altogether the Aristotelian “decision of sense.” Hence ab-sense beyond the opposition of sense/nonsense and also beyond *hors-sens* (cf. Cassin 2012: 180–181), a point that Badiou concurs with.

23 One can further recall the reading of Poe’s “The Purloined Letter” in early Lacan, where the ambiguity letter/letter is intended and put to great use. Implicitly, it’s not merely the question of the signifier but of the letter.

References

Badiou, A. 2014. *Le Séminaire – Parménide: L’être 1 – Figure ontologique (1985–1986).* Paris: Fayard.

Badiou, A. and B. Cassin. 2017. *There is No Such Thing as a Sexual Relationship* Translated by Susan Spitzer and Kenneth Reinhardt. New York: Columbia University Press.

Cassin, B. 1995. *L’Effet sophistique*. Paris: Gallimard.

Cassin, B. 2012. *Jacques le sophiste: Lacan, logos et psychanalyse*. Paris: EPEL.

Cassin, B. and M. Narcy. 1998. *La décision du sens. Le livre Gamma de la Métaphysique d’Aristote*. Paris: Vrin.

Dolar, M. 2006. *A Voice and Nothing More*. Cambridge, MA: MIT Press.

Freud, S. 1975. *The Psychopathology of Everyday Life*. Translated by Alan Tyson. London: Penguin.

Lacan, J. 1979. *The Four Fundamental concepts of Psychoanalysis*. Edited by J.-A. Miller and translated by Alan Sheridan. London: Penguin.

Lacan, J. 1998. *On Feminine Sexuality. The Limits of Love and Knowledge. Seminar Book XX, Encore 1972–1973*. Edited by J.-A. Miller and translated by Bruce Fink. New York: W. W. Norton.

Lacan, J. 2001. *Autres écrits*. Paris: Seuil.

Lacan, J. 2006. Écrits. Translated by Bruce Fink. New York: W. W. Norton.

Lacan, J. 2011. *…ou pire, Le séminaire livre XIX*. Edited by J.-A. Miller. Paris: Seuil.

Milner, J.-C. 2017. “Back and Forth from Letter to Homophony.” *Problemi Internatinal* 1(1): 81–98.

Zupančič, A. 2017. *What* is *Sex?* Cambridge, MA: MIT Press.

Žižek, S. 2020. *Sex and The Failed Absolute*. London: Bloomsbury.

CHAPTER 9

Consistency and Contradiction Two Logical Aspects of Truth in Psychoanalysis

Augusto Ismerim

One possible way to investigate the connection between truth, science, and Lacanian psychoanalysis could be analyzing the operations of truth and falsity from a logical point of view. In this chapter, I will examine Lacanian psychoanalysis in respect to two distinct logical manifestations of the idea of truth, one that is more closely linked to psychoanalysis in general and to Lacanian theory in particular, and another that is closer to that of mainstream scientific praxis.

Brazilian Newton da Costa's research famously promoted logical readings of psychoanalytic practice and theory (Da Costa and Forbes 1987; Da Costa 2014). Da Costa takes the occurrence of contradictions in the speech of the analysand to be an incontestable fact, with the problem consisting in the formalization of such a speech—in classical logic, contradictions trivialize a system, rendering it useless (Da Costa 2014). This relates to his innovative research as a logician, showing that it is possible to build logical languages that tolerate the existence of contradicting propositions (Da Costa 1974). Lacan himself was directly interested in the problem of theorizing and formalizing a thought that renounced the imagined Aristotelian principles of noncontradiction, excluded middle, etc. (Milner 1996)—logical principles whose presence or absence differentially structure one's rules for manipulating truth.

My goal is to investigate the existence of an unresolved (or, perhaps, unresolvable) tension between classical and paraconsistent paradigms within psychoanalysis itself. This will also allow for a brief analysis of how this impacts the relation of psychoanalysis to science today. The sheer breadth and depth of the fields involved in the questions undertaken here imply from the start that this paper will be no more than a preliminary essay. Our measure of success is the degree to which the arguments presented have sufficed to persuade the reader that these are matters worthy of further investigation.

I will first discuss some topics in the relation between logic, consistency, and science. How is consistency, the absence of contradiction, relevant in empirical research? Second, nonclassical logics will be discussed, in particular their relevance to psychoanalysis and Lacan, highlighting how contradiction may be logically relevant to psychoanalysis's object and to its theory. Once these steps have been taken, I will examine an early text from Lacan, *Presentation on Psychic Causality* (2006). *Presentation* is a good example of how logically different paradigms of truth are entangled in psychoanalytical matters. Finally, I will briefly analyze the interplay between logic, epistemology, and openness to mainstream science in two different contemporary fields, conventional post-Lacanianism and neuropsychoanalysis. This aims to demonstrate that the discussion of psychoanalysis's epistemology in terms of the opposition between classical and paraconsistent could be relevant today.

Consistency in Science

Truth has been frequently seen as the constitutive aim of inquiry. In that vein, for example, Karl Popper sought to develop theories of "approximate truth" to account for the progress of scientific knowledge. For Popper, better scientific theories are ones that are closer to the truth, even when one can be sure that they are not, themselves, true. The level of verisimilitude of a theory, or how much it is close to the truth, would be explicated in terms of the "content" of a theory: the totality of its logical consequences, which should be divided into a class of true propositions and a class of false propositions (Oddie 2016).

> Ultimately, the idea of verisimilitude is most important in cases where we know that we have to work with theories which are at best approximations—that is to say, theories of which we know that they cannot be true. (This is often the case in the social sciences). In these cases we can still speak of better or worse approximations to the truth (and we therefore do not need to interpret these cases in an instrumentalist sense). (Popper 1962: 235)

That empirical theories can be described as sets of propositions with logical consequences, as Popper's theory implies, is itself no small debate in the philosophy of science. Mosterín (2011: 294) defines theories similarly as "a set of sentences closed under the relation of consequence." Structuralists, such as Moulines, developed new ways of formalizing scientific theories (Moulines 2002), and, today, causal models are used for similar purposes (Hitchcock 2019). I will not, in any case, delve into the details of the comparative study of these approaches. Instead, I wish to underscore the differences between adopting an underlying consistent or inconsistency-tolerant paradigm in the development of empirical theories. These different paradigms will correspond, as mentioned, to different stances toward the workings of truth. In Popper's case, each logical consequence of a given theory must be either true or false. A proposition cannot be "neither true, nor false," much less "both true and false."

In classical logic, contradictions are not allowed. If a proposition is true, then its negation must be false. For example, either neuron *A* fired at time *t*, or it did not. This is a classical reasoning, in the sense that it is in accordance with Aristotelian logical principles. Namely, it agrees with the Law of Non-Contradiction (LNC) and the Law of Excluded Middle (LEM).

> For Aristotle, LNC is understood [...] as a prima facie rejection of the possibility that any predicate F could both hold and not hold of a given subject (at the same time, and in the same respect). In the same way, LEM is [...] the law that for any predicate F and any entity x, x either is F or isn't F. [...] We can translate the Aristotelian language, with some loss of faithfulness, into the standard modern propositional versions in (4) and (5) respectively, ignoring the understood modal and temporal modifications:
>
> (4) LNC: $\neg(\Phi \wedge \neg\Phi)$
>
> (5) LEM: $\Phi \vee \neg\Phi$
>
> Taking LNC and LEM together, we obtain the result that exactly one proposition of the pair $\{\Phi, \neg\Phi\}$ holds, where $\neg$ represents contradictory negation. (Horn 2018)

To embrace consistency is to embrace a certain relation toward truth. Either "P" or "not-P"; every P must be either true or false. Jesús Mosterín, the late Spanish philosopher, argued that the notion of consistency works as a regulatory idea in the development and progress of scientific research. Researchers, he says, are not happy to find that both P and not-P, though this occurs more or less frequently.

One example he discusses is the nineteenth-century debate regarding the age of the Earth. New findings by geologists and evolutionary biologists suggested that Earth had to be billions of years old to account for the results of the slow processes that they had studied. Physicists, on the other hand, estimated from the time that it should take for the Earth to cool down from its molten state an age around twenty million years. Evidently, both propositions could not be true at the same time (or, at least, "true" in a classical sense). The conflict between these two scientific communities ended with the general acceptance of the geologist's and biologist's version. From the point of view of the physicists, a contradiction remained, regarding their prediction and the "observed" result: this meant that their theory had to be revised. "Once radioactivity discovered at the end of the 19th century and its effect added to the calculations, the contradiction was resolved and a deeper understanding of the internal processes of the Earth was achieved." (Mosterín 2011: 302)

For Mosterín, one may almost never know if a theory is consistent, and it is a matter of fact that there are moments in which contradictions are discovered in scientific practice. Still, the dynamics of progress in science depends on a "dissatisfaction with contradiction" (Mosterín 2011: 298). Special relativity and quantum theory may well today be contradictory, but the will to develop a unified theory of physics is the same as the will to solve the contradiction between these two theories. Mosterín hints at the possibility of adopting inconsistency-tolerant logical systems, only to reject it:

> In dealing with inconsistent theories of empirical science, we could replace classical logic with paraconsistent logic. This move would allow us to isolate the found contradictions and so preserve the inconsistent theory from collapse into the whole language. We could continue to use our old theory, even after the red spots of contradiction have appeared on its face. Yes, it is possible, but is it desirable? (Mosterín 2011: 297)
>
> The discovery of a contradiction in empirical science is experienced as a trauma. It produces uneasiness, discomfort and anxiety across the community involved. Caught in this type of conundrum, it is not a way of living with contradiction that scientists are looking for, but a way of jumping out of contradiction. (Mosterín 2011: 305)

If Mosterín gives an adequate account of mainstream scientific practice, then the conclusion must be that nonclassical perspectives, though possible to adopt, remain pointless from the perspective of an evolving empirical theory.

The Strange Science of Inconsistencies

As early as in *The Interpretation of Dreams*, Freud wrote:

> thoughts which are mutually contradictory make no attempt to do away with each other, but persist side by side. They often combine to form condensations, just as though there were no contradiction between them, or arrive at compromises such as our conscious thoughts would never tolerate, but such as are often admitted in our actions. (Freud 2010: 593)

One may think of that experience that is characteristic of a dream: "I saw a woman [...] It was my mother, and wasn't my mother." *Widerspruchslosigkeit* is the German noun denoting the quality of that in which contradictions are absent. In Freud's works, "contradictorinessless" developed from a feature of the primary process into an attribute of the unconscious:

> The nucleus of the Ucs. consists [...] of wishful impulses. These instinctual impulses are co-ordinate with one another, exist side by side without being influenced by one another, and are exempt from mutual contradiction. When two wishful impulses whose aims must appear to us incompatible become simultaneously active, the two impulses do not diminish each other or cancel each other out, but combine to form an intermediate aim, a compromise. There are in this system no negation, no doubt, no degrees of certainty: all this is only introduced by the work of the censorship between the Ucs. and the Pcs. Negation is a substitute, at a higher level, for repression. (Freud 1957: 186–187)

Two "contradictory impulses" could be, for example, the simultaneous wish to kill and to be the loved object of a single other. One possible propositional writing of such an (Oedipal) situation could be to state the simultaneous truth of both statements: "I love him" and "I do not love him (I hate him)." That would amount to asserting the truth of both P and not-P. Therein lies the relevance of paraconsistent systems, systems in which a statement and its negation may both be true at the same time, without resulting in logical collapse.

There are several ways to construct paraconsistent logics, and the field of nonclassical logics today has expanded far beyond its initial coordinates. In some of them, contradictory propositions are merely "isolated" from the rest of the system, which behaves otherwise like a classical one. Da Costa (2014) has affirmed that he thinks such a logic would be insufficient to meet the demands of Lacan's anticonsistency stances—instead, a paraconsistent logic would be needed that includes a true proposition that itself is incompatible with classical logic. At any rate, in all nonclassical logics, the operation of negation and the predicates "true" and "false" will necessarily function differently, in some way, than they do in classical logic. It is adequate to interpret these, then, as "different" concepts of negation and truth in relation to the classical ones—the specificities of this difference will depend on the logical system adopted.

Da Costa has compared the operation of negation in some paraconsistent systems to the concept of negation in psychoanalysis, and his experience with psychoanalysis was one of the reasons which led him to experiment with these systems in the first place.

> I am referring to the analytic discourse as this linguistic interplay between patient and analyst. In this discourse, if the person, for example, describes her dreams, begins to associate, it is evident that there are contradictions; moreover, this discourse is incomplete, and sometimes derogates other logical principles. Nonetheless, there is an underlying logic. (Da Costa 2014: 61)

Da Costa distinguishes between two different objects of analysis: the language of the material the patients bring to analysis (or the language of the conversation between patient and analyst), and the language of psychoanalytic theory. As mentioned above, the first case would clearly demand a nonclassical logic for its formalization. That does not imply necessarily that the same applies to the language of its theory:

> in psychoanalytic theory—I lack the means and the knowledge to currently solve this problem—there may be an underlying logic, psychoanalytic theory's logic, which could be classical, although I have doubts in this respect. If I understood Lacan well, such a logic would be non-classical. But, surely, unconscious logic, or the logic which manifests itself in this interplay between patient and analyst, this informal logic can be formalized through some kind of paraconsistent logic. (Da Costa 2014: 61)

We are now in a position to investigate how Lacanian psychoanalysis behaves regarding classical and paraconsistent theoretical frameworks, specifically by examining how these two dimensions appear within his *Presentation on Psychic Causality*.

Bisecting Truth in Lacan's Presentation

In his *Presentation*, Lacan (2006) puts forward an explanation for the etiology of madness. His discussion includes important moments of psychoanalytic theoretical development—from clinical case analysis to the advancement of universal propositions. Furthermore, the fact that it was presented to an audience of psychiatrists and neurologists (instead of analysts) makes it particularly relevant to probe the relation between psychoanalysis and "mainstream" science.

Already in the beginning of his speech, Lacan says that, by defending his research in a verbal debate, he is "living up to the requirements of truth" (Lacan 2006: 123). Soon after that, he states that Henri Ey's theory "does not possess the characteristics of a true idea" (Lacan 2006: 125). By the end of the speech, he unites Socrates, Descartes, Marx, and Freud as people who "researched with passion to unveil the truth" (Lacan 2006: 157). Truth here appears as important, valuable, and linked to the processes of argumentation and research—somewhere close to the role of a "regulatory idea."

As one might expect, however, not all is straightforward with Lacan. Already in the 1940s, he presents some ideas on the concept of truth that would reverberate through the remainder of his career. He argues that (1) "man's language, the instrument of his lies, is thoroughly ridden with the problem of truth" (Lacan 2006: 136) (a problem that is here linked to the dialectic of the subject's particular and the Other's universal). He also argues that (2) truth is inseparable from the processes of signification for man, and he defines psychology as "the domain of nonsense [...] of everything that forms a knot in discourse" (Lacan 2006: 137). In both propositions lies the idea that contradiction is fundamental to the realm of language.

Furthermore, Lacan argues for a constitutive relation between truth, language, and madness. In general, that means he highlights the semantic and linguistic aspects of mental illness, in both clinical and philosophical dimensions. He presents an outline of his 1932 examination of a case of paranoia, fleshing out biographical and analytic information to defend his claims, and offering as further support a small a piece of literary analysis. One main piece articulating the dimensions of truth, language, and madness is the concept of misrecognition.

> What then is (the phenomenon of) delusional belief? I say that it is misrecognition, with everything this term brings with it by way of an essential antinomy. For to misrecognize presupposes recognition, as is seen in systematic misrecognition, in which case we must certainly admit that what is denied is in some way recognized. (Lacan 2006: 134)

One example he discusses is Molière's hero Alceste, so willing to recognize the vanity and ridiculousness of his others in aristocratic life, and so incapable of seeing it blossom in himself—in his obsession for the Célimène, for instance. So, there is recognition, and there is a negation of that recognition. Or there is negation and nonetheless recognition. This problem of the "incomplete" negation realized by the subject was of major interest for Lacan later. *Verdrängung*, *Verleugnung*, and *Verwerfung* are all forms of negation that still allow some existence to the things negated. This is one more expression of the contradictoriness that is constitutive to language and truth—now in the core of the experience of madness and in the foundations of psychoanalysis.

These points seem to imply that, if there is a logic for truth in Lacan, it should not be classical: paradoxes of truth and lies, dialectics of Hegelian descent, sense always in lack or excess, nonrecognition supposing recognition, the subject's modes of partial negation.

Perhaps more curious is how some of Lacan's propositions resonate with scientific parlance both in methods and goals. The analyst stresses how the problem of signification arises at once from medical and clinical considerations and likens the structure of the madman's knowledge to an anatomy, which can be and has been outlined. He also supplements his arguments for the causality of (mis)recognition with direct appeal to scientific studies of pigeons and grasshoppers, who mutate on sight of specific stimuli.

But it is in the advancement of causal relations that Lacan is most interested in "living up to the requirements of truth" (Lacan 2006: 123). He argues extensively on the processes of identification and recognition, to conclude that the turning point of madness "lies in the mediacy or immediacy of the identification" (Lacan 2006: 140). An unmediated identification, that is, an identification that is too appealing to the subject, one in which the subject "really believes"; that is proposed to be a main ingredient in the causality of madness.

> [T]he essential misrecognition involved in madness is situated at just such a point, as my patient made perfectly clear. This misrecognition can be seen in the revolt through which the madman seeks to impose the law of his heart onto what seems to him to be the havoc [*désordre*] of the world. [...] It is an insane enterprise, rather, in that the subject does not recognize in this havoc the very manifestation of his actual being, or that what he experiences as the law of his heart is but the inverted and virtual image of that same being. He thus doubly misrecognizes it, precisely so as to split its actuality from its virtuality. (Lacan 2006: 140)

After that, he expands this causality of recognition by elaborating the concept of "imago," which he uses to describe the causal transformations undergone in narcissism and in the Oedipal complex. Eventually, he comes as far as warning against the possibility of technical production of madness, based on the causal knowledge his research presents.

> In concluding, I hope that this brief discourse on the imago will strike you, not as an ironic challenge, but as a genuine threat to man. For, while our ability to realize that the imago's unquantifiable distance and freedom's minute blade are decisive in madness does not yet allow us to cure it, the time is perhaps not far off when such knowledge will allow us to induce it. While nothing can guarantee that we will not get lost in a free movement toward truth, a little nudge will suffice to ensure that we change truth into madness. Then we will have moved from the domain of metaphysical causality, which one can deride, to that of scientific technique, which is no laughing matter. (Lacan 2006: 156)

Here, one may probe the relation between consistency in theoretical systems and Lacan's thought. Where do consistent-like functionings of truth seem to emerge within psychoanalytic thought? In its clinical-empirical dimension. Lacan, by the end of his *Presentation*, affirms that he treated the Aimee material with the respect it deserved as a case. Is he not then affirming that his analysis is in some way consistent with the clinical observations? In this piece of psychoanalytic theory, some distinctions are proposed that allow no "excluded middle," and they have diagnostic relevance. Either the subject's identification is mediate or it is immediate (it is mediate *or* it is not mediate), and this distinction in truth value should be consistent with our observations of cases of madness.

Consider, instead of the role of identification in madness, the later model of a structural difference between psychosis and neurosis. In this conception of psychosis, which Lacan developed in the 1950s, the difference between psychotic subjects and nonpsychotic subjects lies on whether the "name of the father" has been inscribed as a signifier (Guéguen 2013; Pontes and Calazans 2017). This is an affair that allows no excluded middle, no contradiction. Quite the contrary—structurally, it is exact. To think, at once, that "P is psychotic" and "P is neurotic" are both true, would have to be read either as a difficulty in diagnosis or as a novel theoretical proposal.

> If Lacan introduces the subject in such a way as to gear it into mechanisms, it is because he holds the subject he has to deal with in the psychoanalytic experience to be entirely calculable. (Jacques-Allain Miller, unpublished, as cited in Guéguen 2013: 72)

This model, which is at least partially still adopted today (Pontes and Calazans 2017), entails a number of propositions; for example, when questioned about certain matters (say, lack or subjective division), the neurotic patient will respond in a certain way, and the psychotic one will respond differently. This is all the more pressing when the direction of the treatment is in consideration: the same intervention that would produce a clinically desirable effect in one case could produce an undesirable effect in the other. Making approximate predictions such as these is part of an analyst's daily practice. It might well be the case that such predictive propositions are in part what makes clinical practice possible. Aren't they consistent with observations, or should they be? To what extent do they reject the principle of noncontradiction? More precisely, what are the roles played by classical and paraconsistent paradigms of truth in Lacanian clinical practice?

First, I am suggesting that one can find within the text of this Lacan, and perhaps in psychoanalytic practice in general, certain components that apparently depend on some consistency-building process to be meaningful. This points to a specific manner of operating with the concept of truth, logically, which is the same one to be found in mainstream science. On the other hand, as was clear since its birth, psychoanalysis is inherently related to operating with (or within) contradiction. Lacan sought to show that the departure from classical logic is, or must be, built into the actual psychoanalytic theory (Da Costa 2014).

In this way, one can see that there is a tension between a certain paraconsistent operation of truth—to which Lacanian psychoanalysis gives a refined treatment—and the presence of "vectors of consistency" lurking in psychoanalytic thought: in the development of theories, in causal propositions, and in case construction. Such considerations frame the question of psychoanalysis's position in relation to science.

The Contemporary Debate

Considering, now, the contemporary dimension of the tension discussed above, its expression is in two main "figures." One may be called conventional post-Lacanianism. The other is Lacanian neuropsychoanalysis.

Conventional post-Lacanianism often continued the strategy employed by Lacan, aiming to develop an epistemology that has as one of its central concerns the peculiar behavior of truth in the psychoanalytic domain. These authors tend to emphasize psychoanalysis's incommensurable differences in relation to science. They most often depart either from Lacan's "Science and Truth," building their arguments on the differential presence of the divided subject in and out of psychoanalysis, or, instead, from the hyper-formalization of algorithmic theories, such as the four discourses and the formulas of sexuation.

In the first case, the split subject is the protagonist of an irreparable inconsistency, and it is the benchmark for a new conception and organization of the sciences:

> while modern science can be characterized by its attempt to exclude the subject through an always-failed process of suturing, psychoanalysis brings it into its fold, making it precisely what it operates on. [...] If anything, this account suggests that Lacanian psychoanalysis may furnish modern scientific practice with an insight which, if incorporated, may lead to a changed ethical relation between the scientist and his or her work. This is because psychoanalytic praxis incorporates a further dimension of at least equal importance, namely the ethical dimension of the singular subject's truth. One could say that the incorporation of this latter dimension into science itself would involve nothing short of its radical reconceptualization. Such an incorporation, in other words, would constitute a necessary condition for science to become capable of including psychoanalysis within its ambit. (Glynos 2002)

The second case, in turn, may be understood by a reference to Jean-Claude Milner's conception of Lacan's "second classicism." That would be a period in the analyst's epistemology that proposes precisely that fragmented and local mathemes are the means to building a consistency-independent theory. Bourbaki relied on "simple literal consistency," that is, on the consistency generated by the rules of letter manipulation. Lacan, drawing from formal dispositions, adds the caveat that literal consistency does not exist: "letterness" and consistency are from different orders. In this manner, math would supply Lacan with the materials for a nonclassical theory:

> Psychoanalysis's general problem is, let us remember, that there is thought which does not correspond to the imagined and qualitative criteria of thought (coherence, excluded middle, discursivity, negation, etc.; in sum: Aristotle). [...] Psychoanalysis must, therefore, build a theory of thought which integrates, not as an adventitious extension, but as constitutive property, thinking disjoined from imaginary regulations. [...] In the second classicism, homogeneity is broken. Only math remains, and it remains only in its hyper-Bourbakian reading. That is the greatest axis of a theory of non-imaginary thought. (Milner 1996: 111)

Neuropsychoanalysis, on the other hand, is concerned with the consistency between psychoanalytic propositions and the findings from the neighboring scientific fields. Neuropsychoanalysis can be defined as the movement, in psychoanalysis and in neurocognitive science, that claims that combining the knowledge developed in both domains is the proper way to move forward scientifically. The Neuropsychoanalysis Association, the largest organization dedicated to the field, informs about its magazine:

> *Neuropsychoanalysis* publishes papers at the intersection of psychoanalysis and the neurosciences. Our journal was founded on the assumption that these two historically divided disciplines are ultimately pursuing the same task, namely, 'attempt[ing] to make the complications of mental functioning intelligible by dissecting the function and assigning its different constituents to different component parts of the [mental] apparatus' (Freud 1900a: 536). Although the fields have approached this task from radically different perspectives, the underlying commonalities have become increasingly evident as neuroscientists have begun to investigate those 'complications of mental functioning' that were traditionally the preserve of psychoanalysts, such as emotion, unconscious cognition, and interpersonal processes. Neuropsychoanalysis provides an arena for integrating the explosion of neuroscientific insights into existing psychoanalytic theories and models, and for enriching behavioral and cognitive neuroscience, neurology, neuropsychology and related fields with the dynamic perspectives of psychoanalytic thought and practice. (NPSA, 2018)

As a rule, in neuropsychoanalysis, it is considered valid to turn to evidence from neurology or cognitive science in the investigation of the causal propositions that are discussed in psychoanalytic theory. Some researchers wish to present interactions between physiology and subjectivity—for example, analyzing neurologic patients (Kaplan-Solms and Solms 2002)—and others seek underlying neural mechanisms to account for psychoanalytic predictions (for instance, Howard Shevrin's seminal research on the neural mechanisms of repression [Shevrin et al. 2013]).

Within neuropsychoanalysis, Lacanians are not so frequently found, but the field has seen some production in the last decade. Ariane Bazan, notably, has written multiple papers juxtaposing descriptions of neural pathways and vocabulary from the French school of psychoanalysis. In her and Sandrine Detandt's provocatively named "On the Physiology of Jouissance," for example, they proposed a relation between neurocognitive reward systems and Lacan's formulation of the paradoxical satisfaction subjects find "beyond the pleasure principle."

> We conclude that jouissance could be described as an accumulation of body tension, fuelling for action, but continuously balancing between reward and anxiety, and both marking the physiology of the body with the history of its commemoration and arising from this inscription as a constant push to act and to repeat. Moreover, it seems that the mesolimbic accumbens dopaminergic pathway is a reasonable candidate for its underlying physiological architecture. (Bazan and Detandt 2013: 1)

Neuroscientific theories, in general, would like to be consistent with the current physiological models used to explain the causal functioning of brain cells and brain tissues. By extension, when neural or neurocognitive science seeks to give explanations about "mental" processes—that is, processes related to subjective experience and to intentional content—they would like to make these consistent with the physiological models too. Neuropsychoanalysis is concerned with similar problems.

We can also note that the straightforward way through which the fields connect is precisely through the postulated consistencies. It is the clinical aspects of jouissance that can be modeled by Bazan's work—the expected repetitions, the possible counterfactuals, and so on—and not Lacan's "anthropology," so to speak, of being in language.

It is as if these researchers asked: If psychoanalysis is consistent with observations, shouldn't it be consistent with broader empirical models too? And, a lot of the time, the psychoanalyst's answer is more or less: in making psychoanalysis consistent with the natural sciences, they are inconsistent with the very paraconsistency that is proper to psychoanalysis. My suggestion would be that the relations between the paraconsistent and the consistent operations within psychoanalysis itself are not clear enough.

One interesting aspect of neuropsychoanalysis comes about when it attempts to develop causal accounts of the peculiar linguistic properties that give rise to the functions of negativity and contradictoriness one finds in Lacan. Bazan herself has papers commenting on how findings on the neural processing of language could explain the intrinsic ambiguity of words and language in general (Bazan et. al 2002; Bazan 2011). This approach could potentially use classical neural and cognitive theories to ground an entire universe of nonclassical language-structured experience.

On the other side of the board, there are researchers such as Adrian Johnston, the American philosopher, who claim that the true Lacanian consequence is that nature itself is inconsistent (2013). By making inconsistency the foundation of existence in general, however, it might be the case that what results is the problem of explaining the consistency science *does* find in nature.

When one speaks of two logical systems that must be somehow connected, it is reasonable that one approach would be trying to derive one system from the other. To derive the nonconsistency of words from the consistency of neurons (Bazan's paper) or to derive the consistency of some causal processes from the nonconsistency of nature (Johnston's purported problem): the significance of both approaches would be in trying to show how one functioning of truth could give rise to another one, different from itself.

Conclusions

In this exercise, I attempted to show how two logical aspects, classical and nonclassical, might be difficult to untangle in psychoanalysis. To contrast a "need to value consistency" with a "need to reject consistency" seems to offer one a logical frame for thinking through a variety of problems within psychoanalysis itself, as well as problems in psychoanalysis's relation with its neighboring fields.

Consistency has a role in the development of empirical theories that is present in the analytic field—in diagnosis and in case construction, for example. The daily practice of the psychoanalyst comprehends a dynamic evaluation of clinical hypothesis that mimics in small scale the process of scientific development. Analysts must develop consistent clinical descriptions to guide their work, and must be able to distinguish clinical doubt from theoretical inadequacies. Outside each analyst's clinic, the collective debate on how to interpret and solve the perceived contradictions between clinical data and theory is, in principle, one of the ways psychoanalytic theory moves forward. One can imagine that a concrete and detailed study combining history and epistemology on this matter should bring about a clearer picture of the role consistency has played in psychoanalytic theoretical development. Equally pressing, it would seem, is the development of an "empirical psychoanalytic epistemology": an investigation of how individual psychoanalysts reason about their cases—of when and how classical logic is used in actual clinical psychoanalytic thought.

Psychoanalysis, however, is inseparable from the work with contradiction. Dream reports, the content of analytical sessions, the functioning of primary processes, the rules of the unconscious system, and incomplete negations, paradoxes, and dialectics all lay bare the insufficiency of Aristotle's principles for psychoanalytic phenomena. However, the extent to which deviation from classical logic is necessary in psychoanalytic theory remains an open question. Though this point apparently has not received much attention, Da Costa implies that, while Freud's theory was classical, although dealing with nonclassical objects, Lacan tried to build a nonclassical theory for psychoanalysis. If accepted, this idea puts the discontinuities between Freud and Lacan in sharp relief. This opens up the question whether we should follow one path or another, which, in turn, would demand a more detailed understanding of the logical functioning of theories when dealing with nonclassical objects (this, at least, one can assert psychoanalysis does).

The reading of Lacan's *Presentation on Psychic Causality* presented here aimed to demonstrate the coexistence of classical and nonclassical logical paradigms in psychoanalytic thought. Likewise, investigating the contemporary debate highlighted how radical this problematic can become, each approach (consistency-oriented neuropsychoanalysis and anticonsistency-oriented conventional Lacanianism) attempting to govern psychoanalysis in its own terms. The question of psychoanalysis's position in relation to science can be accessed by the mapping the split strategies within the psychoanalytic field itself, and this split in turn can be shown to depend to some extend on logical matters. Thus, to build a successful dialogue between psychoanalysis and science (and, between neuropsychoanalysis and conventional post-Lacanianism) would likely undertake the development of some response to a logical dimension of disagreement.

As of paths forward, quasi-naturalist research on the neurocognitive origins of pervasive negativity and contradiction in linguistic organization—and, thus, in linguistically structured human experience—might be a surprisingly elegant way to solve some of the problems here advanced. But this is speculating. Perhaps, a prior question is: What would solving, or preserving, the contradiction between consistency and contradictoriness in psychoanalysis mean? The entire issue remains open to contradictions: to those one must embrace, to those one must dissolve, or both.

References

Bazan, A. 2011. "Phantoms in the Voice: A Neuropsychoanalytic Hypothesis on the Structure of the Unconscious." *Neuropsychoanalysis* 13(2): 161–176.

Bazan, A. and S. Detandt. 2013. "On the Physiology of Jouissance: Interpreting the Mesolimbic Dopaminergic Reward Functions from a Psychoanalytic Perspective." *Frontiers in Human Neuroscience*, *7*: 709.

Bazan, A. et al. 2002. "Language as the Source of Human Unconscious Processes." *Evolution and Cognition 8*(2): 164–171.

Da Costa, N. and J. Forbes. 1987. "Sobre psicanálise e lógica." *Revista Brasileira do Campo Freudiano* 1: 103–111.

Da Costa, N. 2014. Interviewed by O. A. Cesarotto and M. P. S. Leite. *Leitura Flutuante 2*(6): 51–77.

Da Costa, N. C. 1974. "On the Theory of Inconsistent Formal Systems." *Notre Dame Journal of Formal Logic* 15(4): 497–510.

Freud, S. 2010. *The Interpretation of Dreams.* New York: Basic Books.

Freud, S. 1957. "The Unconscious." *The Standard Edition* 14. London: 159–204.

Glynos, J. 2002. "Psychoanalysis Operates upon the Subject of Science: Lacan between Science and Ethics." In *Lacan & Science*, edited by J. Glynos and Y. Stavrakakis. London, Karnac: 51–88.

Guéguen, P. G. 2013. "Who Is Mad and Who Is Not? On Differential Diagnosis in Psychoanalysis." *Culture/Clinic: Applied Lacanian Psychoanalysis* 1: 66–85.

Hitchcock, C. 2019. "Causal Models." In *Stanford Encyclopedia of Philosophy* (Summer 2019 Edition).

Horn, L. C. 2018. "Contradiction." In *Stanford Encyclopedia of Philosophy* (Winter 2018 Edition).

Johnston, A. 2013. *Prolegomena to Any Future Materialism: The Outcome of Contemporary French Philosophy.* Evanston, Northwestern University Press.

Kaplan-Solms, K. and M. Solms. 2002. *Clinical Studies in Neuropsychoanalysis: Introduction to a Depth Neuropsychology.* New York, Other Press LLC.

Lacan, J. 2006. "Presentation on Psychic Causality." In Écrits: The first complete edition in English. New York, W.W. Norton & Company.

Milner, J. C. 1996. *A obra clara.* Rio de Janeiro: Jorge Zahar.

Mosterín, J. 2011. "The Role of Consistency in Empirical Science." *Manuscrito* 34(1): 293–305.

Moulines, C. U. 2002. "Introduction: Structuralism as a Program for Modelling Theoretical Science." *Synthese*: 1–11.

NPSA. 2021. "The Journal." Retrieved from http://npsa-association.org/the-journal/. Accessed 6 October 2021.

Oddie, G. 2016. "Truthlikeness." In *Stanford Encyclopedia of Philosophy* (Winter 2016 Edition).

Pontes, S. and R. Calazans. 2017. "The Structuralist Legacy in Lacan: Clinical and Diagnostic of Psychosis." *Psicologia: Ciência e Profissão* 37(3): 738.

Popper, K. 1962. *Conjectures and Refutations: The Growth of Scientific Knowledge.* London: Routledge.

Shevrin, H. et al. 2013. "Subliminal Unconscious Conflict Alpha Power Inhibits Supraliminal Conscious Symptom Experience." *Frontiers in Human Neuroscience* 7: 544.

Chapter 10

On Saying More than One Knows
Psychoanalysis, Truth, and Subjectivity

Jasper Feyaerts

Introduction

In *The Question of Lay Analysis* from 1926, a text intended as an exposition of the peculiarities of psychoanalytic treatment before an imaginary "impartial person," Freud lets his interlocutor make the following observation:

> You assume that every neurotic has something oppressing him, some secret. And by getting him to tell you about it you relieve his oppression and do him good. That of course, is the principle of confession, which the Catholic Church has used from time immemorial in order to make secure its dominance over people's minds. (Freud 1926: 189)

Freud responds to this, to distinguish the originality of his talking cure from the Catholic principle of confession, "In confession the sinner tells what he knows; in analysis, the neurotic has to tell *more*" (Freud 1926: 189). This is an instructive proposal, but a fairly ambiguous therapeutic precept, to say the least.

Is Freud suggesting that one should tell things one doesn't know, but merely pretends to know? Say, for example, by telling, in a pretentious anticipation of the psychoanalytic insight, that I actually secretly enjoy what I complain about? On closer inspection, this cannot be the case, because by telling what one doesn't know *as if* one knows, one tells precisely what one knew all along: I already know that I am telling more than I actually know, in other words, that I know nothing about my secret enjoyment. As Sartre would say, consciousness of telling what I do not know is already accompanied by a nonthetic consciousness of my pretending that I do not know. So while I can deceive the analyst by telling what I pretend to know but do not know, it seems that I cannot deceive myself with respect to the knowledge of my ignorance. On this account, pretense is necessarily intersubjective: in the absence of an other for whom I can pretend to know, or even pretend to pretend to know, the iteration of pretense collapses into the primitive project of Sartrean "bad faith." Obviously, the situation will not be not altered by subsequently telling that I was merely pretending to know, because this would lead us back the principle of confession.

But perhaps we can get closer to the Freudian injunction by leaving behind our folk-psychological intuitions according to which speech is merely a verbal mirroring of our anterior knowledge of an "intentional state." Instead of that idealistic *méconnaissance*, we should turn the tables and recognize that there are no determinate intentional states, no knowledge of my subjective condition, prior to the occurrence of a verbal expression (see Dennett 1991, chapter 8). Thus considered, expression establishes *nachträglich*: what "will have been" the knowledge of my neurotic predicament. But yet again, on closer inspection, this cannot be sufficient, because although the order of the terms got reversed in this materialistic proposal (i.e., from knowledge determining expression to expression determining knowledge), I nevertheless still tell precisely what I know. That is, although I now no longer know before actually telling it, my telling does not outstrip my knowledge. What I say still matches exactly the knowledge of the intentional state I am in, because my speech fully determines any knowledge I might have of myself. Hence, judged according to Freudian standards, I still remain a sinner engaged in confession.

Enunciation versus Enunciated

From the provisional analysis just offered, it has become clear that, to be able to maintain the Freudian precept without succumbing to either bad faith or confession, the subjective logic subtending my speech should satisfy at least two minimal conditions:

(1) I should tell more than I know

(2) without knowing that I am about to tell more than I know.

Formulated in Lacanian terms: there should be a difference between the enunciated content (*sujèt de l'énoncé*) and the position of enunciation (*sujèt de l'énonciation*). More precisely, what is said on the level of the enunciated content should differ from the position of enunciation (i.e., condition 1), *in such a way* that this difference was neither expected nor predictable in advance from the position of enunciation (i.e., condition 2). For example, imagine a modest person posing a question during a lecture, prefaced by the remark "my question is probably not that interesting but …," and then imagine his reaction when the addressee immediately interrupts to respond that it would then be best to move on to the next question… By being insulted, Lacan would say, "the subject receives its own message in an inverted form" (2006[1956]: 30). It was not that he already accounted for his own position of enunciation and was merely pretending to be the modest fool at the level of his statement. No, in this case, the feeling of being insulted is the phenomenological correlate and witness of the truth of its own enunciation, in other words, that of being superior. From this short example and the minimal definition of the unconscious above, some further important consequences follow.

Unconsciousness, Truth, Subjectivity

First, the unconscious is necessarily performative, because it can only arise in and by an act of speech. This means that there "is" no unconscious, no substantial unconscious reality, independent from the performative (f)act of telling more than one knows. The unconscious is not, to use Husserl's expression, "a little tag-end of the world" (1995: 30), nor of any kind of "underworld." It is made existent or "realized" within the very opposition that is temporally established *in actu* between the performative and constative levels of speech.[1]

Second, while being performative, it is nonetheless impossible to perform, in exactly the same way, because it is impossible, for example, to be "spontaneously spontaneous." Yet, despite being impossible to perform, it is at the same time impossible to avoid: according to Lacan (2006[1964]: 834), the speaking subject constantly announces its elusive dimension on the level of enunciation without even wanting or noticing it. Consequently, one could say that, confronted with the Freudian directive to tell more than one knows, it is always a matter of "too little" and "too much." "Too little," because I necessarily fail to uphold the directive whenever I consciously try or want to: within the field of conscious intention, I always end up with what I knew already. "Too much," because I am constitutively unable to avoid telling more than I know, even in the case that I try to avoid telling more than I know precisely by telling more than I know. That is, in getting ahead of myself by telling more than I actually know—say, for example, in commenting on some absurd obsession by adding the remark "that it surely has something to do with my unconscious," I always already unwittingly indicate a position of enunciation irreducible to this lofty self-accusation. In this case it is possible that I want to be ahead of myself to remain ahead of you, anxiously closing off any possible interpretation the analyst might make in my stead. In sum, regardless of my conscious intentions—to put it in Kantian terms—the "I desire" of enunciation *will* be able to accompany all of my representations, although it is not a position I can willfully adopt.

Third, to account for this performative fact of telling more than one knows in terms of its putative truth conditions, a specific psychoanalytic version of the Cartesian-Husserlian procedures of (i) *epoché* and (ii) *reduction* is called for. As Freud put it (1911: 225): "one is bound to employ the currency that is in use in the country one is exploring—in our case a neurotic currency." According to Lacan, this Freudian currency should be conceived along "a line of research which is not characterized by the same style as other sciences. Its domain is that of the truth of the subject" (Lacan 1988: 20–21). Furthermore, this

> quest for truth is not entirely reducible to the objective, and indeed objectifying, research of the normal scientific method. It is a matter of the realization of the truth of the subject, as a specific dimension which must be detached in its originality from the notion of reality. (Lacan 1988: 21)

Let us take the example above—the comment "it surely has something to do with my unconscious"—to clarify Lacan's remarks.

What matters in a psychoanalytic approach of subjective truth in such an utterance is of course not it's apparent truth value with regard to empirical data—in this case, whether I am right in claiming that my obsessive idea has something to do with my unconscious. It might be true—and in our example, it is indeed true—but the enunciated content is not taken as a representation of an unconscious reality, nor is its truth value conceived in terms of a representational correspondence theory of truth. This suspension or bracketing of the objective truth claim of the enunciated content—in Lacan's terms, "the detachment from the notion of reality"—is what we could call, in line with the phenomenological neutralization of the naturalistic attitude, a "psychoanalytic epoché." Similar to Descartes's famous transition in the *Second Meditation* from "I am now seeing light, hearing a noise, feeling heat" to "I certainly *seem* to see, to hear, and to be warmed" (Descartes 1996: 19), the psychoanalytic epoché would take the form of a transition from

> it surely has something to do with my unconscious → to: said [it surely has something to do with my unconscious]

What falls within the scope of such a subtractive "said" operator is an objective judgment regarding my neurotic condition. Its conceptual content is dependent upon, because it is identical to, the conceptual content of the objective truth claim, commitment to which the operator then "brackets" and suspends by only focusing on what is said. Contrary to a common reading of the Cartesian and phenomenological theses, however, to suspend objective commitment by an epoché of this sort is not, for psychoanalytic theory, to move from objectivity to subjectivity. More precisely, the subjectivity at which one arrives through a suspension of objectivity is not exhaustive for the kind of subjectivity that is at stake in psychoanalysis. Surely, by disregarding any possible relation the enunciated content could have to the reality of which it speaks, we move from an objective truth claim concerning the nature of my obsession "as it is in itself" to a corresponding trivial truth claim, in other words, that it *seems* or *appears* to me that "it surely has something to do with my unconscious." On this account, for every objective truth claim, in which I am invariably fallible—whether or not it has something to do with my unconscious—there would be a corresponding subjective truth claim, in which I am infallible, a truth claim fulfilled by the sheer fact that I claim so—that it seems to me that it has something to do with my unconscious. Yet again, and as shown in the previous analysis, this Cartesian indubitability would not be able to stand the Freudian-Lacanian test for subjective truth. While it is indeed not a matter anymore of the "objective research of the scientific method" (cf. Lacan 1988: 21), my telling that "it surely has something to do with my unconscious," because it appears or seems to me that way is still not a realization of the truth of the subject in the psychoanalytic sense.[2]

What is needed to account for this specific psychoanalytic dimension is a second procedure described above as *reduction*. What counts in this reduction of the enunciated content is not its representational adequacy with regard to the objective nature of my symptom, nor the subjective nature of how it appears to me, but the relation to its *condition of production*. It tries to answer the question in what way the content of my enunciation is related to its position of enunciation. In Lacan's elusive phrasing: "The point is not to know whether I speak of myself in a way that conforms to what I am, but rather to know whether, when I speak of myself, I am the same as the self of whom I speak" (2006[1957]: 430). Applied to our example, the point is not to know whether the proposition "this surely has something to do with my unconscious" conforms to what I am, but rather to know, when saying this, in what way the act of saying is related to what is said. Like the method of reduction in Husserlian phenomenology, a (transcendental) correlation is presupposed between what is said about myself—the "noematic" enunciated subject—and the one who is saying this—the "noetic" subject of enunciation, but, unlike the former, the psychoanalytic correlation is always a *failed* correlation. Not in some Schillerian existential sense in which words always fail to articulate the pristine kernel of my being—cf. *Spricht die Seele, so spricht ach! Schon die Seele nicht mehr*—but in a much more subversive and precise sense: words *always* succeed in articulating the Real of my desire, but *never* in the right place. Again, in the example, while seeming to talk about myself by commenting on my obsession, I did in fact talk about myself in showing that I—not you—will be the one who is able to disclose the truth of my obsession. This, then, is the proper form of the psychoanalytic correlation between the subject of enunciation and its enunciated double: I did not speak about myself where I thought I was speaking; I speak about myself where I did not think I was speaking. And together with this formal delineation of the disjunctive logic subtending the speaking subject in psychoanalysis is the precise locus of its "truth" as strictly codetermined by this form: I always speak the truth about myself, whatever that truth may be, where I did not think I was speaking.

Fourth and finally, what marks the difference between the representational *knowledge* of my obsessive nature put forth in the proposition "this surely has something to do with my unconscious" and the obsessive *truth* expressed in my act of saying it, in other words, before the analyst got the chance? Did I say more than I knew if this "more" turns out to be exactly what I said all along? Indeed, in both cases, so it seems, I told the truth, apparently disconfirming our previous disjunctive definition of subjective truth. The only possible way to resolve this apparent contradiction and to prevent collapsing the difference between knowledge and truth in a redundant tautology is by regarding the first representational proposition as an illusion in the precise Freudian sense. Freud writes:

> An illusion is not the same thing as an error; nor is it necessarily an error. [...] What is characteristic of illusions is that they are derived from human wishes. [...] Illusions need not necessarily be false—that is to say, unrealizable or in contradiction to reality. [...] Thus we call a belief an illusion when a wish fulfillment is a prominent factor in its motivation, and in doing so we disregard its relations to reality, just as the illusion itself sets no store by verification. (Freud 1927: 30–31)

Like in Freud's example (1927) of a middle-class girl who thinks that she will marry a prince—an idea that, however unlikely, may turn out to be true—the proposition "this surely has something to do with my unconscious," despite being true, still remains an illusion, because it is rooted in my obsessive desire to obliterate the position of the analyst. That is, while seeming to refer to myself as an empirical object-in-the-world from a pure and uncontaminated transcendental point of enunciation—as in Eugen Fink's figure of the "unbeteiligte und uninteressierte Zuschauer" (1995)— I overlook the fact that this transcendental speech act *is already obsessive*. Consequently, one completely misunderstands this illusionary (Freud) or imaginary (Lacan) idea with regard to my obsession if one confirms or criticizes it for its (in)adequacy at the constative level. At this level, the idea is indeed adequate to its object, but what counts is the fact that, at the performative level, this is not its object at all. At this level, it serves a different function than that of merely reporting knowledge about myself and, furthermore, it does not cease to fulfill this function when I happen to speak the truth. As in Spinoza's theory of imagination, it is only error, but not (my obsessive) desire, that is removed by the emergence of knowledge: "No positive quality possessed by a false idea is removed by the presence of what is true, in virtue of its being true." (Spinoza 1955: 191)

The disjunctive correlation between representational knowledge and performative truth in psychoanalytic theory is therefore essentially marked by what the classical psychiatrist Eugen Bleuler (1950) aptly described as a "double orientation" or "double bookkeeping."[3] That is, on the constative level, I can know that my obsession is absurd, that it "surely has something to do with my unconscious," and maintain an appropriate distance toward the obsessive absurdity. Like in Sartre's reformulation of the Cartesian cogito,[4] there is a minimal and ideal distance—*un néant*—between the reflecting I that says "it surely has something to do with my unconscious" and the reflected I that is described as obsessive. It is this reflexive negativity within the immanence of my own self-relation that allows me to negate any supposed coincidence of myself with the obsession. As Sartre put it: "To believe is to know that one believes, and to know that one believes is no longer to believe" (1958: 69). However, if, on this level, to believe is effectively no longer to believe, that is to say, if the obsession is an illusion by which I don't get duped and which I can maintain as an objective semblance, at the level of my performative position, I nevertheless *act* as if I did not know it. At its most basic level, Bleulerian "double bookkeeping" in the disjunctive correlation between knowledge and truth entails that I do not have to believe the obsessive belief for the belief to be effective. In other words, believing is indeed no longer to believe, *mais ça n'empêche pas d'éxister*.

The concept of imaginary misrecognition therefore does not refer to the possible sense or nonsense of what I claim at the level of my statement. It is not a measure of the difference between what I say and what is effectively the case—what I misrecognize, what I effectively overlook, is the illusion that is already on *this* side of reality, the reality that, in this case, structures my performative position as such. "Subject of the unconscious" designates in the end that figure who is incapable of taking itself into account in advance. Every saying is, for such a subject, an immediate showing of how it is reflexively inscribed toward what it says. For that reason, the Lacanian subject is not to be considered as something to which I have to return in authentic way by, for example, confessing what I feel or think or by being faithful to the private depths of my soul. For Lacan, "subject" designates that which will return all by itself.

Notes

1 Cf. Lacan's: "Ontically, then, the unconscious is the elusive" (1973[1964]: 32); "The gap of the unconscious may be said to be pre-ontological [...], it does not lend itself to ontology. It is neither being, nor non-being, but the unrealized" (Ibid.: 30–31)

2 For more on the relation between Lacanian psychoanalysis and transcendental phenomenology on the question of "appearance," see Feyaerts and Vanheule (2015).

3 The concept of "double bookkeeping" was originally used by Eugen Bleuler to designate the peculiar "double" attitude schizophrenic patients maintain towards their delusions and hallucinations. On the one hand, they seem to be profoundly occupied with their fantastic delusions, holding them with an unshakeable degree of certainty irrespective of clear empirical proof to the contrary. On the other hand, despite the indubitable nature of their delusional experience, they nevertheless do not *act* as if they mistook their delusions for reality. Bleuler writes: "Kings and Emperors, Popes and Redeemers engage, for the most part, in quite banal work, provided they have any energy at all for activity. This is true not only of patients in institutions, but also of those who are completely free. None of our generals has ever attempted to act in accordance with his imaginary rank and station" (1950: 129). Interestingly, what we have here in Bleuler's account of the "double orientation" in schizophrenia seems to be a precise inversion of the disjunctive relation between knowledge and truth in our own account. Whereas in Bleuler's description schizophrenics do not act on beliefs, they nevertheless hold to be most certain; in our case, we precisely act on those beliefs that we do not really believe.

4 Cf. Sartre: "Now, my reflecting consciousness does not take itself for an object when I effect the Cogito. What it affirms concerns the reflected consciousness. Insofar as my reflecting consciousness is consciousness of itself, it is non-positional consciousness. It becomes positional only by directing itself upon the reflected consciousness which itself was not a positional consciousness of itself before being reflected. Thus the consciousness which says I Think is precisely not the consciousness which thinks" (2004: 44).

References

Bleuler, E. *Dementia Praecox or the Group of Schizophrenias*. New York, NY: International University Press, 1950.

Descartes, R. (1996). *Meditations on First Philosophy*. Cambridge: Cambridge University Press.

Feyaerts, J. and Vanheule, S. (2015). How to return to subjectivity: Natorp, Husserl, and Lacan on the limits of reflection. *Theory & Psychology* 25 (6): 753–774.

Fink, E. (1995). *Sixth Cartesian Meditation: The Idea of a Transcendental Theory of Method*. Bloomington: Indiana University Press.

Freud, S. (1911). Formulations on the Two Principles of Mental Functioning. *The Standard Edition* 12: 218–226.

Freud, S. (1927). The Future of an Illusion. *The Standard Edition* 21: 5–56.

Husserl, E. (1995). *Cartesian meditations: An introduction to phenomenology*. Dordrecht: Kluwer Academic Publishers.

Lacan, J. (1964). *The Seminar 1964, Book XI, The Four Fundamental Concepts of Psychoanalysis*. New York: Karnac, 1973.

Lacan, J. (1988). *The Seminar 1954–1955, Book II, The Ego in Freud's Theory and in the Technique of Psychoanalysis*. Cambridge: Cambridge University Press.

Lacan, J. (1956). "Seminar on "The Purloined Letter," in J. Lacan and J-A. Miller (Eds.), É*crits*. New York and London: W.W. Norton, 2006: 6–50.

Lacan, J. (1957). "The Instance of the Letter in the Unconscious," in J. Lacan and J-A. Miller (Eds.), *Écrits*. New York and London: W.W. Norton, 2006: 412–444.

Lacan, J. (1964). "Position of the Unconscious," in J. Lacan and J-A. Miller (Eds.), *Écrits*. New York and London: W.W. Norton, 2006: 703–721.

Lacan, J. (1988) *The Seminar 1954–1955, Book II, The Ego in Freud's Theory and in the Technique of Psychoanalysis*. Cambridge: Cambridge University Press.

Sartre, J.P. (1958). *Being and Nothingness: An Essay on Phenomenological Ontology*. London: Methuen.

Sartre, J.P. (2004). *The Transcendence of the Ego: A sketch for a phenomenological description*. London and New York: Routledge.

Spinoza, B. (1955). *On the Improvement of the Understanding. The Ethics. Correspondence*. New York: Dover Publications.

PART 3

Toward a Psychoanalytic Politics of Truth

Chapter 11

The Politics of Truth and Its Transformation in Neoliberalism
The Subject-Supposed-to-Know in Algorithmic Times

Nelson da Silva Junior

During the most recent elections in Brazil, a series of disturbing phenomena came to light: the polarization of the Brazilian population into two large blocks, the dissemination of verbal and physical violence, the normalization of prejudice, segregation, and exclusion. There was a contempt for reflection and debate as ways to reconcile differences. In their place, a kind of legitimacy of verbal and physical aggression against those considered as incarnations of moral and sexual corruption of order, family, and economic progress emerged. Finally, it is worth emphasizing the presence of a leader with authoritarian attitudes and discourses, often contradictory, with homophobic, misogynistic, and racist statements, with Manichean narratives capable of mobilizing the masses, and who ended up winning the elections by popular vote: the Captain Jair Messias Bolsonaro. His name and rank were in perfect continuity with the military and religious references of his campaign.

Conservatism and moralism as differential elements that weighed on the popular vote seem to be a disturbing nostalgia for the period of the Brazilian military dictatorship. Hannah Arendt presents the book *The Origins of Totalitarianism* as an attempt to answer the questions of her generation before the horrors of the Second World War: What had happened? How could that have happened? (Arendt 2000: 339–340) A reminder that the function of the intellectual is to try to respond to the "current," that is, to what is presented as incomprehensible in society.

This work is an attempt to understand at least part of what is happening in this current form of mass mobilization. In my view, it inaugurates a new form of social management of truth. To contextualize this form, I will start from what Foucault understood as the "politics of truth," because such mobilization has been inseparable from a new modality of dissemination of knowledge among the masses. Next, I will bring to light the main differences between the traditional modes of mass communication and the current ones, based on social networks and their technology. This technology allows an unprecedented individualization of power relations and is, today, inseparable from the neoliberal form of governmentality. In conclusion, I propose to understand this mode of discursive manipulation as complementary to rhetoric, but different from it. It is, in my view, a fundamentally pragmatic form of manipulation.

In 1976, Michel Foucault published a short text on how the political function of the intellectual had changed over the twentieth century (Foucault 2017[1976]). This change is illustrated by Foucault with two different types of intellectuals based on their relation to politics. In the late nineteenth century, and until the Second World War, the intellectual was a free and morally engaged subject that embodied the universal conscience. They would not be confounded with other educated people whose occupations implied scientific knowledge, such as the physician or the engineer. Instead, they had, in general, an education in law, and used to pronounce their opinions and were heard every time social issues, discussions on universal and humanist values, such as justice, crimes, and their proper punishment would appear. The mid-twentieth century brought about another kind of intellectual, the one Foucault calls the specific one, who was heard for their knowledge on specific matters, mostly on technical issues and whose effects would concern everyone, such as atomic energy and its risks. Contrary to the universal one, the specific intellectual is specialized and has deep knowledge of a few objective problems. However, this limited knowledge is precisely what supports their opinion when general problems come about. This change was the result of the development of technological structures that brought about a new form of political power whose agents were the scientists.

Foucault's approach to truth is inspired by Nietzsche's critique of Western idealism: truth is not considered as a transcendent and/or absolute reality. On the contrary, truth is thought of as a radically worldly and contingent social creation, inseparable from power and political ambitions that are historically situated. In this sense, every society, according to Foucault, has its *general politics of truth*: the types of discourse that it accepts as true, its mechanisms and ways to distinguish true and false statements, techniques and procedures to achieve truth, and the status of those who are allowed to say it. In our society, the political economy of truth is historically marked by five traits: the scientific discourse is the legitimate form of truth; truth is constantly demanded and used by politics and economy; truth is abundantly diffused and consumed; it is mostly produced under the control of large political and economic institutions such as universities, the armed forces, and so on; and, finally, truth is in the core of political debate and social confrontations (Foucault 2017[1976]: 112–113).

This description may still appear valid today, because scientists and universities continue to be considered the most legitimate agents of truth discourses. Their productions still arouse interests within the political and economic domains and are more than ever object of extended diffusion, of consumerism and intense social debates. Nevertheless, I would like to draw attention to the fact that the *political regime of truth* in our society has undergone important changes since Foucault's text. This was due not only to something Foucault didn't have access to—namely, the advent of the internet—but mostly to its intertwined functioning within the neoliberal politics throughout the world.

First, the production of truth is no longer exclusively under the control of universities and state institutions. Private corporations have since extended their funds to research and development, fostering knowledge production precisely tailored to their market needs. The diffusion of research achievements or its failures has also changed, but in opposite directions. On the one hand, with the advent of the internet, scientific knowledge seems to have been finally rendered accessible to everyone on the planet. Indeed, one could say that we live in an unprecedented time of *democracy of truth*. On the other hand, the diffusion of knowledge has gradually become more akin to the diffusion of advertisement, both because of its simplified language form as well as its consumption-enhancing role. In this sense, the traditional social agents endowed with the discourse of truth, such as scientists and universities, were also affected by the same economic logic that shaped scientific truths. They don't speak for themselves anymore, because their testimony is no longer a free one, and their opinions are requested only under heavy market constraints. They are invited only as legitimizing actors, like film stars are called to support the sale of products. Now, this doesn't mean that the specific intellectual has become just a puppet at the service of marketing professionals. They still have the essential task of producing effective and complex technologies. In other words, they are still responsible for the production of truths. It is their legitimizing and diffusing role on truth matters that has changed. First, they have lost the privilege of giving the *last word* on the matters of their domain. Not only has the internet become an almost infinite source of instant knowledge but also the digital environment offers a myriad of different points of view opposite to theirs. This entails perhaps what can be considered as the most important change in the *truth regime* of our society: with so much information, with such contradictory material, it is now up to the consumer to decide what can or cannot be considered true. The current legitimizer agent in the new economy of truth of our society is, in fact, the layperson.

Compared to the specific intellectual, laypeople do not produce truths, but they usually decide what facts and ideas they will believe to be true. Another difference is that their knowledge domain is not a specific one like that of the specific intellectual, but rather a universal one. Finally, there has been a contrary movement in what Foucault names the "rarefaction of truth." This expression is, in fact, a literal one: he indicated the scarcity of occurrences of statements commonly held as true in our society. Whereas these occasions were then sparse, because they depended on the acknowledgment of a few number of respected researchers, these circumstances have become inflated, incessant, and widespread, because everyone is now endowed with the ability to discern the truth.

The digital environment out of which laypeople drag their knowledge is not the natural field of their own experience—far from it. Due to the highly developed algorithmic technology, this environment is carefully and thoroughly controlled. This means that the common person, the internet user, is split into a double situation: on the one hand, they act freely and choose the trustworthiness of information they have access to without noticeable constraints. On the other hand, the environment from which they acquire information sets is the result of a precisely designed and personalized process of selection. Here, we are faced with an indirect form of power: the power over the possible actions of the other. This kind of individualized power in our society was interpreted by Foucault as a *pastoral power*, an expression that was chosen after the kind of control developed by the early Christian monastic tradition. Digital technology became a powerful political tool in the neoliberal economy, because it enables the shepherding of large numbers of well-fit and customized-free individuals. To properly fathom how this personage appears and engages in the new truth regime of our society, we can start with a comparison with a predecessor, the traditional receiver of mass media.

This will allow us to discern the more general structures of this new technology and its application to the pastoral modality of power, whose first diagnosis was made by Foucault. If the common person is artificially elevated to the new subject-supposed-to-know in neoliberalism, it is first necessary to understand how this occurs, and then to think about what this reveals of the general strategy of power in neoliberalism.

The Mutation of Pragmatics in Media: From the Passive Mass to the Free Individual

Mass communication grew exponentially throughout the twentieth century due to the technical advances with extended reach and/or high capacity of reproduction. Marshal McLuhan, for example, had already spoken of media transforming the planet into a global village back in the 1970s. Although this expression has become even truer today, because communication networks have spread a much finer mesh around the globe, two different functions of communication are at play in each of these moments. A radical change occurs in the logic of communication with the advent of new technologies such as personal computers, the internet, and smartphones.

In traditional media channels, such as radio, television, and print newspapers, the same information was bound for all. The transmitting device was essentially dynamic concerning a mass of static viewers, fixed recipients of an incessant flow of information. This structural passivity of the viewer can be considered the mark of submission in the logic of mass media, because they are powerless to interact with the information to which they has access. Now, in the internet environment, both the device and the user are essentially dynamic. This may give the impression that the viewer is less passive in this context, but, in fact, they are in an even more unfavorable relationship than before, concerning the freedom of interaction with the information they receive. This apparent contradiction between user dynamics and their unfavorable position becomes clearer if we think that the current media devices are active computer programs. Such programs provide new information to the user from an algorithmic analysis of the breaks in their search patterns. Thus, an unusual search for airline tickets on Google will produce the emergence of dozens of on-screen tour packages. In this way, the user experience is that of a comfortable anticipation of the world to their interests. The user's freedom, however, is far less than that of the television viewer; it is precisely in their *innovative actions*, in the changing of their pursuits and interests, that the user contributes to their mapping and isolation in new sets of possibilities of action.

The modalities of social experience that this new information technology offers can no longer be understood in the old paradigm of mass communication. In the latter case, the same message was transmitted simultaneously to a large number of people, mobilizing affections and thoughts in unison. Currently, the plurality of web television unites people in segmented groups, producing aesthetic affinities in a much more specific manner. The most powerful instruments of social interaction today are undoubtedly social media. Through Facebook and Instagram, everyone can have the sensation of seeing and being seen by everyone else. However, this overall experience is biased. The groups to which each user is invited to belong, follow, in their constitution, the same selection logic that information technology uses in drawing their profile. One of the effects of this type of grouping is the collective legitimating of the information received by the user, leveraging the persuasive effectiveness of any information. Another effect is that of a progressive isolation between different clusters, because the information to which each group has access are hardly accessible to others. Not only is there no discussion between opposing segments, but they are isolated and have no access to the same information nor the same fake news. This facilitates group constitution in opposition to others, in the well-known logic of narcissism of small differences (Freud 1982[1930]).

Another particularly effective aspect of emotional appeal completes this process in the relationship between leaders and their interlocutors, namely, the creation of an apparent closeness between leaders and followers. Trump, for example, broke ground in a new method of communicating with the population by using Twitter. Jair Bolsonaro, on the other hand, privileged WhatsApp in his communications with the population during his election campaign, and this style has been continued throughout his government. Statements, which in traditional politics would be considered as "breaches of protocol," are a specific style of government made through communication. The voter's or citizen's experience tends to be an intimate one with their leader, which in turn legitimizes the truthfulness of the leader's statements. By comparing the information they receive directly from their leader with those they receive through traditional means of communication, disagreements tend to be systematically interpreted as manipulation made by the opposition. The discrepancy of information within the media itself is thus integrated with the practices of intentional disinformation known as fake news. The leader's periodic disrespect for institutions also gains space in this environment. Indeed, the rise of the hero begins precisely with their contempt for the situation. This technique proves to be very effective, despite disrespectful statements being systematically followed by denial of the same. In this case, the effect of the contradictions is not mistrust, but something closer to what Orwell described in his critical parable to Soviet totalitarianism, *Nighteen Eighty-Four*, as the *doublethink*. In analytical terms, the psychic defense at stake is that of refusal, whose ultimate formalization is the statement: "Yes, I know, but still..."

As described by Freud, the circle of truth closes around each group and its leader. Within the groups, identifications are reinforced by the exclusion of threatening differences and also by the creation of new enemies. However, something else is at stake, namely, the participation of technical instruments in this process of producing groups, simplifying truths, and reducing discursive logic to simple negations. This technical element did not exist until recently in mass communication. The algorithmic production of a specific information set for each individual and simultaneously for their groups calls for a new conceptual approach to the type of power at play, different from that used by the traditional means of communication.

The Pastoral Power, the Other Side of Biopolitics

Let us begin with the singling out of the control actions on each individual. According to Foucault, this is not a recent technique in the practices of power. Regardless of the high degree of technological refinement at play in social networks and media today, its origin can be found in the model of the shepherd and their flock employed by the Christian monastic tradition.

Foucault underlines the differences between the form of collective government according to the pastoral power and that of Greek politics. The polis's government was impersonal in the sense that the ruler was replaceable over time. In the case of pastoral power, the government implies a maximum individualization: the shepherd is responsible not only for the flock as a whole but for each sheep. For this reason, the pastor of Christian souls must know the thoughts of every one of their believers: "it is not possible to exercise this form of power without knowing what goes on through people's minds, without exploiting their souls without forcing them to reveal their innermost secrets" (Foucault 2017[1982]: 1048).

Michel Foucault, in the final period of his work, works simultaneously on two fronts of his research on power: that of self-government and that of the government of others. These two fronts, apparently independent of each other, had, however, a relationship between them, which he called *governmentality*. The latter is a neologism that marks the mentalities, and therefore the psychism, as an object of the chiasm between the government of others and the government of oneself: "I call it 'governmentality,' he writes, to the encounter between the techniques of domination exercised over others and the techniques of oneself" (Foucault 207[1982]: 1604).

Most of the time, the author's definition of governmentality emphasizes only the first of the elements of this meeting, the government of others. For example, in the 1977–1978 course Sécurité, Territoire, Population (Foucault 2004[1977–1978]), Foucault defines governmentality as

> the set made up of institutions, procedures, analyzes and reflections, calculations and practices that make it possible to exercise this very specific, though very complex, form of power that has the population as its main target, [which] has the political economy as its main form of knowledge, and [and which] has the security devices as its essential technical instrument. (Foucault 2004[1977–1978]: 111)

Many of Foucault's texts and conferences portray the history of the articulation between the rationality of governments in the seventeenth and eighteenth centuries, namely, the reason of state, and the emergence of a new way of conceiving of the population and individuals. Far from the current negative sense, linked to the legitimacy of the state to act independently of the laws in certain situations judged as a national threat, the reason of state indicated a new way of thinking the latter as an end in itself, and no longer as an instrument for the prince. The reason of state was articulated to new forms of knowledge, such as statistics, as well as to new control practices such as public policies. The latter, significantly, were called at the time by the name of *police*, which dealt with the various aspects of the then incipient administration of the population, that is, its health, its education, its commercial relations, its morality, and its religion. But each one of these new perspectives of social life aimed at it only as a means of growth and strengthening of the state. The population is now seen as one of the resources and riches of the state, and the police as the way to manage this wealth to multiply it. Life as *bios* acquires a political meaning here, hence the term biopolitics. In biopolitics, an instrumental rationality defines the population as life, the state as an end, and the police as a means. At the same time, the human sciences are born as the psychological facet of knowledge in this instrumentalization of the population, articulated to administrative practices.

It is in this general context of Foucault's project, that is, of thinking our society as a complex combination of "techniques of individualization and procedures of totalization," that it makes sense to isolate the psychism as an object of power. On one occasion, Foucault refers to this combination as "truly demonic" (Foucault 2017[1979]: 966)

The advent of pastoral techniques in the algorithmic universe of social media was not witnessed by Foucault. Through them, the technology of pastoral power has reached levels of articulation of totalizing social management procedures that are probably more demonic than those of his time. It can be understood that the totalizing procedures of our time are those of neoliberalism. Of course, governmentality, according to Foucault, is not limited to the neoliberal way of population management, which is only its present form. But we are immersed in this form, and it uses the pastoral power, which it has available, in its best interest. The updating of the pastoral power on the internet articulates with surprising perfection the principles of totalization of the neoliberal project to which it is associated.

Currently, neoliberalism is characterized by two aspects. First, the questioning of the idea that the state is an unquestionable necessity, which marks its difference with the previous form, grounded on the idea of state as an end in itself. Second, it promotes the logic of maximizing benefits and reducing costs as a universal principle of action of political reason. These two aspects of neoliberalism are homologous to the idea that subjects be radically free. Gary Becker, a Nobel laureate in economics, argues that any human behavior should always be considered as a "rational choice between excluding objectives having the maximization of objectives as a goal" (Becker 1990: 5).

However, Becker does not problematize the set of choices available to this so-called free subject. A closer analysis of this set would easily demonstrate that, in the end, it is a tightly controlled freedom. For example, in the case of the algorithmic functioning of the new social media, the irreconcilable objectives offered to the rational choice of individuals are subject to a refined control. The same could be said about the individual's rational choices in the world today. Thus, the rationale of an apparent paradox of neoliberalism can be seen, namely, that of being simultaneously, a theory of social management based on individual freedom and one that places itself as totally compatible with authoritarian and violent governments, as clearly shown in Pinochet's "inaugural experiment" in Chile.

Language as the Possible Field of Action of Subjects

The Foucauldian perspective of neoliberal governmentality stresses precisely this: power relations can only occur with subjects who act as if they were free. Since the advent of biopolitics, Foucault says, governing has become a way to structure the possible field of action of others, both present and future (Foucault 2017[1982]: 1055). This implies defining devices, frames, environments, and norms in which human beings will understand themselves as free. Therefore, the specificity of the performative project of neoliberalism in the set of forms of governmentality is made clear. No one evidenced this more than Margaret Thatcher when she stated: "Economics is the method, but the goal is to transform the spirit." (Harvey 2013: 32) In other words, if the goal is the conduct of each individual's action within the general conduct of the population, this depends on considering and educating each individual as a free and rational subject. By controlling the discursive, legal, and moral framework of the subjects considered as units of cost-benefit analysis, it is possible to say that the devices of neoliberalism are forms of production of subjectivities that work on an ontological level. In effect, as Laval precisely underlines, this "is not primarily an ideology. It is, above all, a technology of power" (Laval 2018: 42).

To conclude these reflections, I would still like to highlight two points. The first point concerns a transformation in the discursive strategy of domination, which begins to work essentially in the field of pragmatics. The rhetoric of authoritarian leaders and, to use a particularly happy expression proposed by Ian Parker, their "calculated stupidity," remains fundamentally the same as described by the founders of the Frankfurt School.

Horkheimer and Adorno saw in Freudian psychoanalysis a strong ally in the understanding of advertising in culture and politics. In his empirical research on anti-Semitism, Adorno broadened the interpretations of the Freudian mass psychology and described new rhetorical elements: the small great man, the lowering of inhibitions, the nobility of sacrifice, the indetermination of the cause to be defended, the limitation of argumentation to repetition to a restricted group of clichés, etc. (Adorno 2015[1951]).

It should also be remembered that Adorno differentiates with surgical precision the psychoanalytic approach and the sociological interpretation itself in the understanding of the mass phenomenon. For him, even though there is always a spontaneous propensity for fascism in all the masses "the manipulation of the unconscious is indispensable for the updating of its potential." (Adorno 2015[1951]: 185). Thus, Adorno maintains that "fascism as such is not a psychological problem." (Adorno 2015[1951]: 185). Fascism only "defines a psychological area that can be successfully exploited by the forces that promote it for reasons of self-interest" (Adorno 2015[1951]: 186).

Adorno understands such an appropriation of psychoanalytic concepts by the cultural and political industry as an anesthetic of the "revolutionary potential of the masses." Considering that psychoanalysis aims to emancipate the subject from the heteronomous laws of the unconscious, Adorno describes the cultural industry as a kind of "reverse psychoanalysis." He therefore reaffirms the relevance of the Freudian theory of power, as well as the efficacy of the semantic register in which it is in force. But he also includes it in a broader dimension of language, properly pragmatic, in which the technology of communication institutes forms of power capable of absorbing and using in its favor the concepts of psychoanalysis, annulling its critical potential.

In my view, the approach of this form of domination from the Foucauldian point of view confirms Adorno's shift to the pragmatics in the interpretation of the mass-mobilization phenomena. However, his conceptual tools go even further in the importance of a reflection on power from the point of view of language as an element that precedes subjects. Language is the socializing environment par excellence, and as such, it is also within this possible field that subjects and their actions can be better controlled. According to Foucault, the main object of his work was to try to "produce a history of the modes of subjectivation of the human being in our culture [in other words,] the modes of objectification that transform human beings into subjects" (Foucault 2017[1982]: 1042). In this sense, he considers discourses, disciplines, and practices as essentially performative forces of knowledge and power that socialize subjects by objectifying them. This way of transforming human beings can be seen as being on different grounds from rhetoric and persuasion. In the modes of subjectivation, subjects and their consciousness are thought of as the effects of discourses, disciplines, and practices, devices fundamentally open to historical contingency. In other words, the Foucauldian perspective, based on an essentially pragmatic approach to discourses, suggests that an analysis of power in the neoliberal key emphasizes a properly performative level of its functioning, where language precedes subjects and their social relations.

This allows us to conclude by emphasizing the centrality of language in a critical view of alienating discourses and their techniques. Syntax, semantics, and pragmatics can be seen as contours capable of tracing differences in forms of power that are reached by language and which not only persuade and are a part of, but that constitute subjects and social relations. Power in neoliberal governmentality is not only updated by a semantics centered on the paternal figure, following the Freudian hypothesis on mass psychology, nor in a syntax of instrumental reason of planetary dimensions, as shown by the Frankfurtian school. It infiltrates more subtly into the structures of language that define the essence of subjects and their social relations.

The second point concerns the transformation of the politics of truth under the neoliberal regime by elevating the layperson to the place of the subject-supposed-to-know. After the universal intellectual, after the specific intellectual, truth is today legitimized by the common person. But this is not achieved simply through a mere rhetorical conviction of the common person of their intellectual excellence. On the contrary, their ascension to the place of supposedly knowing subject depends on a refined control of the social structures of recognition of their new position, that is, of their most immediate discursive environment. As Foucault affirms, it is a truly demonic technological evolution, capable of articulating total forms of management, of biopolitical amplitude, with individualized forms of surveillance, which silently conduct their conclusions, guaranteeing their impression of autonomy and discovery.

This privileged access to the truth produced no longer by rhetorical persuasion, but by the performative character of pastoral power, has its price. The main difference, from the point of view of discursive interactions, is that rhetoric admits what might be called a *logomachy*, this is a war of words, wherein the opponents legitimately recognize themselves as such. Already in the performative moment of domination, the common people, duly elevated to the place of knowing, feel that they must protect the truth without submitting to such a war of words. Not by chance, the information they get about the world and society always takes the same form: "You were being deceived." In 1973, in his seminar on The Psychiatric Power, Foucault demonstrates how truth in medicine progressively passes from a revelation regime, that is, from a sporadic event to a demonstration regime. Now, in the algorithmic domination of neoliberal politics, truth as demonstration is again reabsorbed by the regime of truth as revelation. The experience of knowing the truth of the common person is not separable from that of having been deceived, which allows us to consider this knowledge as essentially paranoid. Indeed, aggressiveness thus begins to mediate social relations around the holding of truth. It is no accident that the revisionism of history and the denialism of the spherical geography of the Earth are points of honor for the new subject-supposed-to-know, because, in paranoid knowledge, all that is common sense, all established knowledge, must be put under suspicion.

References

Adorno, T. W. (1951) Teoria freudiana e o padrão da propaganda fascista. In: *Ensaios sobre psicologia social e psicanálise.* São Paulo: Editora Unesp, 2015.

Arendt, H. (2000). *As origens do totalitarismo.* São Paulo: Cia das Letras.

Becker, G. (1990). *The Economic Approach to Human Behavior.* Chicago: The University of Chicago Press.

Freud, S. (1930) *Das Unbehagen in der Kultur.* Studienausgabe. Frankfurt: Fisher Taschenbuch Verlag, 1982.

Foucault, M. (1976), La fonction politique de l'intellectuel, in: *Dits et Écrits.* II, 1976–1988, Paris: Gallimard, 2017: 109–114.

Foucault, M. (1977–1978) *Sécurité, Territoire, Population, Cours au Collège de France.* Paris: EHSS/Seuil/Gallimard, 2004.

Foucault, M. (1982) "Le sujet et le pouvoir." In: *Dits et Écrits.* II, 1976–1988, Paris: Gallimard, 2017:1048.

Harvey, D. (2013). *Neoliberalismo: História e Implicações.* São Paulo: Ed. Loyola.

Laval, C. (2018). *Foucault, Bourdieu et la question néolibérale.* Paris: Éditions La Découverte.

Chapter 12

Resistance and Truth
Between Psychoanalysis and Politics

Paulo Beer

Truth has been a central issue of psychoanalytic thinking and its clinic since the beginning. While Freud was unable to straightforwardly "believe" his patients' narratives nor his own interpretations (Freud 1986[1897]), he never displayed any kind of cynical or skeptical approach, insisting on the pertinence of "truth" in most part of his work. This, however, did not stop him from defining truth in different ways throughout his work. The same might be affirmed about Lacan, who emphasized "truth" as a key element of his rationality (Lacan 1998[1951]; 1998[1956]; Johnston 2017), yet while subverting its common meaning. Lacan leaves no doubt that truth plays a crucial role in psychoanalytical treatment, because it is considered the central axis around which an analysis orbits (Lacan 1998[1951]: 215).

However, if a rigorous reading of canonical psychoanalysts shows that truth is indeed an inescapable (or even irrepressible) element of psychoanalytic practice, this has not prevented a particular kind of critique according to which psychoanalytic truth is some sort of malleable narrative in the hands of the analyst. This critique entails that psychoanalysts transform what are at first rather unspecific demands (from the part of the analysands) in accord with psychoanalytic theory, thereby actually creating the very problems psychoanalysis would search to resolve through treatment. This form of critique may be found, for example, in Adolf Grünbaum's famous work on *The Foundations of Psychoanalysis* (Grünbaum 1984), which perhaps constitutes one of the most important and serious critiques psychoanalysis has ever received. A recurrent and disputable point of this sort of critical argumentation revolves around one of the central psychoanalytic concepts—often taken as a static oppositional counterpart to the idea of truth: resistance.

However, for several reasons, such an easy opposition is hardly tenable. First, one should consider that both notions of truth and resistance are employed in many different fields and with diverse meanings, sometimes even in antagonistic ways: one understanding, inspired by the work of Michel Foucault, for example, speaks about resistance as a "resistance to power" (Mackenzie 2018). Here, one might point out that, even within psychoanalysis, this concept has already been offered a different understanding, namely, as a form of power enactment, which is the opposite of how Foucault would define resistance. Moreover, this critique of the concept of resistance as an adequation tool has already been addressed by Freud himself (2018[1937]). Nevertheless, this critique has survived in the work and thought of other psychoanalysts, such as Kohut (1979), not to mention several critiques from revisionists or foes (Meyer 2005).

The persistence of this sort of critique, which Freud addresses in his "Constructions in Analysis" (1937a), might result from the fact that resistance is not considered unequivocally within psychoanalysis, hence leading to possibly different conceptions. The same could be pointed out about truth, because it is held as a central notion in both psychoanalysis and political philosophy (Mackenzie 2018) and is hence subject to varying approaches and understandings. This conceptual complexity likewise reinforces the difficulty of defining a stable relation between resistance and truth, rendering it inimical to fast and easy formulas like "resistance and truth are always on the same side" or "are always opposed to each other." In fact, precisely because these two concepts carry a wide variety of diverging meanings, to consider their mutual articulation demands an explicit consideration of their polysemic nature.

Furthermore, it is crucial to realize that this discussion is not limited to a mere question of technique, because it combines a clinical quarrel with an inseparable political dimension related to its possible use as a tool for oppression. Therefore, approaching truth and resistance not only implies the complexity of multifaceted notions, but actually requires it. In other words, it is impossible to advance this discussion without transiting between different fields of thought, in the same way as holding to their possible definitions and proposing static and inert relations would be an unfruitful effort. Instead, to access the complexity of resistance and truth, one should recognize their dynamic interaction. Without this recognition, psychoanalytic theory would be grossly distorted and a powerful debate prematurely reduced.

This chapter will focus on the proposed dynamic relation between truth and resistance. I will argue that a close reading of their appearance in psychoanalytic discussions demonstrates that truth and resistance should be understood in a dialectical way.

Resistance Is More than an Obstacle

The notion of resistance is immediately relevant already in the beginning of Freud's work. For example, in the "case Elisabeth" (Breuer and Freud 1895), resistance is presented as an obstacle against the psychoanalytic cure, a force opposing attempts at change. This notion of resistance plays a central role in psychoanalytic treatment, represented by the claim, for example, that resistance would get stronger as the treatment gets closer to the main repressed material. At different moments in Freud's work, there is a close link between repressed material and truth, even though truth is also not an unequivocal notion.

This nonunivocity might be due to the different ways Freud treats the matter of truth. Truth is present in symptoms and delusions (1907) and could be therapeutically mobilized. From this perspective, different conceptions of truth are proposed, such as historical truth (Freud 2018[1937])—articulated with respect to the possibility of creating a narrative of past events—which is itself different form "material truth," something that would be inaccessible in its completeness (Ambra and Paulon 2018). These are only a few examples, given that, throughout the presence of truth in symptoms and its possibilities of reconstruction in analysis, there is a central conception of truth related to the "truth of desire" (Johnston 2017), something widely referred to by Lacan and central to his developments on the subject, as will be presented later.

In general terms, truth in Freudian theory is conceived as one of two pathogenic causes (Silva Junior 2017). The first pathogenic cause relates to the renunciation of erotic drive, a necessary abnegation for the constitution of civilization that could also be understood—in a Lacanian reading—as the insufficiency of language in dealing with the body. The first pathogenic cause is therefore not only related to renunciation but to an essential suffering caused by an original impossibility. The second pathogenic cause would be linked to truth in its historical form: the suffering caused by the unavoidable loss that is present in any attempt at reconstruction or communication of that more original truth. If there would be a first cause intrinsic to the process of civilization and therefore one that is impossible to avoid and difficult to treat (Silva Junior 2017), the second could be made a target within treatment. In this sense, Freud conceived truth as both a pathogenic center and a therapeutic horizon. Furthermore, truth could would be articulated to the first pathogenic center, because collective narratives and social discourses (such as moral demands, sexual restriction, etc.), beyond causing distress by drive renunciation, might also deepen this suffering through limiting people's relationship with their historical truth and desires: "This is the second source of suffering in Freudian theory: the relationship of subjects with truth might potentialize or attenuate the suffering originated in the structural impasse between nature and culture." (Silva Junior 2017: 138–139)

Resuming the articulation with resistance, it is possible to think of two different paths: resistance would be triggered by the approximation of historical truth—mobilized through the analyst's constructions—and when an interpretation gets close to the truth of the desire. In both paths, there would hence be a resistance to truth. In this sense, however, while resistance might be seen as an obstacle, it is nonetheless also a sign, something that gets stronger when truth is approached.

In further developments, Freud affirms that resistance is not only a sign but also a necessary stage within psychoanalytical treatment. Rather than an obstacle that should be avoided, resistance is something that must be worked through, without which no treatment could have an enduring effect. As Freud writes:

> This working-through of the resistances may in practice turn out to be an arduous task for the subject of the analysis and a trial of patience for the analyst. Nevertheless it is a part of the work which effects the greatest changes in the patient and which distinguishes analytic treatment from any kind of treatment by suggestion. From a theoretical point of view one may correlate it with the 'abreacting' of the quotas of affect strangulated by repression—an abreaction without which hypnotic treatment remained ineffective. (Freud 1914: 155)

Resistance is not just an obstacle, then, but a necessary element of psychoanalytic treatment. It also marks the difference with hypnosis and constitutes the core of the refusal of suggestion. Its overcoming is something that takes time, a process with which the patient must become acquainted to be able to work through and to defy resistance and continue the analysis (Freud 1914). As Freud affirms in the same text:

> Only where the resistance is at its height can the analyst, working in common with his patient, discover the repressed instinctual impulses which are feeding the resistance; and it is this kind of experience which convinces the patient of the existence and power of such impulses. (Freud 1914: 155).

In this passage, there are two interesting points that should be considered. The first one is that resistance is fed by repressed instinctual impulses; the second one is the idea that the analyst should work together with the analysand to deal with resistance.

The first point—the idea that repressed drives feed resistance—is interesting insofar as it blurs the initial opposition between resistance and truth. Resuming the path that links truth to desire and therefore to repression and drive, there is a mixed origin when we consider that repression also bares some truth: the truth of the impossibility of dealing with drive and desire. Freud considers repression as an effect of the psychic apparatus's immaturity to deal with too complex and invested drives and desires or traumas, for example (Freud 1905). Thus, beyond the truth that is repressed, there is also the truth of repression itself, of that very impossibility.

Therefore, if resistance is a defense against the work on experiences that were too much to be confronted, it should be considered as a reactualization of the truth of impossibility, of suffering and anguish. In this sense, resistance might also be linked to repetition compulsion, because it repeats defensive patterns that trouble psychoanalytic treatment. This is one of Freud's further developments, arising from affirming diverse approaches to resistance from a metapsychological point of view (i.e., considering different sorts of resistance depending if they are linked to the ego, the id, or superego). So, if one might initially focus on resistance *to* truth, now it is also possible to consider the truth *of* resistance.

The second point, which starts from the assertion that the analyst and patient must deal with it together, takes us back to "Constructions in Analysis" (1937a). In this text, Freud replies to a critique suggesting that the notion of resistance would be some sort of "joker" in psychoanalytical treatment, a card that might be played whenever the analyst is questioned (or, in his works, as flipping a coin: "heads I'm right, tails you're wrong").

Refusing a construction proposed by the analyst might hence be the consequence of three different causes: (a) the analyst might actually be wrong (which is not a problem unless the mistake is frequent); (b) resistance in the "classical" form of an issue that must be worked through, as previously presented; (c) the refusal as indicating an incompleteness, suggesting that the construction is true, but that there is still some truth missing.

It is important to acknowledge that Freud does not consider the first nor the last cases as resistance, even if it is possible to think that they are somehow concerned with truth (the first as a negation of something wrong, the second as the affirmation of incompleteness). As for the second case, it is possible to consider that it assembles both "the truth of resistance" and "resistance to truth," in line with what Freud had already established regarding an affectively invested negation of an intellectual representation (Freud 1925).

Nevertheless, the third case also reveals a form of affectively invested negation, not linked to resistance as something that would directly confront the course of therapy but linked to the incompleteness of truth. It nevertheless does not consist of any kind of passive incompleteness, in other words, the mere recognition that something might be missing; it appears in the form of negation, something active and affectively invested. Moreover, if the attempts to define truth always carry this dimension of incompleteness, it is possible to consider it as a characteristic of truth itself (which is present, for example, in the necessary difference between historical truth and material truth).

Additionally, if this negation is not understood as an obstacle to treatment, it surely has the function of resisting to something: perhaps the opposite of what would be entailed by the traditional idea of resistance, in other words, being a limit to the illusion of producing a full or whole understanding of the unconscious. It is perhaps not by chance that Freud develops the idea of possible limits to an analysis in "Analysis Terminable and Interminable" (1937b), a crucial text contemporary to "Constructions". The case of negation invested by the necessary incompleteness might therefore be understood, in a second moment, as the emergence of truth as knowledge limitation. In that sense, a third form of articulation would become possible: together with "the truth *of* resistance" and "resistance *to* truth," there would also be a "truth *as* resistance."

One could think, however, that this is already a Lacanian reading of Freud. While there is no doubt that it is an important part of Lacan's "return to Freud," the idea can also be retrieved from the Freudian corpus. Apart from what Freud suggested regarding the inherent limitations of psychoanalysis in "Analysis Terminable and Interminable" (Freud 1937b), there is a last element in "Constructions" (Freud 1937a) that must be considered. Freud specifically emphasizes that, while some patients fail to remember the historical truth mobilized by a construction (or even deny its accuracy), the construction might still have the same effect as when historical truth is actually recaptured. This observation is compatible with Freud's affirmations about the unavoidable distortion of truth and the tension between historical and material truth (Ambra and Paulon 2018). Yet it is also compatible with the Lacanian reading of truth as something that touches the impossible (Lacan 2003[1973]), but still retains value.

While Freud does not abandon the idea that there is some trace of material truth in historical truth, neither does he affirm that the latter might completely represent the first. In any case, if a construction has the same effect of lifting repression (and therefore "accessing truth"), this might be understood as something that questions the historical necessity of truth itself. It is no coincidence that this text will be a central piece in Lacan's return to Freud, which includes a conceptual reorganization of the understanding of truth.

A Speaking Truth

As is well known, Lacan considers the question of truth from different approaches and produces various definitions. However, from the central affirmation according to which "truth speaks" (Lacan 2006[1955]), all the subsequent forms of truth in Lacan's work always aim at the appearance of something new, something that was uncounted for and that somehow entails a tensioned relationship with previous stabilizing ideas (or identifications, narratives, objects of desire, etc.). This tension offers a common line to other delimitations of truth, be it truth as equivoque (Lacan 1992[1969–1970]), truth as impossible (2003[1972]), or truth as having the structure of a fiction (2007[1953]), for example. On the other hand, Lacan also developed some important remarks about resistance, within a new conceptual framework that goes beyond these two notions: resistance and truth gain a different sense together with the notions of interpretation, knowledge, transfer, and the unconscious, among others.

It is worth considering, however, that the centrality of the debate regarding resistance predominantly features at the beginning of his seminars. Although posterior to the start of his return to Freud—as some elements were already present in previous texts (including his "linguistic turn," decisively presented in his *Rome's Discourse* some months before)— one should recognize the effects of this conceptual and clinical reorganization on the notions of truth and resistance.

It is well known that his seminar of 1953–1954 was dedicated to Freud's writings on technique, starting with a clear critique of what was defined as the "analysis of resistances." If one of our points of departure is the understanding of psychoanalytic treatment—and in particular the concept of resistance—as a possible practice of domination or normalization, it is important to notice that this debate was already present at an initial moment of Lacanian discussions. In this regard, it is possible to highlight Jean Hyppolite's intervention in Lacan's seminar: after resuming Freud's proposition that suggestion would leave the patient in an objectified position, Hyppolite wonders that, if clinical practice might be understood as a form of domination enabled by specific ways in which the notion of resistance is employed (as a way of overcoming the subject's refusal), the result could in fact be a more aggressive form of domination compared to suggestion:

> Whereas in the Freudian domination, it is the vanquishing of a subject, a being who still has self-awareness. Hence there is a stronger will for domination in the domination of the resistance to be conquered than in the simple and straightforward suppression of this resistance—without being able to draw from that the conclusion that Freud wanted to dominate the world. (Hyppolite in Lacan 1991[1953–1954]: 27–28)

This sort of political comment on the psychoanalytic clinic is not surprising, because the French psychoanalytic scene (and Lacan in particular) had been deeply influenced by the work of Georges Politzer, especially by his book *A Critique of the Foundations of Psychology* (1994[1928]). In this book, Politzer's Marxist critique of psychology was still compatible with a certain ideal about what psychoanalysis could offer (which demanded abandoning Freudian metapsychology though), a hope discarded in his late writings (Politzer 2017[1939]; Bianco 2017). In the psychoanalytic field itself, a critical approach to the power of the analyst was already proposed by Ferenczi, who possibly influenced Lacan (Ferenczi 1930). The result is that this sort of critique is clearly present in Lacan's thinking, in what we could call a reformist rather than a revolutionary reading of Freud. In fact, Lacan focused on defending Freud against misleading post-Freudian readings, searching the Freudian writings to support one's position. This might be seen in the sequence of his reply to Hyppolite; Lacan affirms that he does not believe that "the theoretical promulgation of the notion of resistance can be used as a pretext for making this accusation against Freud, an accusation which goes radically against the liberating effect of his work and of his therapeutic activity" (Lacan 1991[1953–1954]: 28).

As mentioned above, Lacan implies that this kind of accusation is rather the result of a misunderstanding committed by post-Freudian theories that transformed Freud's considerations about defenses into a programmatic and misleading "analysis of resistances." This misunderstanding would result in a psychoanalytic practice that employs much more rigid interpretations and forces them on analysands. Lacan affirms that this results from a misunderstanding of resistance: not something to be confronted or explained, but a sign of proximity to truth accompanied by anguish, indicating the analysand's difficulty in facing truth. A moment when the analysand calls for the presence of the analyst, as a witness.

One of the possible outcomes of this misunderstanding is that it establishes a bypass to the relation with the analyst, in line with the Freudian affirmation that transference is the result of resistance. That "*ego* to *ego*" relation would work as an instance of alienation when, by identifying himself with his conscious self, the analysand can avoid their unconscious truth. To provide an interpretation of this avoidance in the sense of offering an explanation would only further reaffirm this alienation, producing a further distancing from truth. This is the point where Lacan offers a different idea of interpretation, in which the void is underlined, emphasizing the "lack of being" as the political horizon of psychoanalytic practice (Lacan 2006[1958]). This idea of interpretation also requires a different understanding of transference and repetition, resulting in the famous proposition of two different types of repetition ten years later in Lacan's seminar on *The Fundamental Concepts of Psychoanalysis* (Lacan 2008[1964]). This conceptual reorganization also leads to the well-known dictum according to which resistance is always resistance from the analyst (Lacan 1998[1958]). At this point, the idea of the opposition between truth and knowledge was already present in Lacanian thought: it was possible to affirm that the analyst's knowledge works as resistance when silencing or suturing the subject's division between knowledge and truth.

Here, we already have reasons to consider resistance as much more than a simple obstacle to treatment, but as an essential part of truth. Considering the presence of anguish and the understanding of interpretation as an intervention that goes toward the void rather than an explicative act, this new conception of truth holds on to the idea that that the unconscious does not express but reveals itself. Beyond the Heideggerian influence that might be seen in this moment (which would be discarded some years later), there is also a strong presence of Hegelian dialectics in the articulation of truth and its denial as constituent parts of the same movement. This has the immediate effect of resuming the discussion about truth and negation, together with the differentiation and opposition between truth and knowledge. It is worth remembering that, at this moment, Lacan was still working with the notion of "full speech" as something that approaches truth. Nevertheless, through his critique of forcing analysands into interpretations, the opposition between truth and knowledge gains centrality and remains even after Lacan abandoned the notion of full speech.

The best example is the way Lacan treats Ernst Kris's case (Lacan 1986[1953–1954]; 1998[1958]). In this case, a patient who had the fantasy of stealing others' ideas affirms, in a session, that the research he was willing to publish had already been published as a treatise, which contained his basic idea. Kris confronted the patient, asking for details that revealed the it was not the same basic idea. Kris not only said that the fantasy was unfounded because the ideas were not the same, but he also interpreted the patient's narrative, emphasizing the link with his father and grandfather's history. Following that interpretation, the patient tells the analyst that, after sessions, he usually goes to a street known for its restaurants and stares at the menus looking for his preferred dish: "fresh brains". Kris took it as a sign of the accuracy of his interpretation, affirming that it revealed the impulse to devour. Once it was made conscious, the patient would be able to surpass it and perform his intellectual activity as he was supposed to.

Lacan refers to this case in the seminar (1986[1953–1954]) and then again in the text about the direction of the treatment (1998[1958]). He does not question the interpretation's accuracy, yet he affirms that what Kris considers a confirmation of an analytical work, he takes as an acting-out on the part of the patient. In this key moment filled with anguish and closeness to truth, Lacan asserts that the interpretation goes against the unconscious's revelation, thus damaging the established transference and producing the acting-out. According to Lacan, the chief mistake was to consider the symptom as an expression of the will to steal ideas (or to devour) and not as the impossibility of having his own ideas. The latter would more properly contain the negativity of desire, which should be the permanent horizon of any interpretation: because there is no object adequate to desire, interpretation should not offer explanations (knowledge), in order to avoid the illusion that it would be feasible to know a possible or satisfactory object of desire. On the contrary, the interpretation should carry that impossibility, thus presenting a "negative" appeal that would lead to the truth of desire, which is this everlasting unsatisfaction.

Therefore, the Lacanian critique of "analysis of resistance" is located in a conceptual reorganization that includes notions as resistance, truth, knowledge, language, interpretation, and desire. This developed over the following years in Lacan's work, always directed toward a liberating horizon, and he often chose normalizing practices as something that should be confronted. This might be seen, for example, in his reference to Canguilhem's image of psychology as "a toboggan from the Pantheon to the Prefecture of Police" (Lacan 2006[1966]: 750). This account shows the constellation of themes mobilized from a specific question where psychoanalytical treatment shows its unavoidable and intimate connection to politics: "is psychoanalysis a domination practice"?

As we have seen, this question is brought up by the notion of resistance, inevitably calling for a consideration of truth. It is through this conceptual reorganization that the popular notion of resistance as "resistance to power" is incorporated in the notion(s) of truth, articulated in regard to desire and the unconscious.

In a later seminar, Lacan (1988[1959–1960]) resumes this discussion in a more assertive fashion, defining psychoanalytic ethics as "the ethics of desire."

This proposition, elaborated later on in the text "Kant with Sade" (2006[1963]), entails that there is no absolute moral ground that could be used to distinguish right from wrong. Formulated by Lacan in the famous "there is no Other of the Other," this absence of warranty emphasizes desire as the central issue in ethics. The critique of clinical normativity implies the refusal of any model or idea of health within a psychoanalytic horizon. Furthermore, the formula "there is no Other of the Other" unfolds in another version, "there is no truth of the truth."

This last version is articulated in relation to the "absence of metalanguage" in its epistemological sense, from where Lacan reaffirmed his critique against logical positivism (Lacan 2006[1966]). A detailed examination shows, however, that it also carries an ontological dimension that points to the notion of truth as a limit concept between clinic and politics. Here, one must consider three assumptions about truth (Iannini 2012): (1) there is truth; (2) there is no truth of truth; (3) truth speaks. The last one recalls, as argued before, that truth is not a qualifier or a parameter, but something active, an operation. Lacan plays with Erasmus of Rotterdam to affirm "I, the truth, I speak" (1998[1955]). In 1965, during the seminar session that would result in the famous text "Science and Truth" (2006[1966]), Lacan offers a further elaboration it by emphasizing "truth is as cause": the cause of neurotic suffering, among other things.

At this moment, truth as cause is also opposed to knowledge, as indicated by the reference to the Möbius strip. The main idea is that, besides the fact that truth causes and speaks for itself, it can never be fully spoken, never fully reduced or stabilized as knowledge. At this point, Lacan no longer embraces the idea of full speech; he takes to its limits the idea that there is no essence to be revealed. Negativity thus plays a central role in his conceptual economy, because a part of the unconscious itself would be impossible to render conscious (Safatle 2014).

Therefore, when something is presented as knowledge, truth would be defined as what is not contained in that knowledge. This is the point where the articulation with desire's negativity can be found (Safatle 2014). From that moment, however, the notion of truth becomes even more radical, changing from incompleteness to impossibility. The way in which Lacan talks about truth shows this radicalization: truth opposes knowledge; truth resists knowledge. In 1969, during his seminar *The Other Side of Psychoanalysis* (1992[1969–1970]), truth was placed in the spot marked by impossibility, and this became a crucial idea in considering the analyst's discourse as the reverse of the master's discourse. Consequently, psychoanalysis should always be opposed to domination in a broad sense, as might be seen in Lacan's interaction with students in which he affirms his reluctance about the events in May 1968: for Lacan, the revolutionaries were looking for a mentor, a new master.

Truth as Resistance

Returning to our initial question regarding the potential of domination within psychoanalysis, embodied by the notion of resistance, we can affirm that this sort of critique has not only been animating debates early on in the history of psychoanalysis but also that an accurate examination shows that the understanding of this concept as an instrument for domination would be a misemployment of a theoretical and clinical tool.

First, the critique ignores the constitutive complexity of Freud's work regarding this notion. If resistance might easily be approached to a problem linked to the question of truth, it is not possible to sustain an inert opposition between them. On the one hand, resistance carries itself some quantum of truth: it is the very reason why some processes are hindered, that is, the avoidance of truth also carries the truth of the anguish or of the distress coupled with what is to be avoided. If it is possible to think about that avoidance as "resistance to truth," this other complementary side is what we have called the "truth of resistance."

As I have argued, this recognition was already present in Freud and was later resumed by Lacan in his critique of post-Freudian psychoanalytical practice referred to as "analysis of resistance." This critique is based on Freud's idea that the conflictual dimension present in approaching highly affective charged representations is constitutive of psychoanalytical treatment itself. This is clear in Freud's *Negation* (1925), a text focused on by Lacan after Hyppolite's intervention regarding psychoanalysis's domination potential. In this process, the specific interest in negation constitutes a cornerstone of Lacanian thinking, assembling different threads that will be carefully developed in the following years. This development always replies to that initial critique, to the constant attention regarding psychoanalysis's liberating horizon.

In this sense, if restricted to resistance as an obstacle to treatment, Lacan straightforwardly affirms that it is something enacted by the analyst, not the analysand. This constitutes a first response to the question of domination. However, it is not the only response, given that Lacan understands resistance also as something linked to the negation of an affectively invested representation that cannot be admitted by the self (Lacan 1991[1953–1954]; Freud 1925; Safatle 2014).

This negation is closely articulated with the notion of truth, in a way in which it seems that truth wholly absorbs this kind of understanding of resistance. However, the assimilation of resistance with truth is made through a conceptual amplification: the affective response to any stabilized enunciated demonstrates a radical understanding in terms of which truth is always the possible negation of any enunciated; in the same way that any affirmation of an object of desire carries the possibility of its negation (Safatle 2014). This is the point from which a third articulation of resistance and truth becomes possible, where truth entails resistance to the idea that a final form of desire, of the self, of knowledge would exist. Therefore, the articulation between truth and resistance only leads to the rigid conclusion of resistance as a tool of domination within a particularly reductive reading; as I set out to demonstrate, such notions demand a wider understanding that articulates their dynamic intertwinement, because each particular understanding produces a retroactive effect on the other dialectical notion. In general terms, articulating truth and resistance shows itself to be foremost a critical procedure, leading to the idea of "resistance to power." And, in this dynamic construction, truth resists.

References

Ambra, P., and Paulon, C. (2018). O analista é o historiador. *Psicologia USP*, 29(3): 412–417. https://doi.org/10.1590/0103–656420180012

Bazan, A. (2017), Alpha synchronization as a brain model for unconscious defense: An overview of the work of Howard Shevrin and his team. *Int J Psychoanal*, 98: 1443–1473. doi:10.1111/1745–8315.12629

Beer, P. (2017). *Psicanálise e ciência: um debate necessário*. São Paulo: Ed. Blucher.

Bianco, G. (2017). Apresentação: o longo fim da psicanálise. In: Politzer, G. O fim da psicanálise [Trans. G. C. O. Silva]. *Lacuna: uma revista de psicanálise*, São Paulo, 3: 14. Disponível em: <https://revistalacuna.com/2017/04/28/n3–14/>

Brakel, L. (2015). Critique of Grünbaum's "Critique of psychoanalysis." In S. Boag, L. Brakel and V. Talvitie (eds.). *Philosophy, science, and psychoanalysis: a critical meeting*. London, England: Karnak Books: 59–72.

Breuer, J. and Freud, S. (1895). Studies in Hysteria. *The Standard Edition 9*. London: Hogarth.

Ferenczi, S. (1930) Princípios de relaxamento e neocatarse. [A. Cabral, trans.]. In Psicanálise IV. São Paulo: Martins Fontes, 1992: 53–68.

Freud, S. (1897). Carta de 21 de setembro de 1897. In: Masson, J. *A correspondência completa de Sigmund Freud para Wilhelm Fliess 1887/1904* (V. Ribeiro, trans.). Rio de Janeiro: Imago, 1986.

Freud, S. (1905). Three Essays on Sexuality. *The Standard Edition* 7. London: Hogarth.

Freud, S. (1907). Jensen's "Gradiva." *The Standard Edition 9*. London: Hogarth.

Freud, S. (1914). Remembering, Repeating and Working-trough. *The Standard Edition* 12. London: Hogarth.

Freud, S. (1925). *Negation*. *The Standard Edition* 19. London: Hogarth.

Freud, S. (1937a). Constructions in Analysis. *The Standard Edition*23. London: Hogarth.

Freud, S. (1937b). Analysis Terminable and Interminable. *The Standard Edition* 23. London: Hogarth.

Grünbaum, A. (1984) *The Foundations of Psychoanalysis: a philosophical critique.* Oakland: University of California Press.
Iannini, G. (2012). *Estilo e verdade em Jacques Lacan.* Rio de Janeiro: Ed. Autêntica.
Johnston, A. (2017). *Irrepressible Truth: On Lacan's "The Freudian Thing."* London: Palgrave Macmillan.
Kohut, H. (1979). The Two Analyses of Mr. Z. *Int. J. Psycho-Anal* 60: 3–27
Lacan, J. (1951) Intervenção sobre a transferência. In: *Escritos.* Rio de Janeiro: Jorge Zahar, 1998: 214–225.
Lacan, J. (1953). *O Mito Individual do Neurótico.* Rio de Janeiro: Jorge Zahar Ed, 2007.
Lacan, J. (1953–54). The Seminar, Book I: *Freud's Papers on Technique.* [trans. John Forrester] London, New York: Norton, 1991.
Lacan, J. (1955). The Freudian Thing. In: *Écrits.* London, New York: Norton, 2006.
Lacan, J. (1958). The Direction of the Treatment and the Principles of Its Power. In: *Écrits.* London, New York: Norton, 2006.
Lacan, J. (1959–60). *Seminário VII: A ética da psicanálise.* trans. Vera Ribeiro. Rio de Janeiro: Zahar, 1988.
Lacan, J. (1963). Kant with Sade. In: *Écrits.* London, New York: Norton, 2006.
Lacan, J. (1964). *Seminário, livro 11: os quatro conceitos fundamentais da psicanálise.* Rio de Janeiro, RJ: Jorge Zahar, 2008.
Lacan, J. (1966). Science and Truth. In: *Écrits.* London, New York: Norton, 2006.
Lacan, J. (1969–1970). *O Seminário XVII: o avesso da psicanálise.* Rio de Janeiro: Jorge Zahar, 1992.
Lacan, J. (1972). O aturdito. In: *Outros escritos* [Trans. Vera Ribeiro]. Rio de Janeiro: Zahar, 2003.
Lacan, J. (1973). Televisão. In: *Outros escritos* [Trans. Vera Ribeiro]. Rio de Janeiro: Zahar, 2003.
Frosh, S. (1997). *For and against psychoanalysis.* London: Routledge.
Mackenzie, I. (2018). *Resistance and the politics of truth.* London: Routledge.
Meyer, C. (2005). *O livro negro da psicanálise.* São Paulo: Civilização Brasileira.
Politzer, G. (1928). *Critique of the Foundations of Psychology: The Psychology of Psychoanalysis.* Pittsburgh: Duquesne University Press, 1994.
Politzer, G. (1939). O fim da psicanálise [trans. G. C. O. Silva]. *Lacuna: uma revista de psicanálise,* São Paulo, n. 3, p. 14, 2017. Disponível em: https://revistalacuna.com/2017/04/28/n3-14/.
Safatle, V. (2014). Aquele que diz "não": sobre um modo peculiar de falar de si. In: Freud, S. *A negação.* São Paulo: Cosac Naif.
Silva Junior, N. da (2017). O sofrimento como hífen na teoria social freudiana e sua atualidade. O exemplo das modificações corporais. In: Silva Junior, N.; Zangari, W. (ed.) *A psicologia social e a questão do hífen.* São Paulo: Ed. Blucher, 2017.

Chapter 13

Revolution and Liquidation of Transference The Subjective Destitution as a Procedure of Social Emancipation

Vladimir Safatle

I'm afraid we are not rid of God
because we still have faith in grammar.
Friedrich Nietzsche

In 1967, Lacan presented a fundamental text on psychoanalysis and politics, "Proposition of 9 October 1967 on the Analyst of the School" (*Proposition du Octobre sur le psychanalyste de l'Ecole*) (Lacan 1968b). Faced with the need to justify the function of the Freudian School of Psychoanalysis, an institution that he had created, Lacan presented a political formulation in this text that had as its central axis a reflection on the structure of transference. This focus on transference as a site of politics should not be surprising. Psychoanalysis addresses the processes of the constitution of social ties from the dynamics of identification and argues that there can be no social bond without some form of identification (Freud 1990[1921]). Moreover, identification explains the productive dimension of power—that is, the way in which power produces psychic life, mobilizes affections and demands for love, and constitutes the subjects to which it relates (Butler 1997). Consequently, Lacan's focus on transference allows us to grasp how domination can be overcome. Stated otherwise, transference has real consequences for reflecting on emancipatory processes.[1] If we take into account that power becomes concrete through identification, then all possible emancipation must take the form of a liquidation of transference. This emancipation is a way to understand how ex-timacy works on clinics, and how ex-timacy is a mode of relationship that emerges in clinic through the liquidation of transference and its related process of subjective destitution.

A distinction must be drawn here. Identification shows how social relations are necessarily power relations instituted through repetition. In identifying with something or someone, I assume an implicit development proper to what I have identified with—that is, the structures of my psychic life and its developments will be the reproduction of what I have identified with. In the mirror stage, Lacan argued that to identify with an image is to internalize the history it represents (Lacan 1966: 93–101). That is, all identification is an exercise of power. However, not all power relations are relations of domination. What sustains identification is ultimately given neither by the I nor the other, and both are incapable of mastering it, what is ex-timate to both. There is something circulating in identification processes that cannot be understood as an exercise of domination. Identification occurs on the basis of something that surpasses the will of the subject. Lacan thematizes this process of identification through his theory of object *a*—something that always insists within the relations of power and which makes these relations unsteady, always ready to reverse, to drift off. Fundamentally, a relationship of domination is the expression of the submission of my will to the will of the Other, but there is something in identification that produces bonds without being the expression of my will or the will of the Other. Rather, it is the expression of an unconscious dynamics of affects. Power circulates by expropriating something that can depose it. Consider, for example, the consequences of a statement such as this:

> Thus functions the i(a) with which the ego and his narcissism imagines himself, by making a chasuble of that object a which makes the misery of the subject. This because the (a), cause of desire, for being at the mercy of the Other, anxiety then on occasion, dresses itself contraphobically with the autonomy of the self, as does the hermit crab with any old shell. (Lacan 2001: 262)

Lacan is saying that the ego ideal, which is responsible for the imaginary constitution of the self through narcissistic relations, sustains itself by relying on object *a* to strengthen the discourse of autonomy. The autonomy of the will appears as a defensive discourse against the phobia resulting from the discovery that what constitutes us in our very identity—the images that constitute us—are sustained by something that could bring forth their own dissolution. This is why we can say that what sustains the material reproduction of psychic life, that which allows the constitutive exercise of power relations, can at the same time dissolve the power relations themselves. And if power can control the circulation of these objects that destitute us, it is because it "knows" that the recognition of itself in these objects distresses us.

Power "knows" that freedom distresses us at the same time that it attracts us. If subjects accept servitude, it is because they fear the anxiety that freedom produces, and one of the fundamental things that analysis can provide concerning the exercise of freedom is to lead the subject to put down its counterphobic defenses. The anxiety of freedom does not arise from the transcendent possibility of doing and desiring everything, but from the realization that we are acted upon by external causalities that, as Lacan said, are something in us more than ourselves. This Lacanian theme of self-recognition in the object aims to expose the subject to the anguish of knowing that it is moved by causalities that decenter it, causalities deeply rooted in the uncontrolled history of our desires. If freedom were not of such a dramatic nature, the urge to avoid it would not be so constant.

In this sense, the function of the School, as Lacan understands it, was basically to recognize subjects who pass through the liquidation of the transference, leaving behind a form of subjection expressed not only in the supposition of knowledge of the Other but also in the supposition of a knowledge that is constitutive, which would define the modes of self-relation: control, autonomy, deliberation. For this reason, this recognition is not only the guarantee for the constitution of social bonds that are no longer haunted by relations of subjection; it also holds the possibility of the emergence of bonds capable of transforming subjects.

After all, Lacan understood perfectly well that if one goes into analysis, it is because there is an assumption that one can know the truth of one's desire. This assumption of knowledge is not only a cognitive curiosity, a desire to know oneself better; it is an expectation of reconfiguring the structure of practice and care based on self-knowledge. However, this supposed knowledge falters, not by the simple observation of the analyst's ignorance or by the ineffectiveness of the analytic discourse, but by the emergence of an object that sustained the relationship to the Other and which was hitherto veiled. This explains why, in the analyst's discourse, the object occupies the place of an agent. In the analyst's discourse, what is revealed is how the subject's connection with the supposition of knowing was, in fact, a link to an object that caused this subject. Analytical knowledge is realized by its own self-destitution.

To illustrate this point, we can refer to the Lacanian reading of the dialogue between Alcibiades and Socrates in *The Symposium*. In a certain sense, Lacan's reading makes Socrates into the first analyst, just as he makes Socrates's response to Alcibiades's desire the first instance of a lesson on managing transference. In Plato's dialogue, Alcibiades is not just someone who does not know how to govern himself, who is not a master of his own desire. He is also one who hopes to govern the polis, to govern others (Plato 1927). Socrates tries to show Alcibiades that he will not be able to govern the polis before he can govern himself. However, in this context, self-government is not, for Lacan, self-domination through the dynamics of control and self-regulation. In fact, governing oneself is inseparable from the capacity to recognize the remainder that as determining the division of the subject, "brings about his fall from his fantasy and makes him destitute as subject" (Lacan 2001: 252). Socrates shows Alcibiades how there can be no self-government if he is unable to confront the object that causes his desire, a confrontation that produces a traversal of fantasy and a destitution of the subject.

For this reason, Lacan emphasizes the way Socrates says that Alcibiades is wrong about his desire, because it is not exactly Socrates whom Alcibiades desires, but the *agalma* that Socrates wears. Socrates thus makes an operation of separation insofar as he tries to show Alcibiades the distance between the ego ideal and the object that supports it. By exposing this distance, Socrates produces a kind of short circuit in the identification system that has supported Alcibiades's position, because the ego ideal no longer appears, as it appeared before, as the point of transcendence compared to imaginary objects. It appears as an article of clothing that supports the subject by preventing him from confronting an object without place that nevertheless causes him, acts in him, and constitutes him.

For this reason, it is necessary to insist that if knowledge in transference is a supposed knowledge about my desire and what causes it, the analytic process aims to extract the object that causes my desire from the paths of knowledge. Socrates denies knowing anything about the matters of love, which does not mean that he does not know what to do with such matters. It only means that his action is not oriented by deliberation or shared knowledge, which fits within a symbolic structure. His actions are a form of openness that presupposes a destitution of domination, a form of recognition of an external causality, upon which it is useless to seek to defend oneself. Lacan then speaks of an operation of "confronting the truth" that is distinct from the operation of the exercise of knowledge. Here, the distinction between knowledge and truth is fundamental.

Lacan himself acknowledges that this initially seems to mean the impossibility of constituting any form of social bond. As he puts it: "Subjective destitution is written on the entry ticket." And he continues: "Isn't this to provoke horror, indignation, panic or even outrage, in any case give pretext for an objection in principle?" (Lacan 2001: 252) What could be a bond constituted from a liquidation of the transference that seems to preclude all symbolic identification, which can no longer mobilize any phantasmatic production? A type of bond that makes Lacan affirm that

> In this change of tack where the subject sees the assurance he gets from this fantasy, in which each person's window onto the real is constituted, capsize, what can be perceived is that the foothold of desire is nothing but that of a désêtre, disbeing. In this désêtre what is inessential in the supposed subject of knowledge is unveiled, from which the psychoanalyst to come dedicate him- or herself to the agalma of the essence of desire, ready to pay for it through reducing himself, himself and his name, to any given signifier. (Lacan 2001: 252)

This is how Lacan describes the process of the liquidation of the transference. Let us first note how it is a question of breaking down the security provided by fantasy as a window onto the real—that is, by fantasy's framing of the real over a certain distance and in a certain operation. There is a temporality to fantasy, a temporality marked by repetition and the modular updating of the original experiences. What happens at the end of transference is that the subject approaches real, experiencing a temporality outside of the structure. When the security produced by the fantasy falters, desire reveals itself as nothing more than a *désêtre*. This is not exactly a form that reregisters the subject into the ontological security of a being thought through normativity, as a necessity, but rather is a drifting off, a dispossession. Desire is, then, shown to be precisely this drifting off, and in this sense, the time of the real appears adrift. This shift from being to *désêtre* is characteristic of the destitution of the analyst's knowledge (Cotter 1996: 187–194). That is to say, in analysis, the analyst goes through a *désêtre*, which presupposes anguish, and the analysand goes through a subjective destitution, which implies a certain helplessness.

Such destitution can be described as the change in the structure of recognition processes, because what occurs is not a self-recognition in another subject but in an object. Such recognition is made by reducing the name of the subject to any signifier. That is to say the name, which establishes relations of filiation and transmission, and bears the mark of the subject's inscription in the horizon of a family constellation, becomes any signifier, in the sense of a purely contingent inscription, without place in a chain of needs.[2] The symbolic reinscription that the analytic interpretation produces through the mobilization of the frames of relation specific to the Oedipus complex and its normative horizon are destitute in a such way that the name appears as any signifier.

But a central question remains: Why is this process not simply a depressive process, the dead time of melancholia? What makes it a process, on the contrary, of affirming emancipation?

Transference and Emancipation

To answer these questions, let us begin by asking ourselves how to finish a transferential process. Of course, this question can only be answered on a generic level, because the paths of an analysis are always unique. However, this does not mean that the generic level is devoid of importance and interest or that it does not reveal structural traces. We will say, then, that the transfer is liquidated when what Lacan calls the "analytical act" occurs—an act that can answer the general question of emancipation.

Let us first recall some considerations about emancipation as a normative horizon for political struggles. The traditional tendency is to derive discussions about emancipation from the regulatory notion of maturity by generalizing the consequences of the distinction between minority and adulthood. In this understanding, political struggles that are driven by expectations of emancipation are struggles to realize forms of development of an individual capable of self-deliberation and self-affirmation.

However, we must insist that this way of thinking does not allow us to distinguish between emancipation and subjection to disciplinary patterns that are socially required for a conformity to social roles. Exiting the "minority" can be understood as a result of the internalization of systems of judgment and socially accepted actions that are proper to those subjects who are held imputable and responsible. In this context, there is a risk that we will no longer be able to draw minimally operative distinctions between emancipation and mere social adaptation to legal patterns of imputability, or even between recognition, as the establishment of hitherto unpredicated modes of existence, and acknowledgment, as confirmation of potentialities achieved by the current mode of existence. From this arises a problem: a condition of socialization that is historically defined and legally organized turns into an ontologically stable horizon for regulating forms of life. In contradistinction to this, the notion of analytic act allows us to see emancipation as a possibility for the subject to emerge as a normative power capable of producing singularizations. To do so, a structural change in the notion of agency needs to occur.

In this regard, let us remember how Lacan states that the analytic act would be grounded on a "paradoxical structure arising from the fact that the object is active and the subject is subverted," a subversion that is an inscription of the position of the subject in the real (Lacan 2001: 332). We return to this point, because such an idea of an act capable of inscribing the subject in the real is central. It implies that, in producing an act, subjects act from a position that collapses the symbolic order. Therefore, they lose their previous inscription in the symbolic order and the order of knowledge that constituted them. This is why, from a clinical point of view, the concept of analytic act reconfigures the processes of analytical intervention by putting in second place the mechanisms of symbolization through the significant inscription produced by interpretation. From now on, the analysis will not seek, through interpretation, to provide subjects with inscriptions within a regulated framework of conflicts and affiliations. It will confront the subjects with an act that deprives them of such a place.

This explains why, in the device of the analytic act, a force of dissolution and an operation of establishment are linked, and the complexity lies precisely in the understanding of this double movement. It is not possible to think about processes of establishment without answering the question about how dissolutions are carried out. Because there are dissolutions that are only degradations of the previous order, or if we wish, that are mere passage to the act, mere fascination with annihilation that removes from the act every possibility of recognition. For this reason, the classic forms of the *passage a l'act* are linked to suicide.

However, there are dissolutions and landslides that result from the pressures of new orientations. Is one of the fundamental questions that concerns political action not how to make orders collapse? (Lenin 1975) Considering what the experience of revolutions in the twentieth century has shown us, orders can be perpetuated even after they fall, or, rather, they can be perpetuated exactly because they have fallen and have become an implicit mode of existence rather than an explicit one. They may then resurface as a recurrence that reappears when we least expect it, or they may continue to operate in an underground stratum, gradually eroding the new order until it becomes unrecognizable (Freud 1990[1939]). For this reason, the question of the political act as a process of dissolution is of paramount importance.

A Kind of Revolution

This discussion brings us to the power of negation proper to every act. At various times, Lacan brings the analytic act closer to a possible reading of the political concept of revolution. However, a distinction must be made here. On multiple instances, Lacan insisted that "revolution" means, in relation to what we know about astronomical movements, "to return to the same place." In commenting on the Copernican revolution, so often used as a metaphor for epistemic change in philosophy (Kant and criticism as a Copernican revolution) and even in psychoanalysis (Freud and the Copernican revolution of the unconscious), Lacan wondered: "What is revolutionary about refocusing the solar world around the sun?" (Lacan 2001: 420) Because there was no change in the hierarchy, unity, and centrality represented by the notion of spherical motion as a perfect celestial form, the true revolution was in the advent of elliptical movement—that is, the notion of two centers as the form of celestial movements. Hence, if revolution is not the wish to return to the same place, it cannot be separated from a change in the entire structure of knowledge. Revolution is not limited to transformations on the place that each element occupies within a given structure, nor to the placeholders of knowledge and power.

Lacan appeals to poetry to think about the revolution that an analytic experience really entails. In this respect, let us remember a poem dear to Lacan, which he considered an expression of the "general formula of the act" (Lacan 1968a), Arthur Rimbaud's À une raison:

> A tap of your finger on the drum releases all sounds and initiates the new harmony.
> A step of yours is the conscription of the new men and their marching orders.
> You look away: the new love!
> You look back, - the new love!
> 'Change our fates, shoot down the plagues, beginning with time,' the children sing to you.
> 'Build wherever you can the substance of our fortunes and our wishes,' they beg you.
> Arriving from always, you'll go away everywhere (Rimbaud 2011a)

First, it is noteworthy that the general formula of the analytic act is given by a poem—that is, approaching the act and the emergence of another regime of language expressed in the form of the poem. If language appears here in a fundamental position, it is because it decides the form of the experience, the dynamics of our grammars of affects, and the structure of our sensibilities. There is no real revolution without a transformation in the capacity of the enunciation of language.

Second, let's remember the title of the poem, "To a Reason." The general formula of the act is linked to a poem entitled "To a Reason." What is most obvious here is the idea of "*a* reason" and not "*the* reason," as if it were to say "everyone has their reason." But a sentence of this nature generally seems to mean: "there is no reason, because everyone has their own," "there is no truth, because everyone has their own reason." If there is no reason, then there is no ratio, not only in the sense that there is no common measure, but specifically in the sense that there is no generic implication, which is the ground of truth. Every process of truth is a process able to produce a generic implication or universal recognition. If there is no reason, it seems that nothing involves us generically, nothing gives us a common field. There seems to be only one word, one word, and then another word. However, the poem expresses exactly the opposite idea. It is as though the singularity of the experience that produces the body in which a reason bursts through is an experience that can be recognized by everyone—as if what was unveiled was only the opening of a common space that transcends the world.

It is clear that the poem begins with a horizon of war and music, as if the real war was the transformation of language into music. It begins with a drumbeat, announcing creation by breaking the silence with a sound, usually dry, without resonance. But now this absence of resonance is the advent of a new harmony produced by all sounds.

I would like to note, however, an important point here. All sounds played together can only produce a cluster of sounds; they never provide a new harmony. A touch that liberates all sounds can actually be perceived as a sound capable of producing harmony, much like the substance of our fortune and our desires that can be cultivated anywhere. That is to say, we are talking about a relation (because harmony is necessarily a relation) without restriction and without loss, which can potentially operate in a time and space that is now devoid of finite determinations. And as the outbreak of war is transmuted into music, the poem produces the irruption of new men and a new love. This is a new love that needs to be repeated, which is not just said once, but makes us to turn our heads back once more. It is as if love is what must be repeated, as if love would really be the scene of a repetition, or as if love would be what allows repetition to exist in its transformative power.

Like reason, love is a question of relationship and existence in the relationship. Reason is, among other things, a decision about the logical structures of order, identity, difference, and unity—that is, the relation and compatibility between determinations. There is always a ratio resonating in reason. As Rimbaud writes in another poem, "Genie": "love, perfect and reinvented measurement, wonderful and unforeseen reason" (Rimbaud 2011b). There is a time peculiar to love and the dispersion of its act. This time of love founds another reason, as Lacan clearly understood "To a reason": "Love is in this text the sign, pointed as such, of the change of reason." (Lacan 1973: 26) In producing this repetition that denounces the desire for duration, the poem opens to a song. The children not only sing, but they pray, because they feel the urgency of the desires that are cultivated in a place out of place—that is, in a place foreign to the grammar that we use to describe the current state of things, in an "anywhere" out of the world as it is now composed and divided.

An act is always the triggering of another time and another space. That is its function: to allow desire to be cultivated in another time and another space, breaking the hierarchy of places that desacralize distances. In this sense, it is not by chance that Lacan chose Rimbaud to provide a general formula for the analytic act. He is the poet who speaks of a time of revolutions, who writes poems on popular emancipation battles, and who leaves the verse poem behind and makes language into a colorful system through phonetic work with vowels. That is to say, Rimbaud produces a new *aisthesis* in language and expression by exploring significant dimensions elaborated beyond the purely semantic modes of determination. An "eruption of all the senses," as Rimbaud himself says, which is the advent of new constructive principles. Recall that "To a Reason" was written between 1872 and 1873, that is to say, just after the Commune. This gives a concrete expression to who the new men are, those who rise and live in a new harmony.

This must be kept in mind when Lacan says that "the act takes place in a saying and it modifies the subject," or that "the act destitutes in its end the very subject which it establishes" (Lacan 1973: 375). This demonstrates how the analytic act, instead of merely externalizing the subject, modifies it in a paradoxical movement between instauration and destitution. This paradoxical position may explain why "the act is best accomplished by failure," which does not mean that every act is a failure. There is a kind of failure that results from the pressure of the productivity of desire toward new forms. The failed act expresses the failure of the determining force of ordinary language, where one must feel ordinary language fails, confesses its powerlessness, and transmutes its categories. Or, as Lacan said: "My proof only touches on being [*à l'être*] to give it birth from the flaw the being [*l'étant*] produces from being said [*de se dire*]." (1973: 426)

We can now understand the political implication of the concept of the analytic act. It allows us to think about the political notion of revolution beyond its submission to a merely restorative dynamic. The act shows more clearly the true dimension of transformation that a revolutionary action must produce, and it shows how it is related to the modification of the structure of knowledge/power. However, and this is a decisive point, the act does not simply push the knowledge previously assumed by the Other toward a knowledge now present in the consciousness of the subject. It does not imply the reappropriation of knowledge. Reappropriation would only be the reiteration of the same regime of knowledge and action, which has now become available to consciousness. It is useless to praise the praxis if this praxis still depends on the same grammar of knowledge that we have already been subjected to. A grammar composed of the ideals of autonomy, deliberation, choice, and decision necessarily refers to the mode of representation of consciousness. It doesn't matter who actually acts—that is, if one always acts from the same grammar. In any case, it is the grammar that acts; it is the system of rules that acts. An emancipated practice is not the result of the transfer of knowledge. That is, emancipation is not a transfer of knowledge that would allow us to recover the enunciation of knowledge and that would in turn allow us to better deliberate. Let's remember an important statement:

> Thus the being of desire reunites with the being of knowledge and is thereby reborn, in their being bound together in a one-sided strip on which a single lack is inscribed, the one that the agalma sustains. (Lacan 2001: 254)

Desire and knowledge meet as two sides of a Möbius strip. They pass into each other, in a passage that occurs only under the condition of assuming a torsion. This passage is the inscription of a lack, which is not a lack that is simply related to incompleteness or to the subjectivation of castration, understood as the assumption of finitude, but which is the emergence of an object that is not reduced to what a signifying chain represents. When a knowledge of desire is possible, it is only by a torsion that, from the point of view of the present configuration of knowledge, is a lack.

But I would like to insist on a fundamental point. If something is lacking, it's because I do not have it. If the articulation between desire and knowledge inscribes a structural lack, it's because such an articulation points to something that I can never have, which will never be under the sign of my possession, and this is exactly one of the main features of *agalmata*: subjects do not have them, but they support them, which is a totally different matter (Gernet 1982). This is a way of saying that the destitution of knowledge, the condition for the liquidation of the transfer, has the assumption of another word, another relation to language: a language that does not seem to be exactly mine, a knowledge that does not strengthen the illusion of my propriety and domain. Hence, statements such as: "Everything that is unconscious only plays on language effects. It is something that is said, without the subject representing himself or saying it—or knowing what he is saying." (Lacan 2001: 334)

More than being structured as a language, the unconscious is a discourse that lays down the very speech of the subject. It is the emergence of a language that no longer appears as mine. Not only because the subject's utterances are ruled by the involuntary, but mainly because it is no longer the language of meaning and the restoration of properties produced by the dynamics of meaning. This is the language of a truth event.

It should also be noted that, with this, we have said nothing about revolutionary processes in their concrete dimension of unfolding and in their historically situated causality. But what I would insist on is that psychoanalysis can say nothing about them, because they are the objects of history and politics. It can, however, talk about what was once called "the subjects' revolutionary becoming" (Deleuze 2003), that is, the psychic rooting of a desire for revolution that involves the effective transformation of forms of agency. Not only are there historical bases for such a desire, there are also bases for it in the drive. The concrete existence of such a becoming is the necessary opening up of potentialities within social life.

The Religion of Meaning

If we come back to the relationship between language and revolution, we should insist on the specificity of such a Lacanian notion of meaning. After all, what can be a language that is not a language of meaning, but a language of a truth event, as Lacan assumes in speaking of the unconscious? Among the different ways of discussing this complex problem, let us insist on the one that exposes the political dimension of this debate. We can recall what Lacan affirms in a text about the political act of dissolution of an institution that he himself created:

> The international, since such is its name, is no more than the symptom of what Freud expected of it. But it is not what weighs in the balance. It's the Church, the true one, which supports Marxism by giving it new blood [...] with a renewed meaning. Why not psychoanalysis when it turns into meaning? I'm not saying that for a vain joke. The stability of religion comes from the fact that the meaning is always religious. (Lacan 2001: 318)

This is the Lacanian way of saying that the real political problem we face is the resurgence of the theological-political dimension of power.[3] Religion is a means of supporting social bonds through the reduction of political demands to demands for protection, through the constitution of authority by figures of pastoral power. So to say that meaning is always religious means to say that psychoanalysis cannot be reduced to a discourse of confession, because it is not thinkable within the relationships of necessity, of confirmation of the original destiny, or of the substantial unity of redemption. Lacan isn't afraid to speak here of religion, of a type of Marxism, and of the bureaucratization of social ties by an international (in this case, the IPA), which is maintained only out of the fear of the analytic act.

It should also be noted that the ground of religious experience is based on the circulation of a particular notion of time—the time of providence, of redemption. In this context, meaning can only appear as a relation of necessity guaranteed by a ground originally situated. Meaning restores what has been lost, it heals us by returning us to an original ground. Thus, the main contrast is between meaning and event, meaning and truth. If Lacan criticized Marxism, it is because he understood its theory of revolution from a historical eschatology in which the proletariat appears as a finally reconciled subject-object. In this eschatology, every event is canceled under the weight of a time that is none other than the projection of an irresistible realization of progress. This is not the only reading possible of Marx's theory of revolution; however, this is how Lacan understand it. Contrary to this redemptive time, analysis plays on the destitutive time of the cut and of a revolution that can appear as a real space for the event.

But what can psychoanalysis offer to the critique of religion, utopian politics, and the rise of bureaucracy? If we return to the question of how we know that we are not dealing with the "stylization" of a depressive position, we must insist on the relation between act and jouissance. Because what leads to an act of this nature, an act beyond sense, is the displacement and depersonalization that the experience of jouissance necessarily produces. There is always a relation between act and the attempt to transform the impossible of jouissance into the figure of a form of future relation, giving body to the impossible. Thus, in transference, it would not be possible for the subject not to be driven by the emergence of jouissance beyond the forms of the symbolic inscription of desire. This is exactly what allows the liquidation of the transference, its nonconsolidation in a simple relationship of suggestion and dependence.

We can conclude then that, in transference, there is always an emergence of a character without a place of enjoyment (Lacan 2001: 358),[4] as we see, for example, in the oral enjoyment of Ernst Kris's patient, haunted by his desire for plagiarism and his decomposition of the illusions of being author, and in the example of the enjoyment of the Rat Man before the description of Chinese torture. Transference, in its destitution of knowledge, must allow the emergence of such enjoyment, as distressing as it is. It must allow the emergence of an enjoyment that does not function to reassure the subject but to show that there is no place for enjoyment in the administration of life as it happens in the current situation. In fact, psychoanalysis tries to show how the helpless character of this jouissance brings with it a political truth—namely, the fact that the conditions of the material reproduction of the life to which the subject is submitted are only sustained through a desire to not know about this enjoyment. With this enjoyment, it is impossible to do anything, and it is necessary to ruin it and forget it. That is to say, the real nature of this jouissance entails transformations and singular productions and relies on the subject assuming and producing an act which has the form of a noninscription. In this sense, we can understand the importance of a statement such as "enjoyment is what truth finds in resistance to knowledge" (Lacan 2001: 358). If truth is what resists knowledge in the name of enjoyment, then the action of truth will always be a destitution in the name of an impossible situation to come.

The Paradoxes of the Pass

It remains to be seen how we can understand the processes of recognition proper to the end of transference in its generality and supposed universality. Lacan sought to consider this in his discussions of the pass. Such discussions lead us to specific problems of organization and transmission, problems that will prove unsolvable within the Lacanian horizon. This leads Lacan to dissolve his own institution.

Within the project of the Freudian School of Psychoanalysis was the ultimate belief in the return to recognition processes based on the assumption of a certain form of "communication." In this sense, the school should be the place where the liquidation of transfer would be "communicated." "This experience cannot be eluded, its results must be communicated." (Lacan 2001: 255) If the results are to be communicated, it is because the unveiling of the homelessness of jouissance that comes from the dejection of the analyst, and their supposed knowledge doesn't lead us to a position of simple isolation. Lacan will say:

> What does this step, of being made alone, have to do with the one alone that one thinks oneself to be by following him? Did I not trust myself to the analytical experience, that is to say that which has happened to me from the one who sorted things out alone? Should I believe myself to be the only one to have it; so, for whom would I speak? (Lacan 2001: 263)

In this context, Lacan speaks of the founding act of the École Freudienne as the representative of the analytic act. This act is carried out alone, but it can nevertheless constitute a bond presupposed by the demand for "communication." And there must be an extreme tension between enjoyment and communication, a tension that may not really be resolved, which can only end in the dissolution of the space of communication, which is another way of understanding the question of the dissolution of the school. But the dissolution of the space of communication will be, paradoxically, the last wager on the institutional possibility of politics. An institution organized as a field and whirlwind.

Recall here what was at stake in the notion of pass. Under the pass procedure, an end of analysis allows the analysand to "give an account of his analysis" to passers who will then pass it to a jury. The first question concerning this procedure lies in the notion of "give an account." At other times, Lacan spoke of an act that could be "readable" by all. But what kind of speech and full readability is this? What counts here? And for what form of common space? Here lies the full weight of the problem. There is something transmissible at the end of an analysis, but as Lacan says: "How can one recognize a legal status to an experience that one cannot even respond to?" (Lacan 2001: 262) How can one recognize a jouissance that language does not want and seems to know nothing about? Lacan bets on a possible transmission and describes what is fully transmissible—namely, a *matheme*, a term inspired by Lévi-Strauss to describe minimal units of formal articulation of relations presupposed by myths. That is, the speech about analysis should be the constitution of a matheme capable of passing on two levels of transmission. The analytic act seems to take place in the constitution of a matheme.

In fact, there is communication only if we can talk in two levels of transmission. If I tell someone something, and that person cannot tell it to a third person, there is no communication, because there is no guarantee that the initial statement was, in fact, understood. The communication demonstrates that meaning is the perpetuation of reference beyond the modification of its enunciators.

However, the inscription of the act in a transmission should not be its submission to sense, and at this point lies the complexity of the procedure. We may even wonder if this would not necessarily invalidate all communication. Lacan believes that this irreducibility of the act to meaning is the only way to guarantee that we will not return to a "group effect." What underlies the group is the possibility of the unity of reference, and the sharing of modes of interpretation of statements and practices. The group is the ultimate expression of belief in a common grammar and a reference that does not change in the modification of its utterers.

For this reason, we may in fact ask ourselves if the experience of the pass could have a destination other than failure. If the analytical act changes the relationship between subject and language, it is not possible to try to recover communication levels after the liquidation of transference. This experience does not communicate, it drives language beyond communication. The requirement of communication can only be accomplished by adjusting the report of analysis to the previously shared grammatical and coding expectations. This means necessarily the reiteration of the code. This will necessarily reproduce stereotypes of reports and only confirm the singularities of the jouissance of the enunciator, whose proper name guarantees the identifying support of the bond produced by the school, whether this proper name is "Freud" or "Lacan." For a theory that links emancipation with subjective destitution, a "Freudian" school is a contradiction in adjecto, just as a "Freudian" or a "Lacanian" field would be a contradiction.

What drives Lacan to this wager? Lacan's appeal to readability and communication is his way of saying that there is something in the act that has the force of implication; it "de-supposes" knowledge, but it does not abolish the social relationship. Lacan's answer through the pass can only lead to a stalemate, because he himself eventually realized, by arguing to the end, for the dissolution of the school.

However, this impasse has positive political consequences. If the process of political emancipation, a process in which clinical experience in its own way is part of and requires the recognition of the "de-supposition" of knowledge and the advent of new subjects and new relationships enunciated in the singular, then, it isn't the place of psychoanalytic theory to talk about how the relations-to-come will be. The theoretical anticipation of reconciliation is an attempt at reconciliation itself. What theory can do is defend the need for subjective transformations that allow subjects to have the power to revolutionize processes in forms of life. But it cannot anticipate the form and direction of the organizations and practices that will be born out of such transformations. That is, theory can articulate the forms of emergence of new subjects, but it cannot specify the way they will organize after their emergence—that is, if theory wishes to avoid the risk of making the future a mere image of the realization of possibilities immanent to the present. At this point, theory must stop to allow praxis to take place in its multiple and innumerable contextual configurations. Theory becomes normative if it imposes its image on praxis.

This is reminiscent of the need for dynamic organizations, capable of constituting and destituting themselves in a continuous process through the recognition of each new singularity of enjoyment with which they are confronted in processes of liquidation of transference. The act takes its distinguishing characteristic from the social forms that it inhabits. For this reason, Alain Badiou is correct in appointing Lacan as heir to the "destitute operations" of revolutionary processes. But it would still be necessary to remember the importance of thinking about how to integrate these destitutions in the normal functioning of institutions, instead of settling for "anarchist leftism" or "tyrannical anarchism" (Badiou 2013: 153). This is perhaps the meaning of Lacan's ultimate abandonment of the school form and his assumption of a field form based on concepts such as the transience of the group's existence, randomness of relationships between participants, lability, limitation of bureaucratic functioning processes, and absence of hierarchy. No one ever said that such tasks were simple. However, they remain fundamental tasks for thinking about the contemporary political field.

Notes

1 This affirmation goes against propositions about psychoanalytical transference sustained by Michel Foucault (2008), *Psychiatric Power: Lectures at the Collège de France, 1973–1974*, ed. Jacques Lagrange and trans. Graham Burchell (New York: Picador).
2 For the relationship between transference and contingence, see M. David-Ménard (2011) Éloge des hasards dans la vie sexuelle (Paris: Hermann): 199–233.
3 See also Lacan (2015), *The Triumph of Religion* (Cambridge: Polity).
4 Serge Leclaire understands this point when he asks about transference: "Que va-t-on chercher? On l'a dit. Dans l'essence même de la parole qu'est l'articulation littérale, *comment celui qui dit se débat avec sa jouissance?*" Serge Leclaire (1968), *Psychanalyser* (Paris: Seuil): 174.

References

Badiou, A. (2013). *Lacan: l'anti-philosophie*, Paris: Fayard.
Balibar, E. (2017). *The Philosophy of Marx*; London: Verso.
Butler, J. (1997). *The Psychic Life of Power: Theories of Subjection*, Stanford University Press.
Cottet, S. (1996). *Freud et le désir du psychanalyste*, Paris; Seuil.
David-Ménard, M. (2011). Éloge des hasards dans la vie sexuelle, Paris: Hermann.
Deleuze, G. (2003). *Pourparlers,* Paris: Minuit.
Foucault, M. (2008). *Psychiatry Power*, Picador.
Freud, S (1921). *Group psychology and the analysis of the ego*, W.W. Norton, 1990
Freud, S. (1939). "Moses and monotheism," In: *The origin of religion*, New York: Penguin, 1990
Gernet, L. (1982). *Anthropologie de la Grèce antique*, Paris: Flammarion.
Herion, J.-L. (1993). *La cause du désir: l'agalma de Platon à Lacan*, Paris: Point Hors Ligne.
Kant, I. (1993). *Political writings*, Cambridge University Press.
Lacan, J. (1966). É*crits*, Paris: Seuil.

Lacan, J. (1968a). *Séminaire XV, séance du 10/01/68* (mimeo).
Lacan, J. (1968b) Proposition du 9 octobre 1967 sur le psychanalyste de l'Ecole," *Scilicet* 1 (1968): 14–30.
Lacan, J. (1973). *Séminaire XX,* Paris: Seuil.
Lacan, J. (2001). *Autres écrits*, Seuil: Paris.
Lacan, J. (2001b). *Séminaire VIII*, Paris: Seuil.
Lacan, J. (2004). *Séminaire X*, Paris; Seuil.
Lacan, J. (2015). *The Triumph of Religion*, Polity.
Leclaire, S. (1968) *Psychanalyser*, Paris: Seuil.
Lenin, V. (1975). "On the state and revolution," In: *The Lenin Anthology*, W.W. Norton.
Nietzsche, F. (1982). *Twilight of the idols*, New York: Penguin.
Nobus, D. (2000) *Jacques Lacan and the Freudian Oractice of Psychoanalysis*, New York: Routledge.
Plato (1927). *First Alcebiades* In: Plato Loeb Classic Library, Harvard University Press.
Porge, E. (2013). "Clinique de l'acte analytique," *La Clinique Lacanienne*, 2013/1: 35–50.
Rajchman, J. (2013). *Truth and eros: Foucault, Lacan and the Question of Ethics*, New York: Routledge.
Rancière, J. (2004). Disagreement, University of Minnesota Press.
Rimbaud, A (2011a) "To a Reason," trans. John Ashbery, Poetry (April 2011) https://www.poetryfoundation.org/poetrymagazine/poems/54557/to-a-reason.
Rimbaud, A (2011b) "Genie" trans. John Ashbery, Poetry (April 2011). https://www.poetryfoundation.org/poetrymagazine/poems/54559/genie.
Safatle, V. (2006) "Mirror without images: Mimesis and recognition on Lacan and Adorno," *Radical Philosophy*, 19, september/october 2006.
Stalin, J. *Marxism and linguistics* (www.marxism.org).
Žižek, S. (1992). *Enjoy your symptom!,* New York: Routledge.

Chapter 14

Critique of Epistemic Economy (Fragments)

Samo Tomšič

I

The relationship between psychoanalysis and natural sciences is marked by a turbulent history. At its core, we find incompatible answers to the question whether psychoanalysis is (or should become) a "hard science", or whether its concepts of truth and knowledge, its theory of language, or its notion of the unconscious are at all compatible with the predominant standards of scientificity. It is worth recalling that Freud and Lacan had strikingly different, sometimes entirely opposite views on the way psychoanalysis should stand toward the scientific disciplines. Throughout his teaching, Lacan cultivated an ongoing dialogue with natural sciences, while remaining consistently ambiguous toward the role of scientific knowledge and technology in the constitution and transformation of subjectivity. However, despite this ambiguity Lacan never ended up in a Heideggerian type of alarmism regarding the absolute "metaphysical" domination of scientific apparatus; unlike Heidegger, Lacan engaged in a critique of capitalism.

Freud, in contrast, remained a man of *Aufklärung*, insisting on the centrality of natural sciences in the gradual enlightenment of humankind (in *The Future of an Illusion*, he spelled out his conviction that scientific knowledge would ultimately triumph over religious "illusions"); he equally claimed that psychoanalysts had to adopt a scientific worldview and believed that his doctrine of drives (*Trieblehre*) and theory of libido (*Libido-Theorie*) would eventually obtain solid scientific foundations, with thermodynamics and biology serving as the main fields of reference. The terms *Lehre* and *Theorie*, with which Freud epistemologically categorized his engagements with the problematic of drive and of libido, already suggest that he saw his own framings as temporary and pending scientific verification or reformulation. Psychoanalysis then appeared as a kind of transitional science, which does not even deserve to be called science quite yet; it is still a science in the making or an epistemological work in progress.

At the same time, despite Freud's orientation toward natural sciences, his proverbial scientism was rather peculiar and overtly speculative. Suffice to recall his "farfetched speculation" (Freud 2000: 234) from *Beyond the Pleasure Principle*, where the jump from the clinical phenomenon of compulsive repetition to the biological problem of the emergence of life out of inanimate matter leads Freud to his most controversial concept, the death drive. Here, we then have another movement, which seems completely opposite from the quest for solid scientific foundations. Now, these "solid foundations" are pushed beyond themselves, or perhaps better, scientific discoveries are evoked because of their inherent speculative potential, pointing toward a truth that natural sciences themselves seem to ignore. In *Beyond the Pleasure Principle*, Freud therefore does not even try to conceal his attempts to trace the conclusions of the then still young biological insights into the structure of living cells significantly further than any natural scientist would have been willing to do. This speculative move concerns the relation between living organism and its environment, and more specifically what subsequent development in natural sciences would address under the notion of emergence and of "extended organism" (see Scott Turner 2002).

The scandal of Freud's speculative developments lies in the thesis that the jump from physical to biological, from inanimate matter to living matter comprises a primordial drama, equivalent to trauma or catastrophe. Freud explicitly argues that life is a disturbance in matter, which henceforth strives to return to the inanimate state and to re-establish an ideal equilibrium condition. At the same time, life is characterized by resistance against this return; it is systematized disturbance or organized disequilibrium. From the viewpoint of life's self-preservation, trauma also obtains a new signification. It is no longer understood in terms of destabilization of an ideal equilibrium state or corruption of homeostasis, but rather, exemplified on the simplest form of life, as disruption of the unicellular organism's protective shield against the threatening influences of the environment, the violation of the provisory border between the organism's inside and outside. Trauma ultimately stands for the organism's incapacity to filter external stimuli. This scenario moreover complicates the understanding of homeostasis. Rather than being an ideal state, which has been subsequently corrupted by disturbance, homeostasis itself results from a constitutively conflicted state and stands for the economization of disturbances. In other words, homeostasis must be thought of in gradual terms, as a process rather than a state, and moreover as a continuously conflicted process.

This is also the reason why Freud insists that the emergence of life must be seen as an emergence of difference and the reproduction of life as an ongoing process of resistance against the abolition of this difference. The French physiologist Xavier Bichat famously wrote, "*life is a sum of functions that resist death*" (1973: 11). Freud seems to go along with this general definition. However, the thought experiment in *Beyond the Pleasure Principle*, in which Freud invites us to imagine life in the simplest form as a "tiny bubble", makes a small yet crucial step further. Life is reduced to one single function, constitutive resistance, which brings about the very difference between life and death, and consequently between the living organism's inside and outside. As such, however, this constitutive resistance falls neither on the side of life nor on the side of death. The "tiny bubble" is not only the simplest but also a paradoxical form of life, no longer dead and not yet alive, situated in the intermediate zone between life and death, an ontological limbo, where the jump from inanimate to living matter requires us to mobilize the category of undead (a category whose negative prefix "un-" is shared with the unconscious). Freud's tiny bubble is not just any unicellular organism: it comes suspiciously close to a virus; however, one that does not reproduce in living cells, but in inanimate matter, and in doing so triggers a pandemic, in which the mutation and the emergence of life's diversity reflects the constitutive resistance that defines it.

Freud calls his thought experiment a speculation, because he insists on describing vital processes in general. But what he equally does is tell the story of the subject's emergence. It is here that Freud's mobilization of biological knowledge most thoroughly diverges from the scientific framing, thus addressing a truth that natural sciences are not—not necessarily, not primarily—concerned with, a truth that is intimately associated with the antagonism that traverses subjectivized life from within, and more specifically with the link between resistance and trauma.

II

Lacan was aware of this redoubling on the level of truth, which he explicated in his famous writing "Science and Truth"—a title that can also be interpreted as "Science and Subject." In this writing, Lacan develops his provocative thesis that science forecloses the subject and, in doing so, not just de-subjectivizes knowledge, but moreover becomes actively indifferent toward subjectivity and its vicissitudes. In this way, Lacan could introduce a critical twist to Alexandre Koyré's historical epistemology that otherwise guided his engagement with epistemological questions.[1] Koyré proposed a reading of the early modern scientific revolution, according to which the main scientific event (itself spanning the approximate period of two hundred years between Nicolaus Copernicus and Isaac Newton) consisted in the gradual dismantling of the epistemic paradigm of a closed world and its replacement with the infinite universe. In this process, Koyré insists, mathematics became *the* language, in which natural sciences address nature with questions and in which they receive its answers.[2] This means that human categories, and particularly language, this fabric of sense, meaning, and enjoyment, no longer play a significant role in epistemic production, and the scientific conception of the Real becomes increasingly foreign to what human beings (consciously) experience as reality. Koyré's identification of the Real with the impossible—a definition that Lacan eventually adopted—means, the Real is mathematical, whereby the term "impossibility" concerns the fact that mathematics remains a form of language and therefore dependent on human existence. Mathematical objects and formulas do not exist objectively in the Real; nevertheless, they explain it and moreover allow for its active manipulation. This manipulation is sustained by technology, which is ultimately reified mathematics or objectified scientific theory.[3] But who does the manipulation?

Here, Lacan takes a step further from Koyré by accentuating the autonomy and foreignness of scientific discourse. In modernity, mathematics becomes the impossible language of the Real, not simply because it never exists in the Real as such, but because it resists the human subject on whose existence it nevertheless depends. In this respect, mathematics is a "paradoxical" language spoken by *no body*. There is no mathematical *parlêtre*; mathematics is language without a body, which, to repeat, does not prevent it from being materialized. The most important feature of mathematics—for Koyré as well as for someone like Gottlob Frege, for whom mathematics and geometry stood for the emergence of the objective *in* the subjective—is that it exemplifies the peculiar autonomy of the symbolic order. For Lacan, this autonomy is not innocent—it acts back on the human subject, hence it is endowed with material causality.[4] At the core of modern scientific revolution stands the emancipation of mathematics and more generally of epistemic production in natural sciences from the human subject. In the premodern epistemic regime, the human subject was still the ultimate point of reference of scientific knowledge, the point, where this knowledge reached its closure and totalization. With the gradual rejection of the cognizing human subject from the field of knowledge—or at least the degradation of its epistemological role—knowledge became de-totalized, which also means that it became embedded in a process of continuous growth. I will return to this point further below.

Lacan drew his own lessons and conclusions from the natural sciences. Although his positions may have been at times affirmatively speculative, they never downplayed an underlying incompatibility between science and psychoanalysis. In "Science and Truth," Lacan somewhat enigmatically marked the point of divergence by saying that science does not want to know anything about truth as cause: it excludes the causal link between discourse and the unconscious, and along with this rejection, it misrecognizes its own impact on the structure of subjectivity. It is therefore not surprising that the "foreclosed subject" of science—a subject, whose life has been, since early modernity, increasingly determined by scientific knowledge and technology—returns on the couch, in the form of "suffering speech," to put it somewhat pathetically. This suffering speech is the perfect counterpart of mathematical language, because it is inseparable from the speaking body: "The cure is a demand that originates in the voice of the sufferer, of someone who suffers from his body or his thought." (Lacan 1990: 7)

The shift from mathematical language to suffering speech reflects on the terrain of truth, which can be again exemplified by the Freudian analysis of the simplest form of life. To repeat, the Freudian perspective in biological matters is that life is a conflicted process, defined by resistance. But life can be regarded as conflicted only under the condition that there is a subject that is affected by this conflict and capable of articulating their suffering. Or to turn it around, whenever suffering is articulated, this is the sign of a subject. So, if life is a conflicted process, this means that life is comparable to a symptom. The scientific manner of dealing with symptoms is directed toward the abolition of their causes, and thus of the symptoms themselves. For this reason, declaring life a symptom makes no sense from the viewpoint of the life sciences. This is evidently not the case for psychoanalysis, which, as Lacan eventually concluded, does not target the abolition of symptoms, but their transformation. In this setting, the symptom is not simply a sign of malign development, but of an irreversible damage, trauma, or catastrophe, which stands at the origin of the subject's emergence: hence the link between the symptom and truth, or more generally, the notion of symptomatic truth, which could not be further away from the (subjectless) epistemic truth, facticity and information.

III

Lacan made another important critical addition to Koyré's epistemology, which remained focused on the progressive mathematization of physics only. For Aristotle, whose views on the relation between mathematics and physical being remained unchallenged until the Renaissance, no mathematization of earthly movements ("generation and corruption") was possible; only the nature of heavenly movements (the regular and repetitive movements of planets and stars) was considered mathematical and geometrical. Consequently, the dynamic processes in physical being could only be addressed in "human language," in which Aristotle outlined his doctrine of four causes (formal, efficient, material, final), rather than in the "inhuman language" of mathematics and geometry. While Koyré proposed a rigorous, albeit not uncontroversial interpretation of the early modern reinvention of "mathematical Platonism," resulting in the abolition of the divide between the heavenly sphere of being and the earthly sphere of becoming, one crucial thing remained unaddressed: modern science not only succeeded "explaining the real with the impossible" but also and more importantly grounded production of knowledge on the expanding quantification of reality. The extension of geometry and mathematics to dynamic processes in nature inaugurated an epistemic regime, in which growth itself becomes an essential feature of knowledge.

The epistemic process of quantification, today enforced and expanded through digitalization, shows that the modern regime of knowledge is not simply accumulative, as Lacan once remarked, but extractivist, grounded on the interdependency between accumulation and extraction of epistemic value (think of today's data mining, but also, and more fundamentally, on the notion of information). It is thanks to this extractivist tendency that science could undergo a systematic transformation into an epistemic economy, in which continuous growth of knowledge must be sustained. With this focus on the growth of knowledge, the natural sciences structurally intersect with the modern economic regime, in which the link between accumulation and extraction (of surplus value) is equally central:

> I would call the state of knowledge before Descartes pre-accumulative. With Descartes knowledge, scientific knowledge is constituted on the mode of production of knowledge. Just as an essential stage of our structure that one calls social but is in fact metaphysical, and which is called capitalism, is accumulation of capital, the relation of the Cartesian subject to this being, which is affirmed in it, is founded on the accumulation of knowledge. After Descartes knowledge is what serves to make knowledge grow. And this is an entirely different question than that of the truth. (Lacan 1965)

Descartes is not referenced here by chance. His place in the early modern scientific revolution is exceptional insofar as he linked the growth of knowledge with the question of the subject's being. Unlike his scientific predecessors and contemporaries, Descartes expanded the modern regime of knowledge, then still in the process of solidification, to the field of subjectivity (the question of the mind-body-nexus). Descartes's methodological doubt famously played the key role in this expansion. Therein, we can observe both the formation of a regime of knowledge, grounded in continuous growth, expansion and movement, and the increase of subject's certainty. The point of cogito is not only "I think therefore I am," but also, "The more I know the more I am certain to exist." This means that my existence is now entirely dependent on science, or with Lacan's (2006: 106) wording, "we have [...] all embarked upon the discourse of science," which transformed us into one among many sources of epistemic and economic surplus.

In the deduction of the subject of certainty, corresponding to the accumulative regime of knowledge, another type of subject is foreclosed, the one exposed in the process of doubt only, a subject, whose being is far from certainty and stability. Lacan was interested in this divided subject of doubt because of its overtly symptomatic status: on the one hand it conditions the solidification of knowledge and certainty, and on the other hand it must be removed from the expanding field of science should the latter remain solidified. The subject of doubt then does not seem to possess any permanent epistemic value or contribute to the envisaged growth of knowledge. Once science is anchored in certainty and embedded in an open-ended movement of knowledge, the experience of cogito's fading is not simply forgotten; it is ridiculed. As Descartes writes at the end of *Meditations*:

> Accordingly, I should not have any further fears about the falsity of what my senses tell me every day; on the contrary, the exaggerated doubts of the last few days should be dismissed as laughable. This applies especially to the principal reason for doubt, namely my inability to distinguish between being asleep and being awake. (Descartes 1988: 122)

From the viewpoint of the solidified science, where knowledge is already in the process of growth, the initial drama of methodological doubt appears as false and even silly. Dreams do not contain any rational thinking, and the subject incapable of distinguishing between dreams and reality is ultimately no subject at all, or at least not yet. Such doubts may have preceded science, but are no longer valid, and the question is whether they ever were meant seriously in the first place. Only if we understand the final ridicule of doubt as an expression of epistemic resistance against an uncomfortable and conflicted truth of modern science can we conclude that Descartes indeed engaged in more than an innocent thought experiment and encountered in methodological doubt more than he may have asked for.

Contrary to the re-normalizing conclusion of *Meditations*, Descartes's decomposition of appearances that he took for granted demonstrates that the subject thinks most intensively when its certainty is destabilized. The logical conclusion that Lacan's reading seems to draw from Descartes's deduction of cogito is therefore: "I think therefore I fade." It is the fading of being, or more generally the link between thinking and alienation that is the radical lesson of doubt. But again, this lesson is excluded from the field of knowledge, because it suggests that modern science was constituted as an essential source of the subject's alienation, and even as an exploitation of alienation. In short, the modern accumulative regime of knowledge requires alienation in order to make knowledge grow. This explains why Lacan concludes his brief reflection on Descartes's foundation of epistemic economy with the remark that the accumulation of knowledge is concerned with entirely different issues than with the question of truth. Truth relates to cogito's split, uncertainty, and instability, but the regime of knowledge, from which this conflicted truth is rejected, is preoccupied merely with the apparently automatic growth of knowledge. It is knowledge that makes knowledge grow, not the subject.

IV

The accumulative regime of knowledge thus contains a feature that premodernity did not know, "surplus-knowledge" (Milner 2006: 337).[5] This feature is accompanied by the objective appearance of self-moving knowledge – knowledge-breeding knowledge or knowledge *in* the real – which points to another notorious appearance of self-generation and automatic growth, capital as "automatic subject" and the economic scandal of "money-breeding money" (both formulations are adopted from Marx). Thus, one can conclude that "foreclosure of the subject" unites modern science and capitalist economy. Marx's discussion of commodity fetishism in the first volume of *Capital* implicitly made this reproach to the classical political economy. Insofar as it wants to establish itself as a "science of value," political economy must foreclose the subject, which emerges in the process of production of value, the labor process. *Laboro* is, so to speak, Marx's *cogito*, and just like the subject of doubt is the rejected truth of production of knowledge, without being the ultimate source of knowledge, the subject of labor is the rejected truth of production of value, without therefore being its ultimate source either. For Marx, insisting on the sameness of the "two" subjects—the subject of value and the subject of labor—is necessary if one does not want to reproduce the trap, in which political economy walks into, when it attributes to value in the accumulative regime substantial status. Commenting on the circulation M-C-M' (money - commodity - increase of money), Marx writes:

> If we pin down the specific forms of appearance assumed in turn by self-valorizing value in the course of its life, we reach the following elucidation: capital is money, capital is commodities. In truth, however, value is here the subject of a process in which, while constantly assuming the form in turn of money and commodities, it changes its own magnitude, throws off surplus-value from itself considered as original value, and thus valorizes itself independently. For the movement in the course of which it adds surplus-value is its own movement, its valorization is therefore self-valorization. By virtue of being value, it has acquired the occult ability to add value to itself. It brings forth living offspring, or at least lays golden eggs. As the dominant subject [übergreifendes Subjekt] of this process, in which it alternately assumes and loses the form of money and the form of commodities, but preserves and expands itself through all these changes, value requires above all an independent form by means of which its identity with itself may be asserted. (Marx 1990: 225)

Value appears as an *übergreifendes Subjekt*, a term, whose meaning is not only "dominant subject" but also, and more literally, "(self-)exceeding subject": a vital subject, whose self-preserving tendency does not seem to match Bichat's definition of life quoted earlier. The automatic subject is not a "sum of functions, which resist death," but appears to be a single vital function, which presumably begets more life, a life without negativity and without traumatism. Contrary to this vulgar vitalist scenario, Marx's critique attempts to demonstrate that capital is indeed a sum of vital functions of the economic order, which, however, resist the subject as a figure of "death," or more precisely, as a figure of damaged, exploited and exhausted life, out of which surplus value, this apparent self-movement of value in objectified form is extracted. There is no need to recall that the truth of this capitalist occultism is the structural and physical violence of the capitalist extractivist metaphysics, implemented with colonial, sexual, and economic violence. Marx, too, strived to expose the traumatic kernel of the capitalist "culture," an ongoing systemic traumatism that accompanies the generation of value. This link between accumulation and traumatism is ultimately unfolded and narrated in the historical chapters of *Capital*, vol. 1, in which Marx debates the issue of primitive accumulation and of modern colonialism. Marx considered the industrial proletariat to be the privileged social personification of the foreclosed subjectivity, sustaining the modern accumulative and extractivist regime of value. As feminist and anticolonial readings have insisted, this figure of subjectivity must be necessarily expanded with other personifications. Needless to say, Marx's thought only draws its relevance from the gap between the function of foreclosed subject and its social personifications. Only in this manner can a *common* truth resulting from the different historical and contemporary experiences of systemic violence be pinpointed and embedded in an emancipatory movement with the aim of abolishing the modern link between this "polymorph" violence and production of value.

The intersection of scientific and capitalist economy obtained another famous expression in the ideal of mastery and possession of nature, equally preformulated by Descartes in his *Discourse on Method* (see 2006: 51). However, while for Descartes it was still humanity who would eventually come to master and possess nature, the scientific and the economic foreclosure of the subject suggests that humanity ends up on the side of the dominated, while the nexus of knowledge and value solidifies its position of mastery. Furthermore, because science and economy are organized around a surplus-object, whose defining feature is growth, their insatiable demand for more knowledge and value can be associated with a fundamental psychoanalytic concept, the drive.

For Freud, the drive (*Trieb*) describes a force in the subject, which demands constant production of pleasure (*Lustgewinn*, yield in pleasure). This logic is surprisingly anticipated in Marx, who recognized in the movement of value and the dynamic of capital a drive of self-valorization. The accumulative regime of knowledge and the idea of surplus knowledge equally imply the existence of a drive (Feuerbach's *Wissenstrieb*, drive of knowledge), which seems to point beyond the frames of human cognition and pursues its own aim of domination over nature, as Descartes would put it. When it comes to this domination, and the function of scientific knowledge in its enforcement, it was none other than Freud who argued that the drive of mastery and the drive of knowledge stand in direct continuity, an observation he exemplified in obsessional neurosis:

> In particular we often gain an impression that the drive for knowledge [*Wisstrieb*] can actually take the place of sadism in the mechanism of obsessional neurosis. Indeed it is at bottom a sublimated off-shoot [*Sprößling*] of the drive of mastery [*Bemächtigungstrieb*] exalted into something intellectual, and its repudiation in the form of doubt plays a large part in the picture of obsessional neurosis. (Freud 2001: 324)

Lacan himself was highly skeptical toward the notion of a drive of knowledge, because it was initially introduced for describing the force of human curiosity (*Neugierde*) and thus invested with anthropological meaning. At the same time, the drive of knowledge rounds up perfectly Lacan's epistemological observation that the core of modern scientific revolution must be seen as a systematic shift from pre-accumulative to accumulative regime of knowledge. To speak of the drive of knowledge would then again imply exposing the rejection of the subject from the field of science. The subject of cognition, assumed by the philosophical tradition ever since Descartes, then turns out not only as a marker of the rejected subject of doubt but also as a mystification of the link between knowledge and mastery or knowledge and exploitation, brought to the point in the impersonal force of the drive. For Freud, then, the drive of knowledge is an elevated, sublimated form of the drive of mastery, its sophisticated expression. So while Lacan argued for a reading of Kant with Sade, the latter revealed as the hidden, obscene truth of the former, and the Sadean injunction to enjoy even in the cruelest of tortures the perverted truth of the Kantian categorical imperative, then Freud seems to be arguing for something like Descartes with Sade. The evocation of doubt and the mutual feeding of doubt and knowledge, which is at the root of the accumulative regime of knowledge, as well as of the junction between knowledge and domination, points in this direction.

V

A major complication that accompanies the accumulation of knowledge is that its growth is mirrored by the increase of uncertainty and lack of knowledge. Lacan pinpointed this interdependency of surplus and lack, characteristic for the modern libidinal, epistemic, and social economy, by mobilizing the ambiguity of the French term *plus*, which appears most prominently in his neologism *plus-de-jouir* (coined in reference to *plus-value*, surplus value). *Plus-de-jouir* means both "surplus enjoyment" and "no more enjoyment", indicating the intertwining of satisfaction and dissatisfaction that marks the logic of the drive. If science is grounded on the growth of knowledge, the same nexus of "more" and "no more"—knowledge and unknowledge, certainty and uncertainty—emerges at the core of its modus operandi.

The link between surplus and lack may be the driving force of epistemic accumulation, but it can equally be used to undermine or relativize scientific knowledge through deliberately induced doubt or the spread of misinformation or blatant lies. A famous example of such a strategy destined to relativize scientific data is provided by tobacco and oil industry. Meanwhile, the widespread phenomenon of culturally induced ignorance, doubt, or skepticism gave rise to a whole area of research (agnotology), whose first and ultimate object could as well be capitalism itself.[6] In the spread of misinformation, we are indeed dealing with a curious perversion of Cartesian methodological doubt, aiming to keep people in an enduring state of uncertainty. This perversion stretches to the very ground of the accumulative regime of knowledge, subjective alienation, to draw the exact opposite result from Descartes, destabilization of scientific authority, and of knowledge grounded in certainty. The main strategy, then, does not consist in simply refuting the results of scientific research, but rather in planting the seed of doubt that will expose their potential or actual incompleteness.

When doubt is generated, the targeted subjects are not simply placed in the position of ignorance; they are strategically made unknowing, the sites of evacuation of knowledge. As such presumably "empty" subjects or "unwritten sheets of paper" they can become objects of political manipulation and economic exploitation. The "unknown lands" (*terra incognita*) in the maps of early modern colonial explorers exemplify this strategy: "The reconstruction of parts of the globe as uncharted territory is [...] the *production of unknowledge*, the transformation of those parts into potential objects of Western political and economic attention. It is the enabling of colonialism." (Schick 1999: 48–49) As the name "unknown land" suggests, these spaces were not simply unknown to the colonizers, but were considered populated by "ignorant savages," by peoples who were forcefully displaced in the position of nonknowledge in order to be transformed into objects of exploitation. While the psychoanalyst appears in the analysand's transference as a "subject-supposed-to-know," the colonial subject is fabricated as a "subject-supposed-not-to-know," even as a subject who must not know, must be kept in the position of ignorance.

Contemporary neutralization of scientific knowledge and enforcement of unknowledge demonstrates that capitalism in any case does not need a science that is sensitive of its social value. All it requires is self-sufficient and therefore asocial accumulative regime of knowledge – asocial, because insensitive to the consequences of mobilizing scientific knowledge for reproducing a social-economic order that is essentially hostile to sociality. Lacan repeatedly spoke of ignorance as one of the three fundamental passions, next to love and hate, and one could indeed say that the blindness uniting these three passions obtains an entirely new dimension in contemporary generation of unknowledge. One does not have to idealize Descartes, but in his case, doubt still served as a method, which in its own imperfect manner reacted to a crisis of truth and knowledge that inaugurated modernity, envisaging a science, which would not simply accumulate knowledge for the sake of knowledge, but serve "for the preservation of health, which is without doubt the highest good and the foundation of all the other goods of this life" (Descartes 2006: 51), hence an essentially *social* science.

The crisis, to which Descartes reacted, can be pinpointed in Montaigne's skepticism. Montaigne is a curious figure, because he is positioned in the gray zone, when the old scientific and social order was dissolving and the new one only entered its process of birth. Galileo, Descartes, and Newton were yet to come, but the scientific revolution had already begun to shake the assumed completeness and stability of the premodern world picture. Montaigne's doubt is still "pre-accumulative," but it nevertheless exposes the conflicted truth that is announced in doubt and that concerns the alienated subject, sustained by no positive knowledge. To repeat, the Cartesian invention consisted in linking doubt with knowledge. There can be no surplus-knowledge without doubt, whose negativity is economized in a productive manner. But in doing so, modern science is founded on an epistemic amnesia:

> the fact is that science, if one looks at it closely, has no memory. Once constituted, it forgers the circuitous path by which it came into being; otherwise stated, it forgets a dimension of truth that psychoanalysis seriously puts work. (Lacan 2006: 738)[7]

What is forgotten in Descartes is the antagonism between skepticism as a radical position in epistemological matters, which confronts us with subjective alienation in action, and tamed skepticism in methodological doubt, from which the radical experience of alienation is progressively removed, and science forgets the encounter that initiated it. Montaigne's skepticism then retrospectively appears to be a simple rhetoric effect and therefore exaggerated and somewhat excessive opinion, potentially comparable to sophistry.

Psychoanalysis, in turn, mobilizes the conflicted truth of skepticism by returning to the tension between Montaigne's "anti-dialectical" and Descartes's "dialectical" position. In her classic essay "Truth and Politics," Hannah Arendt (2006) reminds us that the antagonism between truth and opinion is equal to the antagonism between dialogue and persuasion, in other words, between dialectic and rhetoric. We are dealing here with two classical manners, in which articulated discourse methodologically—dialectical or poetic method—handles the power of language to not simply represent reality, but moreover actively intervene and transform it. While on the side of dialectics, we have the movement of contradiction—and in this respect the antagonism between dialectical and rhetoric discourse stands for a dialectical division of language; on the side of rhetoric, we find seduction. One could say that psychoanalysis brings together both aspects, the dialectical and the sophistic, the divisive and the seductive: it is both the movement of contradiction between the analyst and the analysand, brought to the point in the phenomenon of transference love and resistance to psychoanalysis (whose expression is again transference), and seduction into speaking and thus uninterrupted work on the problematic nexus of body, enjoyment, and positioning within the symbolic order. Incidentally, in his early seminars, Lacan insisted on the link between the direction of speech in psychoanalysis and the movement of dialectic in Plato's dialogues; whereas in the later years, when he became increasingly interested in the fusion of language and enjoyment, conceptualized under the neologism *lalangue*, he saw in the psychoanalyst "the presence of the sophist in our age." Be it as it may, in this direction of speech, which in the analytic setting, pulls in opposite directions, the main effort consists in working on the problematic, even traumatic history, in which the analysand is embedded. Even though something like knowledge is constantly produced in this process, it is not the central product or aim of this work. Rather than accumulating knowledge of the analysand's history, the analytic work is transformative; its product is change, certainly of the subject's structure, but also of their embedding in the social bond. It is for this reason that Lacan could eventually remark that the aim of psychoanalysis is to find an exit from the capitalist discourse, adding that this will not constitute a progress if it does not happen for all.[8]

In our predicament, when natural sciences and humanities are targeted by populist resentment, conspiracy thinking, and corporate interests, criticizing science might risk creating the wrong impression. Lacan's take on the relation between science and psychoanalysis must not be taken as a rejection of science. He seems instead to point out an ongoing tension that has been characteristic of science throughout modernity. We can observe this tension today in the crisis of scientific authority, which echoes the contradiction we find formulated in Descartes: on the one hand, modern science allows establishing a mastery over nature, and on the other hand, it contains a social value, which allows for emancipation from domination, be it epistemic or economic. It is because of this split that Lacan included science in the list of the Freudian "impossible professions" (governing, educating, analyzing), where the first and ultimate imperative is to create the conditions for transformative work on the social and for disrupting the capitalist link between alienation, exploitation, and production-extraction of surplus. To do so, science would have to reverse the foreclosure of the subject that grounded it. In other words, it would have to overcome its own modernity, without therefore returning to some presumably lost past. The break with the premodern regime of knowledge is irreversible and has had its positive consequences. However, including science among impossible professions means that science must be "made impossible," in other words, continuously antagonized in its integration in the capitalist mode of production. Lacan's implicit suggestion seems to be that this "split of science" can only be achieved in combination with the other three professions, which are all involved in the formation and transformation of subjectivity (and which no less struggle with their conformity with the absolutized capitalist system). If the four professions remain true to their emancipatory horizon, they form an alliance of impossibilities. And politics is ultimately an alliance of impossible positions.

Notes

1 "Science's position is justified by a radical change in the tempo of its progress, by the galloping form of its interference in our world, and by the chain reactions that characterize what one might call the expansions of its energetics. In this situation, what seems radical to me is the modification that has occurred in our subject position, in the sense that it is inaugural therein and that science continues strengthen it ever further. Koyré is my guide here and, as we know, he is still unrecognised." (Lacan 2006: 726–727)

2 See Alexandre Koyré (1973), Études d'histoire de la pensée scientifique (Paris: Gallimard): 83.

3 "all the instruments of astronomy before Galileo were instruments of observation; they were moreover instruments of measurement [...] of simply observable facts. In a sense they were still tools, whereas the Galilean instruments [...] are instruments in the strongest sense of the term: they are incarnations of theory." (Koyré 1973: 59) From this perspective, there is no difference between Galileo's telescope and our contemporary particle collider, even though the latter's appearance is significantly more impressive.

4 As he puts it, modern physics is a discourse with real consequences; for an extensive discussion of this formulation, see Alenka Zupančič (2017: 78–80).

5 The Marxist implications of surplus knowledge were recently elaborated by Slavoj Žižek (2017: 162ff). Jean-Claude Milner, who introduced the term, remarks that, with the solidification of the modern regime of knowledge in "absolute knowledge" (a nod to Hegel, albeit a critical one), knowledge ended up becoming an "idol" (again, fetish).

6 Needless to say, the spread of misinformation—about socialism, climate crisis, minorities, political conflicts, etc.—is a crucial component of the capitalist mode of survival. The term "agnotology" was introduced by the American historian of science Robert N. Proctor.

7 Heidegger addressed this link in his speculative etymology of the word *aletheia*. The Greek term, according to Heidegger, relates to *lethe*, oblivion. Instead of speaking of the relation between words and things, Heidegger conceives truth as interplay of unveiling and veiling. Truth thus involves dynamic and instability. One could say that it emerges and vanishes, and is therefore connected with semblance. Its main action is *fort-da* (to recall the game played by Freud's grandchild).

8 For the rather peculiar context of Lacan's remark, see *Television*: 16, and Jelica Sumic (2000): 133–134.

References

Hannah Arendt, H. (2006). *Between Past and Future,* London: Penguin.

Bichat, X. (1973). *Recherches physiologiques sur la vie et la mort,* Verviers: Éditions Gérard & Co.

Blumenberg, H. (1970). "Neugierde und Wissenstrieb. Supplemente zu Curiositas," in: *Archiv für Begriffsgeschichte* 14: 7–40.

Cassin, B. (2019). *Jacques the Sophist*, New York: Fordham University Press.

Descartes, R. (1988). *Meditations on First Philosophy*, in: *Selected Philosophical Writings*, Cambridge: Cambridge University Press.

Descartes, R. (2006). *Discourse on Method*, Oxford: Oxford University Press.

Freud, S. (2000). *Jenseits des Lustprinzips*, in: *Studienausgabe*, Vol. 3, Frankfurt: Fischer Verlag.

Freud, S. (2001). "The Disposition for Obsessional Neurosis," in: *The Standard Edition of the Complete Psychological Works of Sigmund Freud,* Vol. 12, London: Vintage: 311–326.

Khatib, S. (2021). "The Drive of Capital," in: *Coils of the Serpent* 8: 101–113.

Lacan, J. *Le Séminaire, livre XII, Problèmes cruciaux pour la psychanalyse* (unpublished), 09. June 1965.

Lacan, J. (1990). *Television*, ed. by Joan Copjec, New York: Norton.

Lacan, J. (2006). Écrits, transl. by Bruce Fink, New York: Norton.

Lacan, J. (2006). *Seminar, Book XVII, The Other Side of Psychoanalysis*, New York: Norton.

Marx, K. (1990). *Capital,* Vol. 1, London: Penguin Books.

Schick, I. C. (1999). *The Erotic Margin: Sexuality and Spatiality in Alteritist Discourse,* London: Verson.

Turner, J. C. (2002). *The Extended Organism. The Physiology of Animal-Built Structures*, Cambridge, MA: Harvard University Press.

Sumic, J. (2000). "La politique et la psychanalyse: du pas-tout au pour tous." In *Universel, singulier, sujet.* Paris: Kimé: 129–158.

Zupančič, A. (2017). *What is Sex?*, Cambridge, MA: The MIT Press.

Žižek, S. (2017). *Incontinence of the Void*, Cambridge, MA: The MIT Press.

About the Authors

Augusto Ismerim is a psychoanalyst and researcher from São Paulo, Brazil. Augusto graduated with a bachelor's degree in psychology from the University of São Paulo, where he is currently a master's student advised by Prof. Christian Dunker. He is interested in the connections between Lacanian psychoanalysis, linguistics, natural science, and epistemology.

Carin Franzén is professor in comparative literature at Stockholm University. Her research explores the relations between formations of subjectivity and cultural hegemonies. She has published various articles and books on literature and psychoanalysis as well as on early modern literature. Recent publications include "Lacan and the Archeology of the Subject," in *Analysing the Cultural Unconscious: Science of the Signifier* (ed. Rösing et al., 2020) and "An Antidote to the Crisis of Contemporary Culture: Rereading Kristeva on Duras," in *The Philosophy of Julia Kristeva* (ed. Beardsworth and Auxier, 2020).

Christian Dunker is a psychoanalyst in São Paulo, Brazil. He studied psychology at the University of São Paulo, where he now works as professor of Lacanian studies. Member of the Forum of the Lacanian Field, he studied critical approaches of psychoanalysis in Manchester and participated in different research tracks (philosophy, language sciences, social theory, psychosomatic). He is co-ordinator of the Laboratory of Social Theory, Philosophy and Psychoanalysis at Universidade de São Paulo, Brazil.

Derek Humphreys is associate professor at Université Paris 13, where he teaches clinical psychopathology and psychoanalytic theory and epistemology. He is also research director at Unité Transversale de Recherches en Psychogenèse et Psychopathologie (Campus Condorcet, Paris), where his seminars deal with the concepts of fantasy, playing, contingency, and transference. He has published many articles on psychosomatics, transference, figurability, and contemporary psychoanalytical institutional practices (dispositives). He has been an invited lecturer at Universidad de Chile and Universidad Diego Portales, Chile. His most recent articles are "Modes de présence dans l'intrication pulsionnelle,"

Le Coq-héron 236 (2019) and "Figurabilité filmique: le statut pictographique du cinéma," *Etica y cine* 8 (2018). He is a qualified psychoanalyst in private practice in Paris.

Jasper Feyaerts is a philosopher and doctor of clinical psychology (Ghent University), currently affiliated as a professor at the Department of Psychoanalysis and Clinical Consulting (Ghent University) and a research associate at the Centre for Contextual Psychiatry (KU Leuven). His current research focuses on phenomenological, psychoanalytic, and Wittgensteinean perspectives of subjectivity and psychopathology, in particular the study of schizophrenia.

Laurie Laufer has a psychoanalytic practice in Paris. She is professor at the Department of Psychoanalytic Studies at the University of Paris and director of the Centre de Recherche Psychanalyse Médecine et Société. Her most recent publications include *Murmures de l'art à la psychanalyse* (2021), *Après les Aveux de la chair. Généalogie du sujet, généalogie de la psychanalyse chez Michel Foucault* (with Sandra Boehringer, 2020), and *Vers une psychanalyse émancipée. Renouer avec la subversion* (2022).

Mladen Dolar is a professor and senior research fellow at the Department of Philosophy, University of Ljubljana. His principal areas of research are psychoanalysis, modern French philosophy, German idealism, and art theory. He has lectured extensively at universities in United States and across Europe, and he is the author of over 150 papers in scholarly journals and collected volumes. Apart from fourteen books in Slovene, his book publications include, most notably, *A Voice and Nothing More* (2006, translated into ten languages) and *Opera's Second Death* (with Slavoj Žižek, 2001, also translated into several languages). His new book, *The Riskiest Moment*, is forthcoming with Duke University Press. He is one of the founders of the Ljubljana Lacanian School.

Nelson da Silva Junior is a psychoanalyst with a PhD in fundamental psychopathology from the University of Paris VII. He is a professor at the Institute of Psychology, University of São Paulo; editor-in-chief of *Revista Latinoamericana de Psicopatologia Fundamental*; and co-ordinator of Latesfip, together with Christian Dunker and Vladimir Safatle. He is the author of *Le fictionnel en psychanalyse: une étude à partir de l'œuvre de Fernando Pessoa* (2000) and *Linguagens e pensamento: a lógica na razão e desrazão* (2007), as well as the coeditor of *A Psicologia Social e a Questão do Hífen* (with Zangari, 2017), *Pathologies of the Social* (with Dunker and Safatle, 2018), and *Neoliberalism as* *the Management of Psychic Suffering* (with Dunker and Safatle, 2020). His most recent solo book is *Fernando Pesssoa and Freud: Uncanny Dialogues* (2019).

Nicolas Evzonas (PhD in literature and PhD in psychopathology and psychoanalysis) is a Greek Cypriot Paris-based therapist in private practice. He is a candidate in the French Psychoanalytic Association andassistant professor in clinical psychology at the University of Paris. He has published numerous papers in French, English, Greek, and Portuguese on clinical and applied psychoanalysis as well as essays on films, theater, and literature. He is the author of a forthcoming French book on gender countertransference, the coeditor of a recent issue of *Psychoanalytic Inquiry* on "Sexualities, Gender, Class, and Race: A Psychoanalytic View from France," and the editor of a forthcoming special double issue of *The Psychoanalytic Review* on "Trans* Subjectivities and Countertransference," with a transepistemological and transcultural scope.

Patricia Gherovici, PhD, is a recipient of the 2020 Sigourney Award. Her books include *The Puerto Rican Syndrome* (2003, Gradiva Award and Boyer Prize), *Please Select Your Gender: From the Invention of Hysteria to the Democratizing of Transgenderism* (2010), and *Transgender Psychoanalysis: A Lacanian Perspective on Sexual Difference* (2017). She coedited *Lacan On Madness: Madness Yes You Can't* (with Manya Steinkoler, 2015); *Lacan, Psychoanalysis and Comedy* (with Manya Steinkoler, 2016); and, most recently, *Psychoanalysis in the Barrios: Race, Class, and the Unconscious* (with Chris Christian, 2019, Gradiva Award and the American Board and Academy of Psychoanalysis Book Prize).

Paulo Beer is a psychoanalyst in São Paulo, Brazil. With a master's and PhD in social psychology from the Institute of Psychology, University of São Paulo, he is a researcher at the Laboratory for Social Theory, Philosophy and Psychoanalysis and a member of the International Society of Psychoanalysis and Philosophy. Currently teaching postgraduate courses at the Institute of Psychology at the University of São Paulo, he also teaches psychoanalysis at various psychoanalytic schools. His research areas comprise psychoanalysis, science studies, and social theory. He is currently working on psychoanalytic understandings of negationism. He co-ordinates the Centre for Studies and Therapeutic Practices, which offers psychoanalytic treatment and formation to social movements in Brazil. He is one of the editors of *Lacuna: uma revista de psicanálise*, and he is author of *Psicanálise e ciência: um debate necessário* (2017).

Peter Jansson is a psychoanalyst in Gothenburg, Sweden, where he maintains a private practice in psychotherapy, supervision, and research. He is also a philosopher and a writer. His field of research is the intersection between psychoanalysis and culture (especially art, film, and literature). He has written a book about the Swedish female writer and poet Karin Boye. He is also in the final phase of a larger book about the Polish filmmaker Kieslowski, and he is finalizing his contribution to a forthcoming anthology (in English) devoted to psychoanalytic perspectives on the Swedish film director Ingmar Bergman.

Samo Tomšič obtained his PhD in philosophy at the University of Ljubljana, Slovenia, and is currently a research associate at the Humboldt University Berlin and visiting professor at the University of Fine Arts in Hamburg, Germany. His research areas comprise political philosophy, epistemology, and theory of psychoanalysis. Recent publications include *The Capitalist Unconscious: Marx and Lacan* (2015) and *The Labour of Enjoyment. Toward a Critique of Libidinal Economy* (2019).

Vladimir Safatle is professor of philosophy and psychology at the University of São Paulo, Brazil. He is responsible for the Portuguese edition of *Theodor Adorno's Complete Work*, and he is co-ordinator of the Laboratory of Social Theory, Philosophy and Psychoanalysis. He was an invited professor at the universities of Paris VII, Paris VIII, Toulouse, and Leuven; he was responsible for seminars at the Collège International de Philosophy, and he was a fellow of the Stellenbosch Institute of Advanced Studies, South Africa. He is the author of *La passion du négatif: Lacan et la dialectique* (2010) and several books in Portuguese and Spanish about critical theory, psychoanalysis, politics, and philosophy of music.

www.ingramcontent.com/pod-product-compliance
Ingram Content Group UK Ltd.
Pitfield, Milton Keynes, MK11 3LW, UK
UKHW021846100926
8556IPUK00019B/1079

9 789462 703001